THE DEVELOPMENT AND ORGANIZATION OF MEANING

Drawing from extensive developmental research, this book highlights the significance of meaning in shaping individual worldviews within relationships, from infancy onwards. By focusing on behavior and experience, it reshapes our understanding of pertinent psychological phenomena, tracing the emergence of self, self-regulation, causality comprehension, peer relationships, adolescent experiences, and lifelong adaptation. Using developmental psychology and compelling clinical cases, the authors emphasize the central role of "meaning" as a unifying theme, addressing diverse topics such as resilience, intergenerational behavior patterns, trauma impacts, and existential meaning. Ideal for students and professionals in psychology, counseling, and social work, as well as researchers and clinicians in related fields, this book integrates existing theories and empirical evidence to illuminate various aspects of human development and adaptation.

L. ALAN SROUFE, PhD, Professor Emeritus at the University of Minnesota, is a renowned expert in emotional development and developmental psychopathology. With 8 books and 160 articles on these subjects, he has received numerous awards, including the Distinguished Scientist Award from the Society for Research in Child Development (SRCD) and the Mentor Award from the Developmental Psychology Division of the American Psychological Association.

JUNE SROUFE, PhD, is a family and child therapist who specializes in relationship theory and clinical uses of the Adult Attachment Interview (AAI). With eight published articles, she is recognized for her expertise in family functioning and AAI applications.

THE DEVELOPMENT AND ORGANIZATION OF MEANING

How Individual Worldviews Develop in Relationships

L. ALAN SROUFE AND JUNE SROUFE

Shaftesbury Road, Cambridge CB2 8EA, United Kingdom

One Liberty Plaza, 20th Floor, New York, NY 10006, USA

477 Williamstown Road, Port Melbourne, VIC 3207, Australia

314–321, 3rd Floor, Plot 3, Splendor Forum, Jasola District Centre, New Delhi – 110025, India

103 Penang Road, #05-06/07, Visioncrest Commercial, Singapore 238467

Cambridge University Press is part of Cambridge University Press & Assessment, a department of the University of Cambridge.

We share the University's mission to contribute to society through the pursuit of education, learning and research at the highest international levels of excellence.

www.cambridge.org
Information on this title: www.cambridge.org/9781009385473

DOI: 10.1017/9781009385480

© L. Alan Sroufe and June Sroufe 2025

This publication is in copyright. Subject to statutory exception and to the provisions of relevant collective licensing agreements, no reproduction of any part may take place without the written permission of Cambridge University Press & Assessment.

When citing this work, please include a reference to the DOI 10.1017/9781009385480

First published 2025

A catalogue record for this publication is available from the British Library.

A Cataloging-in-Publication data record for this book is available from the Library of Congress

ISBN 978-1-009-38547-3 Hardback
ISBN 978-1-009-38544-2 Paperback

Cambridge University Press & Assessment has no responsibility for the persistence or accuracy of URLs for external or third-party internet websites referred to in this publication and does not guarantee that any content on such websites is, or will remain, accurate or appropriate.

Contents

Preface	page ix

PART I THE BEGINNINGS OF MEANING

1 **The Place of Meaning** — 3
  The Power of Meaning — 5
  Meaning, Synthesis, and Integration — 6
  Meaning and Behavior — 8
  Conclusion — 9

2 **Four Features of Meaning and Its Development** — 12
  Meaning as an Inherent Human Motive
    and Active Process — 13
  The Dynamic Interplay of Meaning and Experience — 15
  The Social Embeddedness of Meaning — 18
  Acknowledging Culture — 21
  The Place of Meaning — 23

3 **The Cradle of Meaning** — 25
  How Meaning Is Created — 27
  Prototypes for Meaning — 33

4 **Attachment Theory: The Rise of Meaning
  in Psychology** — 35
  Attachment as a Relationship Concept — 37
  The Reality and Power of Relationships — 46

5 **Toddlerhood: The Meaning of Me** — 50
  Guided Self-regulation — 52
  Variations in Toddler Experience — 55
  From Past Meaning to New Meaning — 57
  Taking Meaning Forward — 61
  The Way Development Works — 62

PART II THE GROWTH OF MEANING

6   The Preschooler: The Emergence of the Person   67
    Questions of Meaning   68
    The World of the Preschooler   69
    Deepening Meanings as the Person Emerges   77
    The Way Development Works   83

7   Middle Childhood: Me and My Friends   85
    Major Developments in Middle Childhood   87
    The Inner World: Representations of Self, Family, and Peers   94
    The Consolidation of World Views   99
    Change and Continuity in the Search for Meaning   101

8   Adolescence: Finding Personal Meaning   103
    The Expanding Mind of the Adolescent   105
    Implications for Self and Relationships   107
    Finding Meaning in "Autonomy with Connection"   111
    Opportunities and Vulnerabilities   114

PART III THE ORGANIZED AND ORGANIZING NATURE OF MEANING

9   Meaning as the Currency of Development   119
    What Is Taken Forward   122
    The Way Adaptation Works   125

10   The Role of Meaning in Intergenerational Transmission Effects   128
    Continuity of Parenting across Generations   128
    Continuity of Attachment Relationships across Generations   132
    Processes in Carrying Forward Meaning   139
    The Way Development Works   141

11   Competence, Resilience, and the Fate of Early Experience   143
    Resilience   146
    The Fate of Early Experience following Developmental Change   149
    Continuity, Change, and the Nature of Maladaptation   151

PART IV MEANING AND DISTURBANCE

12   On the Meaningfulness of Disturbance   157
    A Note regarding Blaming Parents   159
    Explaining Common Problems   160

	Viewing Childhood Disorders through the Lens of Meaning	167
	The Meaningfulness of Even Extreme Disturbance	169
	Conclusion	172

13 Trauma and Meaning — 175
    Trauma and Brain Development — 175
    Trauma and Psychological Development — 178
    Trauma and Meaning — 180
    Attachment, Coherence, and Trauma — 182

PART V INTEGRATION AND CONCLUSION

14 Integration — 187
    Meaning through the Lifespan — 190
    Individual Variations in Meaning across Development — 193
    Mature Meaning Systems — 200

15 Conclusion — 201
    Personal Meaning — 204
    In the End — 205

Bibliography — 208
Index — 219

Preface

We are a researcher and a clinician. When we have looked from these different perspectives at the panoply of research in developmental psychology, the literature on psychopathology, and a range of clinical case material, we have been impressed by a unifying theme that underlays all of this work. This is the thread of meaning. Whether trying to explain when infants begin to laugh or what things frighten them, or why toddlers jabber in their cribs, why some preschoolers hover by teachers while others do not, why children with classic autism engage in stereotyped behavior, why some children see relationships with others as unavailable to them or fraught with difficulty, or how all of us see the world in the particular ways we do, the answer always came back to meaning. And, while each clinical case seen over the years was completely unique and presented unique issues, always at the core was the meaning the individuals were making of their experience.

In this book we will explore two central ideas: first, that the organized network of meanings that each of us has is a developmental construction and, second, that understandable principles underlie these constructions. The development of anything – from embryos to brains to the universe – has the same nature. As does everything else, our individual meaning systems evolve, step-by-step, building upon foundations that began to be established in the earliest years of life. This developmental process is complex but understandable.

A great deal is now known about the development of meaning, but it is spread through a diverse and unorganized literature. Our purpose is to summarize much of this knowledge, emphasizing what we have learned first-hand through our clinical work and through the Minnesota Longitudinal Study of Risk and Adaptation. The information will be presented both as general conclusions from research findings and as anecdotes based on the lives of actual children and adults, with names and details altered.

The research findings will refer to group data. This means that, of course, there are individual exceptions to the general statements made. Not every 8-year-old child with a history of extreme rejection draws family figures with their arms pinned at their sides. Not every child with a history of secure attachment becomes a peer leader. Moreover, we have made the choice to present findings without details concerning statistical controls of other factors that were necessarily made. There are no graphs or tables with complex statistical analyses. All of this has been presented previously in numerous books and articles. For interested readers, there is an extensive bibliography at the end of the book that will guide you to the details of the ideas and findings discussed. The evidence for each of the claims made in the book is documented in one or more of the books or papers listed, much of it in three of our previous books: *Emotional Development, The Development of the Person,* and *A Compelling Idea.*

Our goal is to present a readable and compelling account of how individual world views develop, in the hope that researchers will feel inspired to continue the study of deeply psychological topics and clinicians will feel newly supported as they continue to explore meaning systems with their clients.

PART I

The Beginnings of Meaning

CHAPTER 1

The Place of Meaning

A 5-year-old enters the preschool classroom and sees other children jumping around and dancing to music. He approaches a child and invites her to dance with him. She declines, and he goes off into a corner and sulks, staying separate from the others for a lengthy period. A second child enters and approaches the same little girl. She turns him down too. But this second child skips on to another child, who responds to his invitation and the two of them happily join the frolic.

These are remarkably different reactions to what is on the surface the same event. The first child experienced a devastating rejection. The second child did not. In fact, he may not have experienced "rejection" at all. He may have seen the turndown as something about the little girl or simply as not very consequential. The first child experienced another blow to self-esteem, while the self-esteem of the second child likely was enhanced, for he once again experienced that persistence leads to success. This event *meant* something very different to these two children. In fact, it is not possible to fully understand their behavior without taking meaning into account.

How do such profound differences in the meaning of experiences emerge? Are they part of a broader, organized network of meanings? What do they forecast regarding later ways of interpreting experiences? Finally, how does meaning making change with maturation? These developmental questions are of both theoretical and clinical importance. Exploring meaning is crucial for understanding individual personality. It is also at the center of the therapeutic process.

It is clear from the start that meaning is personal. Meaning is subjective. The individual *construes* meaning, based on a particular history of experiences. We see things as *we* are, rather than as *they* are (Nin, 1961). Meaning does not lie in the event itself, but in the interplay of the event, individual history, and the surrounding circumstances.

When there is shared meaning that is because there are shared histories and perspectives.

Meaning is also subjective in the sense that it involves the investment of the individual. A meaningful experience matters to the person. Meaning thus involves emotional as well as cognitive processes. Meaning involves more than the objective facts about any particular event or situation. It is influenced by the person's background mood and what the person feels regarding a particular situation and how these feelings color what is perceived.

Consider the simple example of a town square clock striking 10 times on a sunny morning. Leaving aside the case of human groups who do not artificially mark time by hours, for millions of people this event conveys the shared meaning of mid-morning. For some, of course, this may indicate time for a coffee break, for others a time to begin work or attend a class, or for a religious observance. So there is meaning that derives from culture and society. However, even this simple event can have profoundly different *individual* meanings. If a grown-up child or a parent, unseen for many years, is arriving on a 10:15 train, it may stir eager anticipation, excitement and joy for one or both of the individuals involved. In contrast, if one expects shortly to be taken to the executioner by a guard, dread, resignation, and terror would be expected. In both cases, without doubt, the striking of the clock is meaningful.

All of this is obvious, but meaning is, of course, much more nuanced than this. For our waiting parent or adult child both the meaning and reaction depend on the relationship history, both recent and cumulative. If when they parted, they were in the midst of an argument and the last words heard were, "I never want to see you again," the meaning of the hour would be quite different than if the last words were, "Be safe and know we love you." It also matters whether that argument was imbedded in a longstanding contentious relationship or was an atypical reaction to an acute stress. Is this a dreaded encounter or the fulfillment of a longstanding hope?

The entire developmental history of the individual all the way back to the earliest years and months of life also comes into play, especially experiences promoting or eroding trust. For some of us, fears of abandonment and loss are easily triggered; even the slightest hint of criticism can portend rejection. For others, expectations remain positive even in the face of threat. For some, each potential action must be scrutinized with regard to approval or disapproval from others. Some become anxious when certain feelings arise, regardless of the cause. What situations mean, whether they are seen as threats or opportunities, manageable or overwhelming, depends heavily on our acquired beliefs about our own coping capacities, our expectations regarding the availability of others, and our abilities to tap both internal and external resources.

The Power of Meaning

In her book *The Power of Meaning*, Emily Esfahani Smith (2017) draws on an extensive literature, from existential philosophy to modern social and biological science, to make the case that seeking meaning is the preeminent human motive. We continually need to make sense of our perceptions and to seek order and coherence in our experience. "We have a primal desire to impose order on disorder ... we see faces in the clouds, hear footsteps in the rustling leaves, and detect conspiracies in unrelated events. We are constantly taking pieces of information and adding a layer of meaning to them ..." (p. 104). Human beings seem to be intrinsically motivated to extract meaning from experience. We cannot do otherwise. As cosmologist Neil deGrasse Tyson frequently points out, pattern recognition is in our nature. Human brains appear to be hardwired to seek order and to organize experience.

One example of the way our brains function to maintain organization of experience comes from a study of brain scans of people before and after experiences of low gravity in a space flight. After the low gravity experience, researchers found reduced activity in brain regions involved in "bodily self-consciousness" (images of our body position in the environment). Normally, our brain combines information from systems involving motion, balance, and vision to create a coherent experience. Being in low gravity alters some of these messages, so the brain apparently switches them off in order to fend off the incoherence that would result. Such an idea has striking implications for the clinical phenomenon of dissociation. When children experience chaos, trauma or unfathomable experience, dissociation is a means for maintaining some semblance of order in a disordered world.

Meaning is prominent in what we abstract from our experience. In a study carried out decades ago by John Bransford and Jeffrey Franks (1971), college students were given lengthy paragraphs to read, and then tested regarding them weeks later. They were asked which of two paragraphs was the one read before. One paragraph used vocabulary and wording that overlapped almost completely with the original, but it was constructed such that the meaning was entirely different. The other used virtually all new language but conveyed the same meaning as the original. This was the one uniformly recalled as the same one that had been read before. This launched an entire set of studies regarding the meaning-extracting nature of human cognition.

The motive to seek meaning is rivaled only by the motive to survive, and at times the two motives are related. In "Man's Search for Meaning," Viktor Frankl describes how only searching for and finding meaning enabled people to survive in horrendous concentration camps during World War II. Stripped of all worldly possessions, separated from family, and existing in the harshest of conditions, some were still able to survive starvation and cold because they were able to find something to live for – some meaning for their continued existence. Sometimes this was a loved one whom they could someday care for again. For others it was some task in the future they hoped to undertake, some contribution that they could make to society.

Smith describes studies showing that finding meaning in life also seems to be important for physical health. Even when compared to measures of happiness, degree of meaning in one's life is the stronger predictor of cardiovascular and other aspects of health in large survey studies. As philosophers such as Sartre said, finding meaning is the purpose of life. It also apparently supports a healthy life.

In this book we will explore the nature of meaning making, from the very beginnings of meaning in infancy to the complex networks of meaning in adulthood. We want to understand how meaning making changes with development, and we want to understand how individuals form the particular *organizations* of meaning they do. By this we refer to the broader, integrated worldview of the individual and the unique network of meanings of each person. We believe that these individual organizations of meaning are the outcome of development, emerging from early beginnings and building step by step in a coherent, systematic way. A process in which each phase is built upon what was there before, yet also provides the foundation for what is to come, always characterizes development.

Meaning, Synthesis, and Integration

Meaning is the outcome of a process of synthesis and integration. For decades, psychology has recognized the interplay and reciprocal and cyclical nature of emotion and cognition (e.g., Sroufe, 1996). What one perceives influences what one feels, but at the same time what one feels influences what one sees as well. Affect and cognition are "non-dissociable," as

Piaget (1952) said. There are no cognitions without affect and no affect without cognition. We once said that temperament and experience are not carried in separate suitcases; there is only one suitcase (Sroufe & Fleeson, 1986). The same is true of cognition and emotion.

Moreover, emotional reactions unfold, and they do so in the social context. The same event in one context will entail different percepts and feelings than in another context. Meaning derives from the totality of the synthesized experience. For example, as Dan Siegel (2020) says, emotion is, in fact, a "value system for the appraisal of meaning." It both guides cognition and responds to cognitive interpretations. Even before there is "thought," infants make connections between sensations or actions and emotions, as we will discuss in Chapter 3. Without such an integrated process, meaning will be curtailed, distorted, or even obliterated.

A poignant example is the story of "Elliot" presented by neuroscientist Antonio Damasio (2006). Following surgery for a large frontal lobe tumor, Elliot's perception and logical reasoning were intact. He could perceive and describe in detail the events of his life – losing his job, losing his wife, losing his house, and becoming destitute. But his emotional reactions were completely blunted and not integrated with these perceptions. He felt nothing but indifference in the face of calamity. Without such integration, nothing was of personal significance. It had no meaning

The totality of feelings, cognitions, and awareness of the social context always governs the interpretation of a situation and always guides behavior from the earliest years forward. For example, without an attachment figure present, toddlers are generally not very comfortable playing in a laboratory. With an attachment figure present, they are comfortable, and the play improves noticeably in both amount and quality. Next design the playroom so that a screen blocks the view of the adult from where the toys are placed. Toddlers play dramatically less and spend a good deal of time going to where they can see the parent. They know the parent is there; their memories are fully adequate for that. And what is most noteworthy, without the screen they rarely look at the parent; rather they are reassured by the mere knowledge that they *could* look if they wanted to. The meaning of the whole situation is dramatically changed by the introduction of the screen and the concern it arouses.

Likewise, the reactions of the two children in our opening example cannot be explained by simply considering differences in cognitive ability. As 5-year-old children, these two boys had a common cognitive understanding of what happened. They both knew their request was received, and they both knew it was declined. What differed were the feelings that were activated. These feelings colored their interpretation of the event – the meaning it had *for them*.

Meaning and Behavior

In his book *The Undoing Project*, writer Michael Lewis (2016) summarizes the groundbreaking work of cognitive psychologists Daniel Kahneman and Amos Tversky. Of greatest interest to us, Lewis traces the evolution of this work across several decades. Even in the early years of their collaboration, the work yielded insights into the complicated workings of the mind. The mind, it seems, *imposes order* on fragments of sensations and experience, rather than the world imposing order on the mind. However, the early work was largely focused on cognitive operations, in that it was concerned with the logical errors that we all make. This was a great contribution, of course, meriting a Nobel Prize in economics for Kahneman following Tversky's death. Nonetheless, important as uncovering these errors was, it made it seem like they were due to simple faults in our cognitive machinery.

Soon they recognized that these errors were systematic and predictable. Then it became clear that more than faulty problem-solving machinery, the difficulty was in the perception of the problem. Increasingly, a role for emotion entered into the work. Decisions made by people, whether in economics, health, or any other human arena, are not simply made via cool calculus, but in terms of feelings as well. For example, it *hurts* more to lose something you already have than lose out on something you simply might get. Thus, people are more cautious with decisions framed in terms of potential loss, even when judgments regarding probable outcomes are not altered. Financial decisions aren't just economic decisions; they are emotional as well. As Lewis concluded, "to create a theory that would predict what people actually did when faced with uncertainty, you had to 'weight' the probabilities the way people did, with emotion" (p. 271). People make decisions and behave in terms of what a problem *means* to them, and what it means is emotional and cognitive in unison.

Kahneman and Tversky came to see that there were good evolutionary reasons for the mind to work the way it does. Avoiding harm and pain were more important to survival than always having the probabilities right. We would add that there are also individual historical reasons for viewing problems the way one does. Exaggerating threat, for example, or totally denying its existence, are the only ways for some children to survive malevolent childhoods, however illogical and maladaptive such perceptions may later appear to the outside. The integration that leads to meaning includes history as well as current events.

So, clearly, personal feelings aroused influence how we perceive things – what we make of them. "We see things as we are, not as they are, as Anais Nin points out." Yet, at the same time, our cognitive activity influences our emotions, and it is this totality that yields the meaning we make of situations. In the famous experiments of Stanley Schacter (1966), for example, some research subjects were given placebo and some were given epinephrine (more commonly known as adrenalin). Adrenalin, of course, speeds up the heart rate and raises blood pressure, among other things. However, the participants were not told that it was adrenalin (which would be expected to make them feel keyed up and even anxious), but rather that it was a new medication, and varying effects of the drug were suggested to different groups. Depending on what they were told (the "cognitive set" provided), the participants had a hugely varied range of behavioral and emotional reactions. Some even became drowsy when that suggestion was made! Moreover, those given the drug had stronger paradoxical reactions than those given placebo; that is, the drug *was* having an effect, but the *interpretation* of the bodily reactions was key. The physiological changes happened for all the subjects given the drug, but it was the integration of the physiological changes and mental activity that determined the particular reactions; that is, what the feelings meant to the person.

Conclusion

Others before us have, of course, taken on the topic of meaning, and we are indebted to them for their insights. Individual variations in meaning making and their embeddedness in social experiences has long been recognized.

One prominent position in this past work is what was called "appraisal theory." For decades, psychologists, such as Magda Arnold, George Mandler, and Richard Lazarus, recognized that different individuals appraise or evaluate situations differently and therefore react to them differently. Mandler (1975) even referred to appraisal as "meaning analysis." All of these theorists acknowledged that emotions influence thought but at the same time they pointed out how interpretations reciprocally impacted emotion. This back-and-forth interaction between emotion and thought is in continuous operation. Appraisal theory was a powerful position, calling our attention to the evaluative component to one's reaction to events. More than the event itself, it is how we appraise or evaluate it that impacts us.

As valuable as it was, we seek to go beyond this work in several ways. First, appraisal theory was focused on the meaning of specific events. We seek to understand the cumulative history of experience – the broader worldview of the person. Everyone puts together a story of their life which is more or less coherent (e.g., McAdams, 2013). It can be called making sense of or coming to an understanding of one's life or finding meaning. It is a, more or less, well organized view of the world and one's self in that world. It is a process that starts early and never ceases. In time, individuals vary greatly in how elaborated and/or coherent the story is. We sought to understand how this happened.

Second, appraisal was at times made to sound like a rational, analytical process. While emotion was seen as an "influence" on cognition, cognitive activities were given priority. But making sense of one's life/existence/experience is always subjective, primarily because the process begins much before conscious awareness of one's self. Before an individual can reflect on any interaction with an important caregiver, countless events have transpired that form the foundation of understanding. Therefore, as one becomes able to reflect upon and put together a story of one's life, there are already deep biases and expectations about the world that color how one thinks about current events. At this level of integration, one cannot separate emotion and cognition. They are, as Piaget said, "non-dissociable."

Related to this, the process of making sense of one's experience occurs on two levels. On one level, one consciously reviews one's experiences and arrives at an acceptable understanding. On another level, there is unconscious integration of experience, through habitual patterning of mind/brain functioning, further aided by the dreams of REM sleep. This is not voluntary and can only be altered through deliberate and sustained effort. Individuals vary greatly in their interest in self-examination and, even then, it can be useful or not.

Finally, we will emphasize the process of development; that is, *how* do individual people come to see the world the way they do. How do they come to engage and appraise different situations in the way they do? The starting point for appraisal theorists was the presence of the individual differences in adulthood. We want to go beyond that. We want to know why there are these differences. The major goals for this book are to answer questions concerning the origins and unfolding of individual differences in appraisal and in unique worldviews.

We have also received inspiration from numerous other scholars who have emphasized the role of social relationships in the development of meaning. Many of these were writing early in the twentieth century, and we will touch on them in the final chapter of the book. One more recent theorist is Robert Kegan (1982). Is his insightful book *The Evolving Self*, Kegan discussed many of the themes that we will also emphasize. He stressed the sociocultural embeddedness of the person from cradle to grave and rejected the idea of the free-standing individual. He also argued that meaning making was a lifelong activity. Meaning was so central in his position that he suggested that "it is not that a person makes meaning, as much as that the activity of being a person is the activity of meaning-making" (p. 11). His theory is clearly developmental, and he cites many of the same authors we will, such as Erik Erikson and John Bowlby.

We embrace Kegan's theoretical viewpoint and his core ideas. Our goal is to put flesh on these theoretical ideas by providing a more detailed, step-by-step account of *how persons in fact* construct the meaning systems they do, as well as to provide the much-needed empirical support for this position. How do some come to see their world as responsive and their actions as potent, while others have negative expectations regarding support and doubt their power to have any impact on their experience? The necessary longitudinal data are now available.

CHAPTER 2

Four Features of Meaning and Its Development

The process of finding and making meaning is complex, nuanced, and multifaceted. Moreover, aspects of this process and its complexity change with development. Age by age, new capacities for meaning making emerge. Likewise, individual systems of meaning evolve based upon individual histories of experience. Still, throughout all of this development there are four features of meaning making that are pervasive. These will be themes carried throughout this book.

The first feature or theme is that humans are inherently motivated to seek meaning. No one has to be taught to seek meaning. Humans seek to find meaning in their experience from the first time they are able to make connections with the environment, and the striving for meaning continues throughout life. Seeking meaning and coherence is a preeminent human motivation

The second theme, which is quite closely related to the first, is that meaning making is an *active* process. Humans impose order on experience. Meaning is always an interaction between events and the people experiencing them.

The third theme concerns the dynamic or "transactional" nature of the development of meaning. Meaning is a product of experience; yet, at the same time, past meanings govern what kinds of experiences are sought, how they are interpreted, and what is extracted from them. This is a cyclical or reciprocal process that goes on throughout individual development.

Finally, fourth, the developmental process underlying meaning making is inextricably social. Comparative psychologist Michael Tomasello, in his marvelous book, *Becoming Human* (2019) and other writings, makes clear that human motivation for connection with others is what most distinguishes us from other animals. Other animals, especially primates, seek joint attention from partners for the purpose of meeting instrumental goals, but it seems that only humans seek joint attention simply in order to have shared experience. Our greatest adaptive advantage is that we evolved to share experience and to collaborate, even with those to whom we are not related (Wilson, 2019).

Meaning as an Inherent Human Motive and Active Process

How do we know that any characteristic is inherently human? Generally there are two lines of argument. The first is that it is universal. It is a characteristic that all humans across all cultures exhibit. The second argument is that it appears very early in life. Both of these criteria are met in the case of seeking meaning. We see signs of striving toward order from the very earliest days of life.

As one example, when researchers put awake and alert newborn infants in a completely darkened room, with absolutely no light, infrared cameras revealed an amazing thing – the infants continually scanned the black surround. There was nothing to be seen, but still they engaged. This is something that infants do universally. They seek to be engaged with the environment. No one has to teach them to do this. It is a stretch to assume that newborns are even capable of extracting meaning, as we would define it; yet such a built-in reflex to engage is a precursor of what we see age by age, as the individual moves from engagement to interest to curiosity and to the search for coherence.

Here is another example: Use a long ribbon to connect the foot of an 8-week-old infant to a mobile. When they kick their feet the mobile will turn. In just a matter of days or even hours they will learn to make the mobile move, and they will do so repeatedly. No one has to reward them for doing this (or even be present). The "reward" is simply in the connection between the infant's activity and the reaction. There is an inherent interest in one's world and an inherent desire to act upon it.

Toddlers in the early phases of language learning reveal another example of early meaning making. There is a common tendency for them to engage in what is called "crib speech." When they awake from a nap, and no one is present, they frequently jabber away. They don't simply make random sounds. In fact, they are playing with what they are just in the process of learning. They may repeat something like, "Ball, ball, yellow ball." Or they may say, "Put this ... up there" over and over. They are *actively* practicing – making sense out of – their language environment. Practicing is a tool for achieving mastery. It is again noteworthy that they do this in the complete absence of external reward.

Or consider the example of two parents pushing their toddlers in strollers from different directions. When they meet and pass by, both of the toddlers' heads whip around as they look at each other. No one has to reward such activity. It is a part of a built-in interest in others "like them" they both have. Surely it is a beginning step in discovering the meaning of who they are.

A final example may be seen in the symbolic play of 3–5-year-olds. Especially in their solitary play, they routinely review and work through themes that are salient and challenging in their current lives. For instance, children in the midst of toilet training will frequently engage in play wherein they change the dolly's diaper, scold the dolly for being wet, and so forth. And all child clinicians are aware of how conflicts with and between parents are acted out in myriad ways in a child's play. Clearly, young children do this because it is one of the tools available to them to make experience meaningful and to thus explore and achieve some mastery in the world and their place in it. The main point here is that again no one needs to instruct or urge preschoolers to engage in this activity. In all cultures, children engage in symbolic play, recapitulating salient experiences.

Each of the examples here illustrates the active nature of meaning making. This is always the case. Consider the following scenario:

> A researcher dangles a brightly colored toy clown on a string in front of a 10-week-old infant. It engages the infant's attention. After 20 or 30 seconds, the researcher removes the clown from sight. She shows it to the infant again the same way, and again the baby looks at the clown. The presentations continue. Then, remarkably, after the fourth or fifth or sixth time, the baby not only looks at the clown but *smiles* at it. It smiles repeatedly for a few presentations and then apparently loses interest and no longer smiles.

This example conveys something very important about the nature of meaning. Obviously, it is not the stimulus of the clown per se that leads to the pleasurable emotional reaction. It is the infant's active interest and mental activity in this experience. The baby does not smile at the first presentation. So an infant at this young age is not smiling because it is a clown, or a toy giraffe, or any other novel object that you could choose. Clearly, the smile derives from the infant's active involvement. After repeated study, the baby with effort can now *recognize* the clown as something familiar. The clown *acquires* meaning through this active engagement, and the smile is part of this acquired meaning. The pleasure derives from the infant's active engagement and connection with the object. Finding pleasure in familiarity promotes further exploration of familiar objects. With repeated trials effort is no longer required. Engagement and connection, critical cores of meaning making, wane.

A somewhat related example is seen in toddler problem-solving tasks. When toddlers solve problems after some work, they frequently smile, again attesting to the meaningfulness of the activity. Most notably, the harder the problem is to solve, the bigger is the smile, as Jerome Kagan (2013) noted in his study of toddlers. The more actively involved the toddler is, the greater their investment, and the more potent is the experience.

The inherent, active tendency to try to make experience meaningful is helpful in explaining much behavior that at first seems paradoxical. As just one example here, it is at first perplexing why young children, who are as mentally able as others, would repeatedly behave in ways at preschool that lead generally warm and supportive teachers to discipline them. There is, of course, the circular argument that they do such things to get attention. But why do they do it that way? A more helpful explanation is that they, like all others, are actively seeking to make this new world understandable. They have no choice about this, such is the nature of human motivation. And what they know from their experience is the behavior–punishment cycle. For them a nonpunitive response is ambiguous or confusing. It makes no sense when they act out and receive no negative response. When they in time hit on the behavior that leads to discipline, they are back in familiar, understandable territory, which gives them some sense of agency and control. The new world becomes coherent, at least to a degree.

The Dynamic Interplay of Meaning and Experience

Development is "cumulative." Each phase of development builds upon what was there before. The issues and experiences of any given age are negotiated and processed based upon meanings derived from preceding history. These new experiences then become part of a new history that frames subsequent development. Because of the nature of development, there is a reciprocal relationship between meaning and experience, described by Arnold Sameroff in terms of a "transactional model" of development. Meaning is based on the history of experiences but meaning is also the core of what is internalized from any new experience and often drives what experiences are sought. An experience, in contrast to an event, is the personal meaning extracted by the individual. Over time individuals play an increasing role in what their experiences are, even though it is also the case that new experiences can change the organized network of meanings. This ongoing, dynamic interaction of meaning and experience is why early experience is so important. Those around the infant often largely determine first meanings. But soon, and increasingly with age, the child will actively seek and find meaning based on their individual history.

This cumulative, transactional nature of development also explains why therapeutic change can be difficult. Experiences are not just laid upon a person; they are in large part created by the person, as they have developed to that point. New relationships, including those with therapists, are seen through the lens of relationship history. Problems are seen through the lens of past experience confronting problems.

Mikel provides an example of the dynamic nature of development. In his early years Mikel experienced a very responsive environment, a kind we will describe more fully in the following chapters. Because of this responsiveness he developed positive expectations regarding himself, others, and relationships. Social encounters were seen as full of potential for enjoyment. Problems were seen as possibilities for mastery, either by himself or, if not, with aid he expected would be available from others. The meaning network he carried forward set him up well for the preschool and the early school years. His needs had been met before, so he expected the new adults in his world to be responsive as well. Partly because of these expectations, Mikel behaved in ways that in fact encouraged teachers and peers to like and support him, which led to deeper, positive social expectations. All was going well.

Then when he was 8-years-old, Mikel's parents got divorced. This of course would be expected to impact Mikel's meaning network, but by itself would not likely undermine the fundamental structure. The positive history would help him retain basic positive expectations about himself and others. However, this was an acrimonious divorce. Partly to punish his ex-wife, Mikel's father moved away, taking Mikel's older brother with him. This was enough to begin shaking Mikel's foundation, leading to a complex picture. When we saw Mikel at age 10, he had become angry and "ready to fight someone." Still, he had much of the self-confidence we had seen at earlier points, was doing well at school, and was popular with the other boys.

But things got worse. As he approached his teenage years, Mikel's mother had become unduly reliant on him and he, we thought appropriately, had begun to push away. Then she suddenly died in a car accident. One can imagine the guilt he felt. On top of everything else this was too much. His view of the world and his place in it dramatically changed. He became depressed and uncommunicative and engaged in some antisocial behavior (although it is noteworthy that this never involved harming or threatening others). Other young people still liked him. They found that "underneath" he was a thoughtful and good person (see Chapter 8). But, from the outside, it seemed that the light had gone out, that he lost his belief in himself and his optimism about the future. Of great clinical significance he said in an interview at age 19 that the death of his mother only bothered him briefly, perhaps a matter of weeks. He could not accept how profoundly meaningful this loss was for him. We found this distancing from his feelings troubling but recognized that it might have been a necessary adaptation at this time to keep some of his historical meaning system intact.

Then, in his twenties, the situation improved. Mikel married a very supportive woman who, while complaining about his emotional guardedness, recognized a good heart. When interviewed at age 26, Mikel was much more open regarding his feelings about the losses he had experienced. When his son was born, he became a devoted and warm father, one of the best we observed. This and many cases we studied revealed the back and forth process between meaning and experience over time. We often saw that those with solid beginnings were able to capitalize on new opportunities – to reconnect with meanings from the past (see Chapter 11). This was certainly true for Mikel.

Systematic research has amply demonstrated these same transactional processes. Some of the most comprehensive work has been done by Grazyna Kochanska and her colleagues at the University of Iowa (e.g., Kochanska et al., 2019). Measures in her early studies included toddler difficult temperament (including anger and other negative emotional reactions), parental coercive discipline, and later child noncompliance and other problems. She found, as others had before, that negative temperament predicted mother coercive behavior which in turn predicted poor child outcomes. The simple conclusion would be that difficult temperament causes harsh parenting and later problems. But she did not stop there. She showed that such a link was only true when there was an earlier history of infant–parent relationship problems; namely, an insecure attachment (see Chapter 4). When there was a secure attachment history, a difficult toddler temperament led to neither parental harsh discipline nor to later child problems. Her most recent work utilized measures of parent and child representation to explain these findings. What does it mean to a parent, for example, when a toddler behaves in a negative manner? How do they see this behavior? It seems that those parents whose infants have insecure attachments with them are "primed" to see even mild negativity as challenging and to react more negatively to it; that is, it means something more negative to them. Likewise, children with histories of insecure attachment expect their parents to react in negative ways and are therefore ready to escalate their negative behavior. Children with secure histories tend not to make such interpretations.

Another illustration of the transactional nature of development comes from the work of Michael MacKenzie and Susan McDonough (2009). They followed the development of a large number of children in the first 30 months of life. They had measures on both infants and their mothers. There were interview measures with the mothers, similar to those of Kochanska, and they measured the amount of crying and fussiness of the infants at ages 7- and 15-months. Then they measured broader aspects of toddler temperament and problem behavior at age 30 months. The results again demonstrated the importance of a longitudinal data base and a transactional view of development, because only the later measure of fussiness at age 15 months predicted 30-month behavior problems. If this had been the only information in the study one might have thought that inborn temperamental differences cause behavior problems. But, as we are seeing, development is more complex than this. The amount of crying at 7 months did *not* predict later behavior problems *or even crying at 15 months*. What did predict crying at 15 months and later problems was *how the parents experienced the crying* of the younger infants; that is how much the crying bothered them, what it *meant* to them. This had no relation to the actual amount of crying. It *was* related to a representational measure of the mothers that captured their expectations of themselves in close relationships. This finding is consistent with other work that showed what expecting mothers expected the temperament of their infants to be in fact predicted later "temperament" (Vaughn & Bost, 1999).

To summarize: The meaning that the parent brings forward from an integration of their own histories of experiences colors their reaction to their young infants crying. These parental reactions – what these infants experience from their parents when they cry – impact later infant behavior. Those infants, whose parents were most bothered by whatever degree of fussing the babies in fact did, cried more later and became more difficult toddlers. This is again the power of meaning, and in particular how meaning systems adults bring forward to their parenting provide the foundation for beginning meaning networks of the child.

The Social Embeddedness of Meaning

Humans are thoroughly social creatures. Meaning is created in social groups, from dyads to families to communities to society as a whole. As evolution scholar David Sloan Wilson (2019) states in his book,

This View of Life, "individuals are products of their social interactions." What are often thought of as individual traits, such as our statures, our physical health, and our personalities, are "the result of social processes that stretch all the way back to when our distant ancestors were born if we take all evolutionary processes into account" (p. 146). We literally become ourselves through others (Vygotsky, 1978). It is in a social setting that one can work toward deeper and fuller understanding. We really can't write our own story alone. We need others to listen, ask questions, and give feedback. That is how we grow.

Social context includes both the general motivation for connection built into our species, as well as processes that develop in the early months that lead to specific attachments. Beyond revealing the role of engagement and the integrated nature of meaning, studies of joy and fear in infancy reveal the incredible power of the social context in determining what events mean. Consider the following example: Someone puts on a colorful human-looking mask and slowly approaches within a few feet of a 10-month-old infant. What will the reaction be? Remarkably, the reaction can be *anything* from stark fear to joyous laughter. It completely depends on how this is done. If the infant gets to watch his or her *parent* put on the mask, and this takes place *in the child's home*, smiling and laughter are by far the most common reaction. If an unfamiliar person dons the mask in an unfamiliar environment, wariness and fear are predominant and virtually certain if an attachment figure is not present.

It is even more complex than this. If the parent puts on the mask first, the infant is subsequently less wary when the stranger does it (and even may smile in the home). In contrast, if the stranger does it first, then parent, the child is less positive toward the parent (and even likely to be wary in the laboratory). Infants are less wary of the masked stranger if they are sitting on the parent's lap, rather than when he or she is in plain view but a few feet away. Clearly, the meaning of this event is not in the mask but is a product of the infant's context-based evaluation of the event. This is a potent situation, involving transformation of familiar and unfamiliar faces. It will engage all infants at this age. But the masked face has different meaning depending on who puts it on, where they put it on, and who puts it on first. When the infant feels secure, this level of arousal is pleasurable; when not feeling secure, it is distressing. Meaning does not lie simply in the objective qualities of an external stimulus or event, or even the amount of excitation it arouses, but in how it is appraised by the infant. This evaluation is largely a product of the social context.

This sensitivity to such aspects of context is itself a developmental outcome. Five-month-olds show none of this range of reactions. Regardless of who puts on the mask, or where it is done, they generally just look at it attentively; then they try to reach and grab it. It is pretty much like they no longer know (or care) who is behind the mask. But well before the end of the first year, all infants show this sensitivity to social context. Likewise, infants in the first few months of life rarely show wariness regarding strangers, but many do at some point in the second half-year. A 5-month-old may, after scrutinizing an unfamiliar face for some time, pucker and begin to cry. In contrast, if a stranger approaches a 10-month old in the laboratory, many are rather quickly wary. Moreover, if the stranger leaves and comes in a second time, these older babies immediately have a negative reaction, even before the approach. The situation has changed from not-knowing-if-I-like-this, to I-know-what-this-is-and-I-*don't*-like-it. The situation has quite specific meaning.

These observations have profound implications. By the end of the first year, the emotional experiences of infants – the meanings of events encountered – are heavily influenced by the surrounding environment, especially social relationships. In many ways, infants are more dependent on external supports than we are as adults. This is because they have less cumulative experience, fewer cognitive capacities, and very limited capacities to fend for themselves. Whether something is threatening, benign, or delightful depends on how comfortable the infant feels in the situation. And it is clear that the dominant source of this comfort is the presence and behavior of caregivers.

The critical role of caregivers in meaning making was amply demonstrated in past studies of what was referred to as "social referencing." In the second year of life, toddlers often look to parents for cues about how to interpret situations. The caregiver's facial expression and voice tone can be used as a guide as to whether something is dangerous or benign, especially in situations that are ambiguous. In one telling study, 15-month-olds were presented with toys that were pleasant, frightening, or ambiguous while in the presence of their mothers (Gunnar & Stone, 1984). The mothers were instructed to present a smiling face or a neutral expression in each case. It turned out that this expression did not matter in the case of the pleasant toy *or* the frightening toy. The toddlers readily grasp the meaning of these, without recourse to maternal cues. They engaged the cuddly toy and shrank back from the frightening toy. It was in the ambiguous situation that they looked to the mother. Those whose mothers were smiling and nodding much more readily engaged and played with the ambiguous toy. This toy meant something different to them than it did to the toddlers whose mothers showed a neutral expression. It remained ambiguous. Other studies showed that a frightened face on the mother inhibited toddler behavior.

Social context, of course, also includes the infant's history, both recent and distant. Infants recently receiving shots at a doctor's office may be more wary in a research lab, even before any procedure. Beyond such particular experiences, the cumulative history of interaction with caregivers plays a critical role. When caregivers are reliable and responsive to infant signals, infants learn over time to have confidence in caregiver availability. They are more readily reassured by the caregiver's presence. When some threat arises, often a look and reassuring nod by the caregiver is all that is needed to change the meaning of the event. More extreme threat, of course, requires physical contact, but such contact is readily reassuring if there is a history of responsive care. What is perceived as threatening, and the degree of threat experienced are in a substantial way influenced by the interactive history between infants and caregivers.

For many infants, by the end of the first year, the presence of the attachment figure means that most situations are safe. Moreover, infants who have experienced reliable responsiveness to their signals of need – those we refer to as secure in their attachment – have a different sense of themselves and their relationship. They know that, if threatened, they can effectively take action and that they can count on the attachment figure to respond (see Chapter 4). This is the core of the network of interpersonal relational meanings that will develop in the following years. To draw upon an idea proposed by Iris Murdoch (1978), we in fact learn to love by being loved.

Acknowledging Culture

This book is focused on the development of individual meaning systems in relationships, primarily within Western, industrialized culture. The impact of culture is outside of its purview. Still, it must be noted that culture has a huge impact on the meaning systems of human groups. Culture, including variations in religion, has a major impact on how humans prioritize activities and events, how they perceive problems and formulate solutions. Culture at all levels, from family to society, is the basis for shared, abstract meanings.

Culture is part of individual inheritance. In modern evolutionary views of the development of the person, it is now well known that information in genes that is passed from parents to children is only one part of the story. It is indeed complicated. Even the impact of genes is impacted by epigenetic factors, including the way in which experience influences gene expression. Beyond all of this, however, more than the human organism has evolved. As explained by David Sloan Wilson (2019), evolution works at multiple levels, from individuals to groups to human culture itself. There is intergenerational transmission of genetic material and intergenerational transmission of cultural practices. In particular, Wilson states that "meaning systems" are the carriers of culture from one generation to the next.

A classic book by Michael Cole and colleagues (1971), titled *The Cultural Context of Learning and Thinking*, illustrates the huge impact of culture on meaning, as well as providing a warning against making value judgments regarding unfamiliar cultures. When young children and adults (Ivy League college students) in the United States were compared in their manner of classifying objects, it was noted that the college students grouped the objects categorically (for example, all of the foods in one category, all the utensils in another), whereas the young children grouped them "functionally"; that is, put a spoon, a bowl, and a fruit together, because you would eat the fruit with the spoon. Because tribal members in a non-industrialized community sorted the way the children did, some had argued that their thinking was therefore "primitive." However, Cole and colleagues did something brilliant – they asked the tribal members why they grouped objects the way they did. The tribal members responded, "because that is the way a wise man would do it." OK, so how then would a foolish man do it? They would group the objects by category. Of course they had the same cognitive equipment as the American college students. Their culture simply led them to prioritize some ways of approaching problems. Psychologists and anthropologists have provided many such examples.

Culture is unquestionably critical in shaping meaning systems of groups and subgroups of humans. A system of morality is created in culture. Consider the prioritizing of intent that arises in the moral judgments of elementary school children. Major developmental theories consider this a normative cognitive achievement. When, for example, middle class children in Western countries are asked whether it is worse to break one dish trying to retrieve a prohibited cookie from a shelf or six dishes trying to set a table as a nice surprise for your mother, they typically say the first is worse, because of the child's intention. Children in a poor, rural Mexican village were found to say the latter is worse. This is not because of a limitation in cognitive development, but because of the meaning of these events in this cultural context. The loss of that many dishes in the context of poverty would mean great economic hardship. The premium on caring for these precious possessions is far greater.

Culturally based prioritization can also appear in cross-cultural studies of self-development. Individuals in all cultural groups of course have all of the same emotional capacities and the common abilities for self-awareness, reflections on the self, and what can be called self-esteem. But what is given priority in self-evaluations may vary, often in terms of a dimension of independence–interdependence. In some cultures individual achievement and success have greater priority, while in others service to others plays a greater role in self-esteem (Marcus & Kitayama, 2010).

Things reported in this book would be at times expected to operate somewhat differently in different cultural contexts, and this needs to be acknowledged. At the same time, studies have shown that many of the findings are robust across cultural groups (Gojman-de-Millan et al., 2017).

The Place of Meaning

The concept of meaning is absolutely critical for our understanding of individual development. A focus on meaning sheds light on why various emotions emerge when they do and why they are expressed when they are; how experiences at one age provide the foundation for the child's adaptation at the next; how early primary relationships influence development as they do; why maladaptive behavior is perpetuated; and what happens to earlier experience following developmental change. Meaning allows researchers to define the essential core of child functioning at each age. Therefore, it guides assessment strategies and informs the construction of measures. Without the focus on meaning, the task of defining continuity in individual development floundered. With a focus on meaning, powerful demonstrations became possible, as will be documented in subsequent chapters.

Understanding the development of meaning and meaning making also helps us understand variations in adult functioning and sheds light on many important clinical phenomena. Thus, it is a key in explaining why some individuals struggle with the basic nature of reality, why others so chronically feel threatened in objectively safe circumstances, why early experience is so powerful in shaping personality, why therapeutic change can be so difficult, how change is nonetheless accomplished, and why some are more resilient than others.

These are all matters we will consider in this book. From cradle to grave, making meaning is a prime human motive. In the following pages we will share what is being discovered about the role of meaning in the developmental process, age by age. We begin in infancy.

CHAPTER 3

The Cradle of Meaning

The capacities to find and make meaning develop, just as do the human fetus, the brain, and everything else in nature. Because a core principle of development is that it is "cumulative," building upon itself, there is a special place for the very earliest phases of life. Experiences in the early months and years of life are the cradle of meaning. To understand how the capacity to make meaning unfolds and how we each come to have the organizations of meaning we have, it is helpful to understand more about the nature of development itself.

René Spitz had a clear grasp of the nature of development, including the development of meaning. Spitz is best known for calling attention to the devastating effects of institutional rearing; in particular the lack of specific, consistently available, caregiving figures. This was in 1950, decades before the critical importance of specific attachment figures was rediscovered in the Romanian orphan studies at the turn of the century. Neither Spitz's concern about institutionalized infants nor his insights concerning development were widely accepted in his day, but they are now, although rarely with an acknowledgment of his role.

The research of Spitz and his colleagues was focused on early development, most heavily on the first 3 months of life. It is in this period, he argued, that the first capacities for meaning making emerged, and they emerged from a period in which there was no true meaning. Before there was meaning, however, there were developmental precursors or "prototypes" which were the foundation for meaning making. A major premise of development is that you can't get something from nothing. Positing that the capacity to find meaning is "simply there" at the beginning is no solution at all. Spitz's idea of developmental prototypes is one path forward.

The development of the meaning-based smile in the early months provides an excellent example of how this works. Newborn infants smile. However, this is not a social behavior and it is not based on meaning. It is a reflex built into the physiology of the newborn. It happens only when they are asleep or drowsy. It is based on a fluctuation of arousal around some low set point. As the infant drifts off to sleep or moves from sleep toward wakefulness, the arousal level crosses a threshold and the smile reflex occurs. You can create these smiles by gently shaking a sleeping baby or by shaking a rattle while the baby sleeps. This brings them toward wakefulness and as they drift back down several of these smiles may occur. These smiles occur even in utero, because they are of brain stem origin. Premature infants exhibit more of these smiles than full-term infants, so it cannot mean the same thing as later smiles. It cannot be that premature babies find more meaning than full-term babies. As the cortex matures, these reflexive smiles steadily decline in all infants over the first 3 months, as do many other newborn reflexes. Because of all of this, it is clear that newborn smiles cannot be based on meaning. It is also worth noting that these smiles do not have all the features of later social smiles. They involve only the twisting up of the lips, not the mouth opening and crinkling of the eyes of full smiles.

What are called "social smiles" or "exogenous smiles" (that is, in response to the outside world) emerge in a fleeting way at 3 or 4 weeks of age and become increasingly prominent in the first 3 months. This increase is an exact mirror image of the decline in reflexive smiles, denoting a brain maturation process. These emerging smiles also then take the form of mature smiles involving mouth and eyes. Meaning is involved in these smiles. Recall the example of the infant smiling at the toy clown following several presentations that we discussed in Chapter 2. That was a smile based on meaning because if we switch objects there is no smile. The babies smile because, as they engage and study the clown repeatedly, *it is their own efforts* that lead to recognition and the smile. Eight to 10 weeks is the same age that infants rather universally smile at human faces. They do this because with some effort they can recognize the face as something familiar. It is indeed meaningful. For this reason it is called a "social smile," although it is shown in many nonsocial situations.

The question now before us is where did this smile based on meaning come from? How did the infant get there? One might suggest that smiles were present all along – that the slight smiles of the newborn simply got "bigger" over time. But this cannot be true. By 10 weeks, infants no longer smile when they are asleep. The newborn smile disappears. Much research shows that newborn sleep smiles originate in the brain stem, whereas social smiles require involvement of the cortex. (Even the rare infants born without a cortex exhibit the newborn smile, but never the later social smile.) The social smile is not simply a big newborn smile; yet Spitz argued that it does derive from the newborn smile. The newborn smile is the developmental prototype – the precursor – for the social smile. It sets a basic physiological pattern from which, however qualitatively different, the social smile emerges. There is the same arousal fluctuation, though in the social smile it is created by the infant's cognitive engagement and processing of an external event. It is a psycho-physiological response, not merely a physiological one. There is meaning and emotion as we define it; yet the basic earlier patterning is maintained.

There are many examples of such developmental prototypes in early development. As just one more, when young infants get excited, they do a kind of rhythmic frog kicking with their legs. Every parent has seen this. This is long before infants can walk, and it is another behavior that drops out over time. But careful study by Esther Thelen (1989) showed that such movements are actually preparation for later crawling and walking, because the exercising and coordination of muscles involved is the pattern that will be drawn upon later, even though such mobility is qualitatively different from early infant kicking.

Progressive movement toward more complex organization and deeper meaning always characterizes development. There is a particular way that development unfolds, centered on qualitative change and reorganization. We are interested in the developmental prototype concept because we believe it applies equally to all social and emotional aspects of the developing person – to how each of us acquired the networks and organization of meaning we have. The nature of the meanings acquired in our earliest relationships provide the pattern for our organization of meaning in childhood, and all of this together shapes our world views in adulthood.

How Meaning Is Created

Meaning is an active process – a creation. The ability to make meaning is itself the outcome of development. Infants are not born making meaning; rather the capacity emerges in the early months of life, largely promoted by social relationships.

There are several reasons for saying that personal meaning does not exist in the newborn period. It is a few months before the frontal cortex and deeper emotional centers in the brain are interconnected (see Chapter 13). Such connections are central for experiences we would define in terms of meaning. Moreover, newborn capacities for memory are quite limited. A certain kind of memory, called *procedural memory*, develops quickly (that is, recognition and internalization of practiced routines) but memory for events begins to emerge in the second half year and is not well developed until much later.

In contrast to young infants, caregivers have an extensive network of established meanings, based on an entire history of experiences from their own earliest years up to the present. They bring this network of meanings to their interactions with infants, often without even being aware that they are doing so. At times this can lead to failures to understand the importance of the infant's behavior or distortions in what a particular behavior means. Of course, it is also history that prepares many caregivers to respond effectively to infant signals. This "asymmetry" in meaning systems, with the infant network of meanings unformed, is why developmental psychologists see parenting and early experience as so important. It is the meaning system of the parents that structures the first meanings of infants and toddlers through their interactions. The baby learns that the world is predictable, or not.

The Early Origins of Meaning

The subjective core of meaning helps us define its early origins. Even newborns listen to sounds and focus their eyes on a target. They cry and, as we have discussed, even smile; yet it is really not accurate to say that there is meaning in the first days of life. For example, while faces and voices attract attention from the alert newborn, so will three dots in a triangle, an array of blinking lights, or virtually any gentle sound. These newborn reactions are not subjective and they do not involve the quality of engagement that happens later. Infants are drawn reflexively to such stimulation. Their reactions do not involve a connection between the individual and a *particular* event. It takes a few weeks for this kind of connection to occur.

The newborn does have a set of inborn and rapidly developing capacities that can contribute to the soon-to-emerge relationship with caregivers. The newborn actively seeks certain sensory experiences. They are attracted to features of the human face. They follow movements with their eyes. They hear well in the higher ranges of human speech (which is why adult "baby talk" is so effective). From this activity, and with further maturation, first meanings emerge. Perhaps most important of all, the young infant is extraordinarily able to detect contingencies; that is, things that follow from their actions. Caregivers are a major source of contingencies. When caregivers respond to infant behaviors time after time, the infant detects a "contingent relationship" between an action and an event, and such events are highly meaningful for the infant.

From the start, caregivers imbue infant behavior with meaning. For example, consider the situation in which the newborn has been fed and, drifting off to sleep, a little reflexive smile appears on the lips. As caregivers, we see the infant as content, even happy. This reflexive behavior is a beautiful thing nature has given us. The meaning we find and attribute to this reflexive smile and other newborn behaviors is the beginning of the process of eventual meaning making by the child. We are responding to what it *will* mean. This is what is meant by the idea that original meanings are co-constructed.

In the following weeks caregivers initiate the infant into the practice of a turn-taking dialog, in a further step of constructing meaning. As described by Berry Brazelton and colleagues (1974), the parent

> holds the infant with her hands, with her eyes, with her voice and smile, and with changes from one modality to another as he habituates to one or another. All of these holding experiences are opportunities for the infant to learn how to contain himself . . . They amount to a kind of learning about the organization of behavior in order to attend. (p. 70)

Research shows that such early interactions are not truly reciprocal; rather caregivers provide scaffolding for the dialog. In our late friend Daniel Stern's (1990) words, "The exchange occurs in overlapping waves, where the mother's smile elicits the infant's, reanimating her next smile at an even higher level" (p. 14). The infant exhibits a behavior and the caregiver responds in such a way as to prompt a further infant response, so that they can go back and forth. When the infant does not follow suit, the caregiver adjusts to respond to the new behavior. For example, a caregiver talking in an animated fashion to a 4-month-old elicits a smile. The caregiver smiles in return with more animation, and the baby vocalizes. The caregiver vocalizes in return. The baby vocalizes again. Back and forth they go until the baby stops and yawns. The caregiver does an exaggerated open mouth in return; then the two look at each other face to face. The infant furls its brow and the caregiver mimics. The infant vocalizes again. The caregiver responds in kind and off they go again. In his insightful book on "The Interpersonal World of the Infant" and other writings, Stern (1985) wrote beautifully about how fitting the infant into a predictable world of action and reaction is critical in the very early stages of self-development. Through such a process the infant develops a primitive and deep sense of being seen, of place, of belonging. This is critically important. Without such experiences the basic sense of reality is compromised.

From the outside, this back and forth truly looks like a reciprocal dance, even though it is managed by the caregiver. Moreover, it is the critical foundation – the "prototype" – for the more genuine reciprocity that emerges in the second half year. By age 10 months, for example, infants will attempt to put the cloth back over a parent's face during a game of peek-a-boo. They even at times initiate games without prompting. They have come to know their role in the dialog. This is the basic nature of the early acquisition of meaning. In the beginning caregivers attribute meaning to infant behaviors or make them meaningful by creating a structure around them. In time the infant plays an increasingly active role, both extracting meaning and creating meaning through its social behaviors.

The very first acquired meanings of the infant are not deliberately sought out by the infant, but simply occur as the result of the lived experience of the infant. Gerald Stechler and Genevieve Carpenter (1967) and Louis Sander (1975) referred to them as sensory-affective, emphasizing the feelings of the infant and the lack of intentionality. We might describe them also in terms of familiarity or repeatability. Regularity and stability in the surround leads to this kind of knowing, and it shows up in physical state regulation. Just like the smile example, when the environment is dependable, organized, and stable, the infant recognizes this patterning as familiar. This is well before the infant has any intentions. This first sense of dependability – the prototype for what can be known – is recorded in procedural memory. This critical "procedural" learning is internalized and carried forward, though it can never be consciously remembered.

Such dependability and stability are out of the infant's hands. Caregivers determine how knowable these early patterns are. The recently born infant brings certain things to the table: An orientation to the surround, the ability to detect changes in the surround, and a remarkable ability to note events that are responsive to their actions. Attuned caregivers respond to infant behaviors from the beginning, long before the infant has any intentional awareness of its actions. Thus, in the early weeks, while infants do not do things on purpose – with the *intent* of making something happen – they can have the experience of things happening in ways that are coordinated with their states and behaviors. The more stable and dependable the caregiving environment is, the smoother is this recognition process.

Even in the second 3 months of life the infant is not yet capable of intentional behavior. By this time, however, infants are alert and awake much of the time, are able to better direct their behavior, and the behavioral repertoire has greatly expanded. Caregivers and infants have learned much about fitting together. Something very critical can now happen. Infant needs and behaviors become easier to read. The attentive and attuned caregiver can know what an infant behavior means, even though the infant really does not. For example, parent and infant are engaged in face-to-face play. Over time the excitement builds up. If the arousal level becomes too high, the infant has a built-in tendency it can now exercise. It turns away. The attuned caregiver can read this as a signal, creating a moment of meaning between them. The caregiver backs off, waiting for the infant to re-engage. In a few moments the infant re-engages and the play continues. A simple thing; yet, when a cumulative experience, the meaning is profound. These are the very roots of the sense of being known and of having agency – the ability to act on the world.

By treating the infant's behavior as a signal, the caregiver is creating the signal–response pattern that becomes a key organizing meaning in development. I have a need. I act on the environment. It responds to my need. Long before the child can know this in an intellectual way, it is an understanding deep in the psyche. Sensitive care is a visceral training program in the capacity to organize and contain behavior.

The Emergence of the Intentional Infant

In the second half-year of life, infants play a dramatically larger role in the creation of meaning. They move toward being co-creators with their caregivers. They not only react to the lead of the caregiver but at times initiate play and other forms of interaction.

In contrast to the first half-year of life, infants in the second-half year clearly have intentions. Distress in the first months of life may build to the point that we describe it as an angry cry, whereas a 9-month-old pursuing an object that has rolled under a sofa may quickly become clearly angry. The baby *wants that* ball. More certain evidence is that infants at this age will change their behavior if a goal is not achieved. If for instance, they want contact, they may vocalize to the caregiver. If there is no response they may call again, cry out, lift up their arms as a signal to be picked up, or, ultimately, crawl over and cling on. Having such intentions means that they can now experience in a more direct way if their signals are effective or not; whether *they* themselves effective or not.

The infant in the second half-year is qualitatively more advanced than the younger infant. Their profound improvements in memory enable them not only to respond to events in terms of past experiences but also to anticipate the future. The infant that laughs uproariously when attempting to stuff a cloth back into his mother's mouth does so because he remembers the incongruity and *anticipates* that he can create the incongruity again. Likewise, the infant that cries immediately the second time a stranger enters the lab remembers what happened before and knows the stranger is going to try to pick him up again (and he does not like it). Past meanings can now influence current meanings, as can expectations about the immediate future. This is a huge developmental leap forward.

Engagement or investment is the core of meaning at any age. What changes with development is what will pull for engagement and the nature of the connection. Compare the difference between a 5-month-old and a 10-month-old in the following example. When parents put a cloth in their mouths in front of a 5-month-old, it will certainly get the infant's attention. The infants will look steadily, then likely grasp the cloth and put it in their own mouth to chew (as they do with most things at this age). The 10-month-old shows a strikingly different reaction. The child likely will look and smile, then grab the cloth from the parent's mouth. Then laughing uproariously, they will try to stuff it back into the parent's mouth. They are not only more strongly engaged, they are making connections far beyond the 5-month-old, and thus the emotion. They grasp the incongruity of the parent doing this unusual behavior and are amused by it, adding to the well of shared positive feelings.

Alternations in the parent's face have great significance to the infant at this age. As noted by scholars as diverse as Freud and Jerome Bruner (2002), infants in the second-half year are universally intrigued and amused by the game of peek-a-boo. As Freud pointed out in describing the "wo" (where) "da" (there) game of his grandchild, the disappearance and reappearance of his mother was of great significance, because of the way the threat of separation is so quickly dissolved. Or, consider another example – why is an infant of this age so delighted by a parent pretending to suck on their baby bottle? What sophisticated thinking! They know that it is *their* bottle and that this is not something usual for the parent to do. The situation is saturated with meaning for the infant. Moreover, all of these types of events have more meaning when the acter is an attachment figure. The hysterical laughter of infants to the peek-a-boo game, to the mother sucking on their baby bottle, or to the parent walking like a penguin is a reflection of the degree of meaningfulness.

These increased capacities are closely tied to the emotional life of the infant. It is in the second half-year that infants become capable of genuine surprise, fear, anger, and attachment. True surprise can appear only when there are clearly developed expectations. An infant in the first 6 months may look at an incongruous event longer, as researchers have shown. It is a kind of "something is up here" response. But the sudden, eyes-wide-open, "whoa, this can't happen response" is only seen by about 10 months of age. When we made a toy disappear through a small trap door on a highchair tray, one infant even pounded on the tray and leaned to look on the floor. This is a leap in understanding and meaning.

This is also one reason that things like mother pretending to suck on the baby's bottle or walking like a penguin are so funny to 10-month-olds. They violate expectations and the baby gets the incongruity. Likewise, fear, in contrast to wariness or distress, requires the evaluation of threat or dislike by the infant. It is not just that I don't get this. I get it and I don't like it. It scares me. Finally, as we will discuss in Chapter 4, attachment is the outcome of a lengthy developmental process, terminating in discriminating particular people, becoming aware of their permanence in one's world, and recognizing their special place in responding to one's intentions. Forming specific attachments really is not possible in the very first months of life.

Prototypes for Meaning

Attentive caregivers respond to the reflexes and other automatic behaviors of infants in the first weeks, treating them as "signals" of needs and desires long before the infant has intentional thought. Across the early weeks, these responses are honed and improved, as caregivers learn to "read" their particular infants. Thereby, they help the infants establish basic patterns of state and arousal regulation. These patterns are early prototypes for meaning making.

The prototypes for meaning making are greatly elaborated in the second half year. While orchestration is still in the hands of caregivers, they now can respond to the more deliberate signals of the infant; that is, to their intentional behavior. The sense that one's purposeful intentions will be responded to positively is a core foundation for basic meanings regarding the emergent self. Across development what will pull for engagement and the nature of the connections that can be made by the child will change dramatically. Meaning making capacities and the network of meanings will greatly expand. But basic prototypes for meaning are often conserved and carried forward from infancy. They provide a core around which the subsequent networks of meaning may be constructed.

Development is very rapid in infancy and throughout the early years of life. And, in the early years especially, this development is scaffolded by the child's primary social relationships. The child's behavior, feelings, and perceptions are centered around these relationships. In addition to physiological maturation of the child, it is these relationships that prompt the rapid growth.

Experiences during this period don't merely set the stage for later meaning making; very new kinds of experiences are now possible and are internalized in a new way. By the end of the first year, the child can recognize the parent as a haven of safety when they are frightened, and thereby acquire the meaning that they are safe, that social relationships are supportive, and that they are effective in coping with fear. Whether angry, afraid, or just generally distressed, they can begin to learn that re-establishing equilibrium is possible. Other infants, of course, can routinely have very different experiences that lead to different foundational beliefs, depending on the quality of the attachment relationship that is being formed. It is to these vital attachment relationships that we turn next.

CHAPTER 4

Attachment Theory
The Rise of Meaning in Psychology

Before the advent of attachment theory, developmental psychology had been in a rather sterile period. All behavior was thought to be the result of simple associative learning or else built up bit by bit through reinforcement of discrete actions. It had even been argued that there was no such thing as personality because people behaved in different ways in different situations (due to varying situational cues and reinforcement contingencies) – so no consistency, no personality. The child's tie to the mother was explained as being due to her association with feeding. And individual "attachment" behaviors (smiling, vocalizing, proximity seeking) were viewed as simply gradually built up through reinforcement by parents. Emotions were explained similarly. If children are frequently angry, then this anger must have been rewarded. There was really no search for the coherent, feeling, thinking person. Such a search was deemed fruitless. Meaning had no place.

There is no need for us to consider extensively the illogic and many flaws in these historical positions. Of course people behave differently in different situations. To behave the same way in all situations would be incoherent. And because individuals *are* coherent there is individual patterning to these variations *across* situations, as Will Fleeson (2001) has shown. As we will discuss in later chapters, one of the key markers of emotional health is the ability to flexibly adjust behavior to the demands and opportunities presented by different situations.

Simple reinforcement is not an adequate account of behavior, though it is the way many specific actions are learned and how, once learned, many specific behaviors are maintained. Reinforcement is powerful, but it does not account for development. Harlow's famous studies with surrogate-raised rhesus monkeys showed that these infants preferred a cloth "mother" they could hug rather than the wire "mother" that fed them. This preference is not well explained by reinforcement. Further, many studies showed that emotions emerge and are expressed without any major role for reinforcement. As presented in Chapter 2, young infants smiled at the toy clown simply after being exposed to it several times, and then stopped smiling after a few more exposures. This is impossible to explain by reinforcement. It is explained because this event acquired meaning through the infant's effort to make sense of it.

Mid-twentieth century paradigms were inadequate for understanding how and why individuals develop the worldviews they do; how a personal network of meanings is formed. Developmental psychology needed a radically different approach. Attachment theory was just that. It was a developmental theory rooted in biology, in which meaning had a central place. Likewise, the methods and research carried out to implement this theory also had meaning at their core.

In this new perspective, attachment is a unique biological system, independent of feeding. As psychoanalyst and scholar John Bowlby pointed out when he formulated attachment theory, humans are born extraordinarily vulnerable and dependent, and they require a long period to mature. They cannot protect themselves. So, in addition to being fed, they urgently need to be protected. The attachment system evolved to solve this problem. Infants are disposed to attract caregiver attention, and later to seek proximity, especially when alarmed. At the same time caregivers are disposed to respond to and protect infants. Without such a system human infants could not survive. Parents do not need to reinforce proximity; this tendency is built into the infant, just as attraction to infants is built into parents. If someone is there to be with the infant in an ongoing way, the infant *will* become attached to that person, even if they are physically mistreated. It is very difficult to explain the attachments of abused children using reinforcement theory. But it is no problem from within the framework of attachment theory. It is a biological imperative. Infants have no choice but to be attached to the individuals who care for them.

This is a powerful biological system. It is why even as adults we at times feel apprehensive when alone. We are more at ease when connected with others. For infants and young children, separation from attachment figures is inherently anxiety provoking, especially in unfamiliar surroundings. These are "natural cues for danger." This is why separating young immigrant children from their parents at the United States–Mexico border, as was done in 2018, was so egregious and immoral. The situation of these children could not have been more unfamiliar. Such separations were certain to be traumatic, with lasting impacts quite possible.

Attachment as a Relationship Concept

In addition to being a concept rooted in biology, attachment is also inherently a relationship concept. It is about a specific emotional connection *between* the infant and a particular caregiver. In fact, Bowlby defined attachment as *the* emotional bond between infant and caregiver. In contrast to the earlier concept of dependency, attachment is not a trait of the infant. Attachments with different parents may be qualitatively distinctive, each being based on the nature of the interactive history. The infant may in some cases even be securely attached with one but anxiously attached to the other. And, of course, primary attachments may be with adoptive parents, grandparents, or others who rear the child. In any case it is based on the building of a relationship over time.

The entire system is governed by an integration of emotion and cognition. Once an attachment relationship has formed, feelings of distress will prompt the infant to seek contact with the attachment figure. Absence of such reactions is an aberration in the developing system.

The attachment relationship is a deeply meaningful relationship. Consider a video of 12-month-old Tina in our observation room, as part of the Minnesota Longitudinal Study of Risk and Adaptation. She is shown on the floor playing with an array of toys, while her mother sits in a chair across the room. Tina picks up several toys, examining them closely, one by one. She next picks up a toy elephant and looks at it intently. Then her eyes widen and a look of wonder and joy spreads across her face. Everyone viewing this video knows exactly what will happen next. She turns and shows the toy to her mother! This pattern of behavior makes visible the intangible – the emotional connection that is the attachment relationship. She remembers and knows full well that her mother is there, and she expects her mother to respond. Her mother nods and smiles back. It is remarkable how automatically the baby shares her joy. This reaction is based upon a history of emotional sharing. Later in this observational session, Tina is distressed following a brief separation. When her mother returns, Tina immediately crawls to her, reaches to be picked up, and plasters her body against her mother. She settles completely and then returns her attention to the room. She knows exactly where her security lies. It is obvious to all observers that this is a special, vital relationship.

Like all relationships, the attachment relationship develops over time. In the early months, both attention and smiles from infants can be elicited from a wide variety of persons. Then infants become more discriminating, with smiles readily elicited by familiar persons and more sober (and perhaps even wary) reactions to unfamiliar persons. Finally, in the second half-year there is an elaborated system of emotions, the concept of person permanence, and the capacity to organize behavior around specific persons. The specific attachment emerges. This is true for all cognitively typical infants in all cultures. Variations in the quality of this relationship depend on the interactive history with the particular caregiver, but all infants become attached to persons who care for them through this process.

Learning is important in this position. But the learning that is emphasized is not the piecemeal learning of specific behaviors; rather, it is learning to organize a diverse array of possible behaviors around the caregiver so as to promote the infant's wellbeing. It is an experiential, procedural learning about relationships. When young infants are picked up and given care when they cry, they do not learn to cry more. They learn that their signals will receive a response. By the end of the first year, when they have other ways to signal needs, they in fact may cry *less* than infants whose early cries were not answered. They have not learned to be "crybabies"; they have learned that their caregivers will respond, that they are potent, and that relationships have a reciprocating nature.

Most infants are "secure" in their attachments. This does not mean that they are tightly attached. All infants raised by someone have durable attachments. It means that these infants are secure in the sense that they are confident in the reliability and responsiveness of the caregiver. They *know* their caregiver is there for them, a consistent source of reassurance and comforting. It also means that the relationship is effective. One can see all of this readily in the infant's behavior. In play, the infant may reach a toy back over the shoulder without even turning to look that the parent will take it. When distressed, the infant immediately seeks out the parent. The infant's confidence allows it to explore away from the caregiver in circumstances of low stress and to be quickly settled and reassured when distressed (so they can return again to exploration). Such a balance between attachment and exploration promotes the development of competence in the world.

Some infants have "anxious" attachments with their caregivers. This means that these infants are not confident regarding the parent's responsiveness to their signals. If parents have been inconsistent or haphazard in care provided, the infant becomes uncertain that the parent will respond should a need arise. The infant must then hover near them and seek reassurance at the slightest provocation. They may well have difficulty truly settling. They often struggle against contact even when they want it.

This is referred to as the "resistant" pattern of attachment, and it rather obviously compromises exploration.

Alternatively, the parent may have been chronically emotionally cold, or chronically rebuffed the infant's bids for close contact, so that the infant learns to stifle attachment needs whenever possible. Beyond being doubtful about parent response, these infants in fact expect that they will *not* respond, especially when tender needs are aroused. Thus, they may fail to go to the parent when stressed. This is the "avoidant" pattern of attachment and compromises exploration in a different way, because the infant has difficulty using the parent as a resource when distressed.

Finally, as described by Mary Main and Erik Hesse, some parents pose an even greater challenge to their infants, because they enter into dissociative states and/or are otherwise directly frightening to their infants. This creates an irresolvable paradox. All human infants are motivated to flee from the source of fear, but, in addition, they are motivated to flee *to* the attachment figure for protection. It is impossible for infants to flee *from* the source of fear and *to* the parent when they are one and the same. This leads to what is called "disorganized" attachment, a pattern that will be discussed fully in later chapters.

Given this perspective on the formation of attachment, there are two central claims made by attachment theory: (1) That patterns of interaction between infant and caregiver become internalized and organized into various patterns of attachment; and (2) these variations in attachment provide the foundation for later personality; that is, the organized meaning system of the individual. Both of these claims have been amply supported by research. As will be discussed next, the concept of meaning is central to the entire process, from defining crucial features of infant–parent interaction, to defining features of attachment and assessing them, and to selecting later outcomes for confirmation of the theory.

Capturing Meaning in Parent–Infant Interaction

Mary Ainsworth, a gifted researcher with a discerning clinical eye, was one of the first to clearly see and describe the nature of the attachment relationship between human infants and their caregivers (Waters et al., 2024). In her work she stressed the importance of looking at patterns of behavior and the surrounding context in order to see the meaning of parent–infant interactions. One of the major findings in attachment research is that differences in quality of an infant's attachment are not well predicted by frequencies of any particular maternal behavior.

How frequently one talks to a baby, how frequently one picks up a baby, or even how much one holds a baby do not predict the degree of attachment security. Rather, the key is the degree to which parental behaviors are sensitive and responsive to the infant's needs and signals and the way in which these behaviors are coordinated with, or interfere with, the flow of the infant's behavior.

When she conducted her field observations in Uganda, Ainsworth's initial plan was to focus solely on how the attachment relationship unfolded. She had expected that all of the infants would be secure in their attachments. After all these mothers routinely carried their babies in slings, and the popular stereotype was that the breast was continuously accessible to infants in that culture. On the surface, therefore, it would seem that responsiveness would be guaranteed. What she in fact found was variation in the degree to which infants were secure or anxious in their attachments. The surprises did not end there. Not only was the stereotype about breastfeeding inaccurate, length of breastfeeding per se was not related to attachment security; rather, most relevant was the degree to which the mother took pleasure in the feedings – what it meant to her.

Moreover, general measures of warmth or quantitative measures such as how much the mother talked to the baby did not forecast security. What mattered most was whether parental behaviors were attuned and responsive to the infant's signals of intent. The sensitive caregiver "... is exquisitely attuned to B's signals; and responds to them promptly and appropriately. She is able to see things from B's point of view; her perceptions of his signals and communications are not distorted by her own needs and defenses" (Ainsworth, 1967, p. 361). Rather than simply doing lots of things, they do the right thing at the right time. Ainsworth also found that these sensitive mothers were excellent observers and reporters regarding their babies. They *knew* their babies and, perhaps most notably, delighted in them. Ainsworth's work was a precursor to the current emphasis in the attachment field on the state of the parent's mind and parent ability to see, reflect on, and attend to the mind of the baby.

Parents described by Ainsworth's scales as sensitive are not only emotionally invested in their infants but are also alert to their signals, accurately interpret the meaning of the behavior, and respond in a congruent manner. Other parents fail to notice the signal, distort its meaning, and/or respond inappropriately or ineffectively. They may simply not do the right things, or they do all of the right things, but not at the right time. The sensitive caregiver "picks up the baby when he seems to wish it and puts him down when he wants to explore." Those with less sensitivity try to "socialize with him when he is hungry, play with him when he is tired, or feed him when he is trying to initiate social interaction." Responses of sensitive caregivers are to "the baby's own timing and not the mother's timing." In short, sensitive caregivers recognize the *meaning* of the infant behavior and respond to that meaning. This is the beginning of deep-seated feelings of being seen and being known in the infant.

In Ainsworth's later Baltimore study there were also many illustrations of the importance of responding to the meaning of the infant's behavior, in contrast to sheer amount of interaction. As a poignant example, mothers of infants later found to have avoidant attachments held their infants on average as much as mothers of those infants later found to be secure. But, specifically, when the infant came to them and *sought* to be picked up and held – that is, signaled its emotional need – these parents often rebuffed them. It is when these infants express need that parents turn them away; at other times they do hold them. A clinical interpretation of this rejecting behavior is that these parents are somehow threatened by the expressions of need, perhaps because to recognize it would be to acknowledge their own unmet needs for nurturance. Because of their potent procedural memories, the infants learn to later withhold their own needs for contact and so fail to go to their mothers when stressed. In the histories of those infants with secure attachments, mothers routinely responded to the baby's desire for contact. These babies later quickly seek and are readily reassured by contact when they are threatened. Picking up a baby who is crying or who has arms outstretched has different meaning than picking up a baby who wants to play. The amount of holding overall may be similar, but there is a great difference in meaning of being held when it suits the parent and being held when it is what the infant needs.

Measuring the Quality of Attachment

This same attention to meaning characterizes Ainsworth's scales for assessing attachment behavior of infants in her laboratory procedure, called the Strange Situation, and in her overall scheme for assessing the quality of the infant–parent attachment. In looking at behavior Ainsworth provided an alternative to either counting frequencies of discrete behaviors (for example, how often an infant looks at the mother) or subjective, overall ratings without specific behavioral referents. Counting specific behaviors, while easy to do, turns out to have limited value in capturing the quality of the relationship and little or no stability across time or situations.

Subjective ratings are largely unreliable. Therefore, a third alternative was needed.

Close, careful observation is at the core of the Ainsworth system, but observers attend to the meaning of behavior in addition to simple occurrence or frequency; that is, one attends to the timing and context of the behavior, including other behaviors that occur with it or before or after it. Ainsworth's scales group infant's behavior as similarly strong or weak based on *similarity of intent*. For example, after a 3-minute separation from the parent in the laboratory, one baby approaches halfway to the adult and then looks up and waits for the parent to come pick them up. Another looks, smiles broadly, vocalizes, and shows a toy but does not immediately approach and does not get picked up. This baby does approach the adult several times over the next few minutes to share a toy or briefly play beside them. As different as these reactions are, they *mean* the same thing in terms of desire for physical contact. Both of these infants show the same moderate degree of need and desire for proximity or contact in this situation (scored 3), and they show no avoidance of the parent. Neither is as strong as the case of an infant who cries, leans forward, and reaches strongly for the parent (clearly indicating a desire to be picked up, even though not approaching) or the infant who *immediately goes the whole way* but then waits for pick-up (both scored 5). Stronger desire for contact is indicated by an infant that fully approaches *and* reaches for pick up (scored 6) or one that goes the whole way and wraps arms around the mother's legs (7, the highest score). It is the infant's desire for proximity and contact that is being scored, not approaching per se. All of these are distinctive from cases in which the infant merely looks at the parent or merely gives a brief smile.

This same approach is used for all of the scales coded in the reunion episodes of Ainsworth's Strange Situation procedure, including the crucial "avoidance" and "resistance" scales. For example, after one of the brief separations in the laboratory room, low level avoidance may be shown by looking at the mother (or other attachment figure) when she comes in, then *briefly looking away*, then becoming responsive; or by *not looking* at the mother briefly and then soon becoming responsive. Both of these examples would be scored 3 because they show the same modest degree of withholding attention; they mean the same thing. A notably higher score (5) would be given to both of the following examples: (a) The infant gives the mother no greeting despite her efforts to gain his attention. After 15 seconds he *does* give her his attention but remains fairly unresponsive; or (b) The infant immediately greets the mother and starts to approach her; then he markedly turns away and ignores her efforts to gain his attention for some time. Again, it is the degree of withholding that is scored, not simply whether the infant greets or not. Neither of these examples is scored as high as the infant who pays little or no attention to the mother for an extended period (scored 6), or the infant that behaves in this way *despite* the mother's strong efforts to gain his attention (7). Note again, that what is being scored is the degree to which the infant is withholding expression of attachment behavior, as well as the role of context. The difference in judging a 6 and a 7 hinges on noting the strength of the mother's efforts, a key part of the context of the withholding behavior.

In contrast to avoidance, resistance refers to fighting against contact with the attachment figure, even though the infant obviously wants it. It is scored with the same attention to meaning. For example, two subtle signs of anger, such as a little kicking of the feet while being held or dropping a toy offered by the mother while in her arms are both scored 3. Repeated rejection of toys shows a higher level of resistance (5), but so too does squirming to be put down after being picked up by the mother, only to seek pick-up again. At this level, it is clear that the infant's anger is interfering with becoming settled. The highest scores are reserved for conspicuous and ongoing anger, such as crying hard and arching the back while being held, strong kicks of the legs, throwing down toys while crying and the like. They are obviously fighting against the contact they need. Different infants will show different combinations of behavior, and it takes weeks of training to do these assessments properly. At the center of the training is what the behavior means. Does the infant's behavior promote or interfere with the contact he needs?

The meaning of behavior, derived from the way it is organized, is also the basis for judging the overall security of the attachment relationship. It is not whether a baby approaches the mother, or cries, or engages in play, but when and how it does these things, what other behaviors are also present, and how behavior shifts across contexts. Each of the babies described when we discussed contact seeking may well be equally secure in their attachments, given that other observations confirm that they are each getting and effectively using *the contact they need*. On the other hand, some babies who have been distressed may start to strongly approach the parent, and then markedly turn away. While this may indicate strong desire for contact, the approach accompanied by the clear turn away means something very different than a moderate interest in contact by itself. The abrupt inhibiting of the approach when an infant has been distressed suggests a withholding of attachment feelings and suggests an avoidant attachment organization.

Judging avoidance requires careful attention to the meaning of the behavior. Specific behaviors that appear quite similar on the surface can mean quite different things. Consider a baby who, after starting to approach the caregiver, veers off to pick up a toy. Is this infant cutting off attention to the caregiver or not? This can only be determined by examining more of the context. If the baby simply goes to the toy, fiddles with it aimlessly with no further attention to the parent, this would be a clear indicator of avoidance. The meaning of the behavior is redirecting the attention away from the attachment figure. On the other hand, were this a toy the pair had been playing with earlier in the session, and if the infant immediately upon getting to the toy picked it up, turned and showed it to the mother with a smile or vocalization, this can all be seen as a continuation of the infant's desire for interaction. In the absence of stress, starting to approach the mother with a toy, then being distracted by another object and veering off to get it to show to the mother does not suggest avoidance or defensiveness, because in this case the infant follows through on his intention to engage the mother.

The central question concerns the infant's confidence in the responsiveness of the caregiver, especially with regard to addressing emotional needs. When an infant is confident that, should some threat arise, it can turn to the caregiver and expect to get the needed support, it is then free to explore the environment. Thus, a secure attachment relationship is effective in promoting exploration, discovery, and learning how to function in the environment. Attachment and exploration are in balance. Given the emphasis on the interplay between exploration and seeking proximity, contact, or reassurance from the caregiver, it is clear why simply examining the frequency of certain behaviors cannot be revealing. Infants that hover by caregivers at all times, and infants who fail to go to them when distressed both compromise exploration. The infant that plays readily in the absence of stress, but actively seeks comforting and support when distressed, is optimally able to explore because it is effective in using the attachment figure to regulate arousal. Moreover, contact seeking can be done in a number of ways (vocalizing, reaching, crawling to the parent). Sometimes even a mere look at the smiling mother will suffice. *What these diverse behaviors have in common is their meaning.* They mean the infant unambivalently desires connection and is able to use that connection in support of exploration.

When playing, some babies engage their parents with frequent showing of toys. This means something very different from hovering and wanting to be picked up in the absence of any external stress. Both infants are attached and interested in their caregivers, but the latter pattern suggests anxiety about the relationship; that is, uncertainty regarding parental availability and responsiveness. It predicts great difficulty settling after the brief separations.

Other babies may play contentedly for some time with only occasional looks at the mother. This relative absence of looking means something very different than looking away from and ignoring mother's offerings right upon reunion when the child has been stressed by separation (behavior not shown to a stranger). In neither case does the baby interact with great frequency with the attachment figure, but only the second failing to look is avoidance, because it reveals a cutting off of feelings at a time when feelings clearly are aroused. Contented play in the absence of stress may simply mean the infant is comfortable. The meaning of being occupied with toys can only be determined by the way the behavior is organized in the rest of the session.

Many 12-month-old babies, including those with clearly secure attachment relationships, attend to and engage a stranger, even smiling and showing toys in the mother's presence before the brief separations. This tells us little. It can mean lack of interest in the mother, but it can also mean that the infant feels comfortable enough to explore and engage the stranger. By itself, it certainly does not indicate an anxious attachment. However, when frightened or distressed, clear preference for the attachment figure should occur. Infants secure in their attachment show a clear preference for interaction and/or contact with attachment figures *when distressed*.

Thus, it is the meaning of the infant's behavior that allows us to judge the quality of the relationship. Remarkably, even though the behavioral repertoire and the cognitive abilities of the infant change dramatically over time, the assessed quality of the attachment often remains the same (Waters, 1978). A 12-month-old is likely to be distressed by the separation and reunion procedures we use, and many will desire ample physical contact upon reunion. If such contact seeking is effective in smoothly alleviating the infant's distress, a secure attachment relationship is reflected. This same child, at 18 months, may be minimally distressed and may simply wish to interact and show toys to the parent. If this is done actively and effectively, promoting exploration, it shows the same secure attachment, even though all of the surface behavior may be different. These behavior profiles have the same meaning; namely that the infant is confident in the availability and support of the parent. While complex, following training such judgments can be made with high reliability using the Ainsworth system.

The Reality and Power of Relationships

A major discovery in the physical world was that the behavior of molecules is not simply determined by the constituent atoms, but rather by the relationships among the atoms as manifest in their particular geometry. Two molecules with the same atoms could have different qualities. Such findings moved physics beyond a purely atomistic view of the world toward a view emphasizing process. In the same way, it is not particular behaviors of the caregiver that lead to a secure attachment but the way the behavior is fitted to the needs, mood, and behavior of the infant. And it is not the set of behaviors manifest by infants that reveals the quality of the attachment, but the way the infant behavior is organized around the caregiver. It is the relationships we are studying, not merely the individuals.

The power of this relationship perspective can be shown by demonstrating the stability of attachment relationships between 12 and 18 months (Waters, 1978). This stability in the quality of the relationship occurred despite the fact that the behavioral repertoire of infants changes dramatically during this period and behavior is expressed quite differently. It is the core meanings of the relationship that are preserved. Infants that were confident in the relationship remain confident though they show this in different ways. The relationship and the meanings can change, of course. Our work showed that, when family stress declined, parents became more responsive and infants became more confident when they had anxious attachments before (Vaughn et al., 1979). (This is one reason we will point out the inadvisability of blaming parents for child problems at various places in this book. The context of parenting must be taken into account.)

As we will discuss more fully in subsequent chapters, it is also the quality of the relationship that predicts later child behavior, not specific behaviors of infants independent of context and meaning. Beyond the behavioral expressions of infant and parent, it is the organization and interplay of their joint behaviors that is most significant. Close relationships show a coherence that at times is even beyond the coherence of the participating individuals. From infant attachment assessments, which focus on how *infants* organize their behavior around caregivers, one can predict later parent behavior, as well as child behavior, and even behavior of parents with subsequent children and behavior of siblings. This is all because the relationship is being captured.

The main point is this: Before there is an organized personality, there is an organized caregiving network around the infant, with attachment figures as the center. It is this organization that is the prototype for what will become the self. This is despite the fact that these early relationship experiences lie outside of consciousness. None of us are able to consciously remember what we experienced in the first 2 years of our lives. It is not just that we are unable to report on our memories. They simply are not there in verbal or symbolic form, but only in the form of emotionally salient procedural memories.

It is not possible to recall any specific instances when you were an infant or young toddler of turning to your parent with apprehension and receiving a smile and nod of reassurance (or not); or of being frightened and seeking and finding contact and comforting or being turned away. It's not possible to remember specific times when joy was shared or you encountered a blank face or even a disdainful look. But the repeating pattern of such events is internalized as a sequence of behavioral and emotional experiences, as a "script" for the self in relationships. This is the power of procedural memory even prior to well-developed, long-term event memory.

The lack of conscious memory certainly does not mean that what we experienced is of no consequence or left no legacy. As we will show in Chapter 10, one can predict how parents will treat their own toddlers based on assessments made when they themselves were 2-years-old, when verbal memory was quite limited. The case can even be made that preverbal experience in ways has more power than later experience. Being unable to consciously remember these experiences means that they cannot be examined or directly modified.

Because development is "cumulative," always building on what was previously there, early experience has a special place in the formation of our inner worldviews. As we will discuss thoroughly in Parts III and IV, changes in world views can happen at any age. For example, in the Minnesota study, we found that when parents reported increases in social support some children who had been anxiously attached as infants were thriving in kindergarten. Nonetheless, certain basic expectations and "attitudes" begin to be laid down in the early years, and these impact how later experiences are engaged, interpreted, and reacted to. Moreover, early experiences exercise a "tuning" effect on the central nervous system itself, conditioning stress reactivity and basic capacities for regulation of arousal.

According to Bowlby, two of the major meanings that come out of infancy concern expectations regarding caregivers and expectations regarding self – two sides of the same coin. If my caregivers have been consistently responsive, I come to expect that they *will be* responsive. Since this is a core of my interpersonal experience, by generalization I will expect responsiveness from others. At the same time, since my caregivers have been responsive to *my actions*, I come to expect that my actions will be effective. This is the very foundation for a more general sense of efficacy or competence, a core meaning that begins to be established even in the first year of life. Since knowledge of caregiver responsiveness grants confidence to explore the environment, emerging competence is also reinforced by experiences of mastery in the object world.

We would add to Bowlby's account that, in learning about self and other, the infant is also evolving a basic understanding about how relationships work. When one is in need the other responds, or, in contrast, when one is in need the other rejects or exploits vulnerability. Again, this is not at first a conscious knowing but a deep emotional knowing. The emotional knowing is the developmental prototype for the later cognitive/emotional knowing. It was this premise that allowed us to predict individual differences in empathy in later years. Through responsiveness to need, one does not learn only the role of the needy one but a pattern of relating.

Thus, among the early core meanings that infants in supportive relationships acquire are that there is predictability in the world, that others can be counted on, that I am able to draw upon others, and that relationships are valuable. When significant others respond accurately to the *meanings* of the infant's intentions and behaviors, this affirms their sense of reality. It is nothing less than the foundation for a solid grasp of reality in later life.

For some infants, of course, experience teaches that the world is unpredictable or predictably rejecting; that others are inconsistently available or perhaps especially unavailable when my needs for tender care are acute; that my efforts to reach out will be frustrated; that I am unworthy of care; or that relationships are fraught with difficulty or even beyond me.

Moreover, for those who have experienced a chronically emotionally unavailable caregiver or who have been repeatedly rebuffed when seeking tender care, there is a tendency to cut themselves off from certain feelings or states, to not attend to them when they arise, and ultimately to even avoid things reminiscent of those states and circumstances that may arouse them. On the other hand, for those who experienced markedly inconsistent, haphazard care, they may be able to attend to states of anxiety, threat, and distress but be unable to reconcile or resolve them so that maturation is compromised. All of this is the legacy of early relationships.

CHAPTER 5

Toddlerhood
The Meaning of Me

A 22-month-old is playing on the floor while his mother is chatting with a neighbor at a coffee table nearby. He makes his way over to some stairs and begins to go up. "Oh no you don't," says his mother as she hurries to retrieve him. Back at the toys, he watches the women briefly, then goes back to the stairs, takes one step up and looks back to his mother. As she stands up, he starts to scramble up the stairs again.

The major developmental task for every child is to discover how the world works and how they are to interact with it; in other words, to develop their own personal sense of reality. In infancy, this centers on learning to trust in caregiver responsiveness and, reciprocally, to establish a core sense that they are worthy of care. In the toddler period this learning takes a notable leap forward, due to the toddler's increased ability to author his or her own actions, their greater understanding of the intentions of others, and an awareness of conflict of others' intentions with their own. To negotiate this period of expanding autonomy, the child is highly dependent on emotional support, limits, and guidance from parents to ensure continued feelings of safety.

There is no doubt that the toddler in the scenario above knew that his mother did not want him to go up the stairs. He tested out what would happen if he did it anyway. This common, everyday situation illustrates each of our four themes regarding meaning. First of all, no one has to train a 2-year-old to explore what will happen if they do something contrary. It is part of the inherent motive to seek meaning, though now at a level far beyond that of an infant. Likewise, seeking meaning remains an active process, but in a new way. After all, we call them "toddlers" because of their greater mobility. They don't wait for experiences to come to them; they go and seek them.

Further, the transactional nature of development – the interplay between meaning and experience – is well revealed by the limit-seeking of the toddler. Depending on how consistent and reliable the caregiver has been historically, the toddler more or less quickly comes to believe that he or she will hold the line now; that is, what the limits provided by the caregiver mean depends on the history of meanings between the two of them. At the same time, caregivers that are clear and firm with toddlers (without being harsh) will actually deepen the trust that the child has in the relationship, either reinforcing or altering past meanings. Likewise, caregivers that are notably haphazard or inconsistent in setting limits may erode credibility that was already established, shaking the child's confidence in the relationship. Such changes in experience can even alter the basic view of reality; that is how things are and my place in that. So past experience shapes what these current experiences mean to the child, while the current experiences mutually impact the developing network of meanings.

Finally, the most important meanings during this and every period are social in nature. The interactions between toddler and caregivers provide the arenas where the most salient meanings occur. The child in our scenario is seeking and incorporating meanings of profound importance.

The toddler period is a critical developmental transition, and this is one reason it is so important for the growth of personal meaning. This is the age when clear signs of self-awareness are apparent. For example, when shown their image in a mirror after someone has surreptitiously rubbed rouge on their nose, 10-month-old infants will simply look, or they might reach for the image in the mirror; toddlers will reach for the nose on their face! They know that it is "me" in the mirror. Such nascent self-awareness opens the door to the first meanings of what it means to *be* you. Can I actively engage the world while still feeling safe? Can I stay regulated or regain regulation following disruption? Can I count on support?

In addition, 2- and 3-year-olds also have a much greater understanding of intent. They *know* when they want something. They can also understand what you want. If an experimenter pretends to be reaching for something just out of reach, the toddler will push it toward them if they can. This is a virtually automatic reaction, so deeply ingrained is the human motivation for connection. This understanding of one's own intentions and the intentions of others profoundly changes relationships. As in our opening example, the toddler understands that his or her own goals may be counter to those of the parent. Thus, they can *deliberately* test out the consequences of contrary behavior.

This is a vulnerable period for the emerging self because the child has limited capacities for distinguishing parental responses to inappropriate *behavior* from general parental disapproval. This is the critical distinction between shame and guilt. With guilt, entailing a recognition of behavior that is violating a standard, there is a redress, including atoning for and changing the behavior. Guilt offers a way back. Four-year-old children can understand this, but toddlers cannot. When it is not the behavior but *you* that are bad, there is no way back; the situation is hopeless. When limits are capricious or harsh, the child can feel shameful and unworthy. This is the only conclusion the young child can reach. When expressions of feelings themselves are punished, the child can learn that feelings are bad and that to have them is to be bad.

Appropriate limits and guidelines, on the other hand, are reassuring to the child. Likewise, when 3-year-olds purposefully perturb the relationship and subsequently get it back in harmony, either through their own or parent initiative, such a process helps children establish what Louis Sander (1975) called "relationship constancy"; that is, the understanding that relationships are durable and can withstand conflict and disruption. This is a critical meaning to take forward. Children's experiences regarding such disruption and repair are, of course, quite variable (see, for example, Gianino & Tronick, 1988).

Guided Self-regulation

> Thus, the child walks with his eyes fixed on the mother's face, not the difficulties in his way. He supports himself by the arms that do not hold him and constantly strives towards the refuge in his mother's embrace, little suspecting that at the very same moment that he is emphasizing his need for her ... he is walking alone.
>
> Soren Kierkegaard (1938, p. 85)

One of the most crucial tasks for toddlers is to acquire some sense of control over feelings and actions. Without this they would simply be buffeted about by their increasingly active engagements and connections with the surround. While they cannot in fact generate all the actual control needed, they can have the *sense* of control when properly supported by caregivers. Such a sense of control will be severely compromised when parents themselves are out of control or tease, punish, or otherwise stimulate a child on the edge of losing control.

The toddler period is a bridge between rather complete parental regulation and later *self-regulation*. During the early months of infancy, regulation is largely in the hands of the caregivers. Young infants have important reflexes (for example, crying when aroused and recoiling from intense stimuli). But they cannot deliberately, explicitly signal their needs. Therefore, parents must interpret behaviors accurately (does that cry mean hunger or a need to be held? Does that turn to the side mean he needs a break?). By responding sensitively and effectively, a degree of emotion regulation can be achieved. As we saw in Chapter 3, in the second 6 months infants have more capacity to intentionally signal their needs (reaching to be picked up, pushing unwanted food away). Still, while regulation is at that point cooperative, parents continue to play the major role, granting meaning to the infant's gestures by responding to them.

It is in the toddler period that children show the first signs of self-regulation. They have a greater capacity to stay organized in the face of challenge and to persist despite difficulties. Even so, this goes forward best with active support and guidance from caregivers. So crucial is this "scaffolding" role of the parent that this period can be referred to as the period of "*guided* self-regulation." The paradox is that only within a supportive framework can the toddler be self-regulated. Yet this guided regulation is the crucial training – the prototype – that allows more genuine self-regulation to unfold. Some children emerge from this period believing they can regulate themselves, while others do not, even though in reality none do it alone. Future challenges, stressful experiences, and difficulties will mean something very different to children with different experiences as toddlers. A different reality is being created.

We know all of this from our longitudinal studies of parents and children. We have investigated both the origins of guided self-regulation and its later consequences. In two of our studies we viewed toddlers and their parents in a toy clean-up situation, to be discussed subsequently, and in tool problem situations of increasing challenge. The first tool problem was easy. There was a toy in a slot between two boards. It was a simple matter to poke out the toy with a stick that was provided. Most 2-year-olds solved it easily without help. Two problems were of intermediate difficulty. Both of these also involving getting toys with sticks, one for example requiring that two sticks be put together end-to-end to make a stick sufficiently long to reach a toy that was inside a tube. The final problem was quite difficult and beyond the ability of any 2-year-old to solve without help. Candy was in the bottom of a large, enclosed Plexiglas box in a cup attached to the end of a long board. There was a hole in the top of the box but the child's arm was too short to reach the candy. To solve the problem the child had to push down on the end of the board to make the candy come up through the hole. Alas, the end of this board was too far away for the child to reach the candy from there. The solution was to weight down the board with a wooden block, found on top of the box, and then go get the candy. This problem has too many steps, and the solution is too far removed from the goal to be understood by the toddler.

At some point in the series of problems, and certainly by this last problem, frustration is certain to build. The candy is tantalizingly just out of reach, and effort after effort will fail. But the child's parent is right there, directed to let the child try first "then give any help she (or he) needs." There is great variety in how this unfolds. Some children, of course, eagerly approach the problem and do try hard to solve it. It turns out that such enthusiasm and persistence are predicted by a history of responsive care. In responding to signals of the infant, infants are given the expectation that their efforts will bear fruit. Thus, they are persistent as toddlers. At the same time, sensitive parents see when the child is becoming too taxed or discouraged, and they take action. They perhaps draw closer (physically and emotionally) and provide a clue that settles and re-engages the child. For example, they may first direct the child to the end of the board that must be pushed down. Later they may say, "Maybe this block can help you." The key is to give just the clues and support needed to keep the child reasonably settled and on task without undercutting the child's own efforts. This maximizes the child's feelings of mastery. Also, responsive parents anticipate serious frustration, stepping in before the child's organization breaks down, because after that point it is very difficult for toddlers to take direction. Thus, sensitive parents take direct action when more subtle help isn't enough. When well-orchestrated, children not only deepen confidence in the parent's availability, they have an experience of solving the problem and of regulating themselves.

Time and again we observed toddlers working hard on the problems, trying one thing, then another, starting to be discouraged or frustrated, receiving help to stay with the task, and renewing their efforts. When they finally retrieved the candy they exclaimed with exuberance, "*I* take it out!" or "*I* did it." And truly in their inner experience *they* did do it. This is what dealing with this challenge meant to them. This is how they see themselves acting in the world. When occurring time and again, what a boost such experiences give to the child's belief that they are effective and that they can maintain control of themselves, all the while, as Kierkegaard said, not really knowing how dependent they had been on parental help. They now have a foundation for finding positive meaning in challenges in the future. It is not surprising that in our study such parental support predicted academic success far into the future and did so better than did parent or child IQ (Sroufe et al., 2005).

Variations in Toddler Experience

Parents by no means need to give perfect assistance. As Erikson (1963) said, children don't become neurotic because of frustration but from a lack of meaning to the frustration. So children can struggle, and parents can sometimes fail to do the right thing. They may be a bit late or early with their input, or their cues may be a bit unclear. But if the support is good enough the child has a positive experience. On the other hand, if support and guidance fall too short of the mark, the child's experience is compromised. Simply taking the easy way out and solving the problem for the child robs them of the opportunity to develop their own sense of agency. Withholding or delaying help too long dooms the child to failure. These are difficult, potentially frustrating tasks. The child cannot solve the most difficult problems alone. When parents fail to help, the child's belief in support and belief in him- or herself is eroded.

At times, it can be even worse. Some parents not only fail to offer help, they may deride the child's efforts or demean the child as a person. This deals a strong blow to the child's self-confidence. In other cases parents become frustrated, angry, and completely unregulated themselves. Since children learn not just from interactions but also from the models they see around them, such an experience curtails even the belief that self-regulation is possible. (It should be noted that our research revealed both historical and contemporary reasons for these lapses in parenting. In general, their own histories were troubled and/or they lacked adequate current supports for parenting.)

In our 2-year assessments we also saw examples of parent–child role reversal and even seductive behavior by parents. By this we mean either that the parent abdicated the parental role or – with some frequency in cases of mothers and boys – the parent actually was physically inappropriate or used sensuality as a means of controlling and manipulating the child. This was best seen in the toy clean-up task that preceded the tool problems. Toddlers of course generally do not want to stop playing with attractive toys and put them away on a shelf. We created this situation purposefully, and we viewed this task as taxing for the parents. But many stayed calm, clear, and firm, perhaps drawing physically nearer to the child to offer a further degree of emotional support. They were encouraging and positive. "That's right. Good job. Now put the barn up there." There frequently were hitches, starts and stops, but the job got done. Such clear, firm limits and support deepen the child's sense of trust.

In contrast, some parents were hapless, perhaps even giving up entirely. "I just can't make him do anything." Such abandonment is a breeding ground for anxiety, because the child is being left with a task that is too big for him- or herself.

Others got embroiled in battles and in the end the pair wound up squabbling like two children. Then there were those that used seduction as a technique. Often this would occur in the midst of a flurry of tactics – bribes, threats, pleas – in the absence of follow through. Then, in the midst of the child's continuing or escalating noncompliance, the mother might say, "Johnnnnnnny, come give momma a kiss," in a very syrupy voice. Then after sensually kissing the child she would coyly plea, "Now put that away for mommy." We also observed lots of inappropriate touching.

There was a striking parallel in these occurrences to the examples we saw of verbal abuse or physical punishment. One would see the tension building in the parent, gradually leaking out more and more through signs of frustration (disdainful sighs, tightened lips, less calm voice) and then the abusive or inappropriate behavior would spill out. It is noteworthy that independent ratings of the mothers exhibiting seductive behavior revealed that they were low on expressed warmth toward the child. Hugging a child who seeks you out when frustrated is simply being supportive. But interrupting a child who is working on a problem in an effort to get him to be affectionate with you, promising him a kiss if he will do what you want, or even grabbing him by the genitals, is seductive, not warm.

These sessions were video recorded with the mother's full knowledge. It is unlikely therefore that they saw anything inappropriate in their behavior. They at times said it was the only way to get the child to behave or simply blamed the child's misbehavior. In the case of seductive behavior, in particular, we often had the impression that they were unaware of what they were doing and would not even know how they had behaved. We believe that this is because such tendencies in the parents have origins from very early in their lives. They are carrying forward systems of meaning that lie outside of their awareness. We will discuss this further in Chapter 10.

These varied experiences for the toddler have notable implications for their emerging networks of meaning and the emerging sense of reality. Children experiencing boundary violations in any form can take forward the belief that it is the child's job to take care of the parents, rather than expecting care themselves. They may also learn that sensuality and sexual expression are tools for manipulating others and that sexuality and disparagement or aggression are connected. Moreover, many forms of boundary violation seriously disrupt regulation, due both to the inherently stimulating quality of many of these behaviors and the timing of their expression. Often the parental behavior occurs precisely at those times when the child is already at the limit of his or her capacities and beginning to lose control. This is when a child especially needs a steady, firm, and calm parental input. Instead, provocative stimulation – teasing, flirting, yelling at, disparaging – shoves them over the edge. It provides a "clinic" for regulation problems. Time and again these children experience that, when arousal is high, they will surely become disorganized, in contrast to those with sensitive parenting who come to believe that they can manage even such situations. So challenge, high arousal, and emotionality come to mean very different things to different children. It was predictable then that boundary violation on the part of parents was shown to be related to symptoms of Attention Deficit/Hyperactivity Disorder in subsequent years (Jacobvitz & Sroufe, 1987).

From Past Meaning to New Meaning

Developmental change is dramatic in the early years. Two-year-olds are qualitatively different than 1 year-olds, given their greatly increased motor skills, emerging language abilities, and sense of self. What is preserved from prior development is not so much ways of behaving but the meaning of past experiences. A child we will call Rafael at age 8 months would always reach both arms up with an exuberant smile when his mother approached. This was an almost automatic response but certainly conveyed an established expectation that his mother would respond. Then, at age 12 months, in the Strange Situation, we saw him manifest a similar meaning in two more advanced ways. First, while playing on the floor by his mother's feet, he picked up a toy and reached it back over his shoulder to his mother without even looking back. He simply knew she was there and would be attentive. Later, when distressed by the separation, he crawled to her at lightning speed and clambered up when she entered the room. These behaviors show a greater sense of purpose and agency but still the same expectation of responsiveness. Then, at age 2 years, the following was observed: Rafael was very good at climbing stairs but not so good at descending. We watched him ably ascend three steps onto a deck and walk rapidly across it. When he approached the other side, he glanced back toward his mother who was watching and said, "help." Rafael then turned his attention back to the steps and approached them, simply *knowing* his mother would assist.

Just as he automatically shared play or pleasure as a 1-year-old, and just as he trusted that contact with his mother would relieve his distress, now he just knew his mother was coming to help. He did not have to fuss or cry out or physically approach his mother. His newly acquired language behavior allowed him to signal his need in a new, advanced way. This is a dramatic development. What is preserved, however, is the meaning of a challenge. As earlier, he believes help is available, that his mother will respond, and that his actions to achieve assistance will be successful. Thus, it is the same relationship as a year before, *in terms of meaning*, but completely transformed in terms of behavior.

Two-year-olds, in general, respond to our laboratory problem situations in terms of previous meanings. Encountering a problem to be solved has different meaning for different toddlers and getting stuck when solving a problem has different meaning. Children who formed secure attachments in infancy, based on responsive care in the first year, enthusiastically engage the tool problems and more readily and effectively draw upon their parents as toddlers. Already by 2 years of age, challenging problems have begun to mean interesting opportunities for some children. They try to solve the problems on their own but, when they do get stuck, they turn to their parents for help. They follow their suggestions, obviously believing in this resource, as Mary Main also found (Main & Weston, 1981).

Of course all 2-year-olds are at times non-compliant, but this should not be the case when parent and child share the same goal. Our child on the stairs in the vignette at the beginning of this chapter may well have a secure history. One cannot know this from a singular example. It may have simply been a normal part of discovering what the rules are. Only if non-compliance is entrenched and supersedes other goals of the child would it suggest a problematic history.

Some children have already acquired doubts about their own capacity and about the helpfulness of parents. Those infants with histories of anxious/resistant attachment are more likely to quickly give up or become frustrated when working on the problems at 2 years of age. They have little belief in their own effectiveness. Likewise, only children who developed the avoidant attachment pattern in infancy (related to parental emotional unavailability and rejection) were ever observed to give up on the parent and seek help with the tool problems from the experimenter sitting across the room. For some toddlers, someone they don't know is a more likely source of help than are their parents.

Parent frustration and withdrawing of support from the child are also predictable from infancy. By assessing the workings of the relationship between infant and parent, one is able to predict the behavior of both partners in the toddler period.

Lest one be too critical of the parents who are struggling, it is important to know that those in our study who engaged in harsh treatment more often had histories of abuse themselves (as well as limited current support), while those mothers who engaged in seductive behavior with their sons had more often experienced sexual exploitation by significant men when they were children. So they took forward their own sense of reality and the meanings from their own childhoods that help was not to be expected, that adults can meet their emotional needs with children and, often, that this is done on a gender basis. These mothers did not use exactly the same behavior with their sons that they had experienced, but they carried forward the pattern of relating.

Further evidence that early-acquired meaning systems are carried forward comes from our follow-up studies of these children across childhood and youth and into adulthood. At age 3½ we saw the children in a series of parent–child teaching tasks and in another problem-solving situation. In the teaching tasks we found similar variation in patterns of care and a degree of consistency with the 2-year measures. Moreover, by studying a large number of siblings we saw how mothers who behaved seductively with sons treated daughters. We proposed a hypothesis that followed directly from family systems theorizing but was explicitly counter to explanations based on fixed traits. Again supported by clinical work, we predicted that mothers who behaved seductively toward sons would explicitly *not* behave seductively toward daughters; rather, they would behave in a hostile, derogating, or derisive way.

The argument was that, since families are coherent, whole systems, when daughters have been sexually or emotionally exploited by father figures, this has implications for other relationships they have experienced (Sroufe & Fleeson, 1988). In particular, it is likely that the father and mother were not meeting each other's needs and that the mother was distant and/or hostile with the daughter (otherwise, the exploitation would not have been accepted or permitted). In the next generation, then, the daughter will not know how to meet her needs with an adult partner, as her own mother did not. She may well be seductive with her son and hostile or derisive toward her own daughter. "In deprecating their daughters they are deprecating themselves, and they are reconstructing a relationship pattern that they know" (Sroufe et al., 1985, p. 319). Our empirical data supported all of these claims.

Age 3½ was also the first time we saw the children face a task without a parent present. This "Barrier Box" task, developed by Jeanne and Jack Block at UC Berkeley, strongly challenged the children. A large Plexiglas box is filled with very attractive toys. The box is locked with strong latches at the bottom of the back side. It is difficult for a 3-year-old to understand a box opening in this odd way and, besides, the latches were very difficult to open. In short, the child really can't get at these wonderful toys and only a few unattractive toys are available outside of the box. For a while, the experimenter claims to be too busy to help them. So we watched what they did as a window to their developing inner beliefs. Some children indeed worked hard and long to try to open the box. They tried one thing; then they tried another. They exerted strong effort, pushing up with their hands on the top of the box. Some even managed their mounting frustration by playing briefly with the available toys, then went back to work. In contrast, others hardly tried at all or gave up quickly after making weak efforts to open the box. (After 10 minutes the experimenter did open the box and allow all the children a play period, with their mothers joining them.)

One informative measure about the developing inner world of the child that we used here was a rating of "agency," which referred to the child's sense of effectiveness or personal power. This reflected the strength and persistence of the child's efforts. It informed us about the child's belief that, if they tried hard, they would succeed. People making these ratings knew nothing about the child's history or current circumstances. Still, this measure was related to the child's history of secure attachment and guided support in the toddler period. Those with positive histories already by age 3 years have a different sense of themselves than those with histories where needs for support have not been adequately met. Problems mean a challenge to them, not a defeat in advance. They believe their actions have power.

It is noteworthy that such differences in the sense of agency, or in the many measures of self-esteem we are to obtain in the following years, may be predicted from experiences when memory capacities are still meager and even before infants have consolidated their attachments to parents. The strongest measure we found from the first 6 months was Ainsworth's measure of parental sensitivity. When principal caregivers are attuned and responsive to the child's behavioral signals, this both helps the infant be emotionally regulated and lays the foundation for a deep belief that one's actions are meaningful, that one can have an impact on the environment, and that one can be effective.

Taking Meaning Forward

We were able to follow more than 100 of the children we had studied since birth into adulthood and see them with their own 2-year-old children in the same toy cleanup and tool problem situations used before. By doing this we didn't have to rely on retrospective accounts of childhood. How these new parents had been treated as toddlers was directly observed. And now different investigators rated how they treated their own children. There was an impressive degree of predictability (Kovan et al., 2009). The general degree of support received as a child predicted support given. In addition, more specific features of parenting were also carried forward, features such as hostility and boundary violations. As expected, it was not specific behaviors like the amount of talking that were carried forward, but it was the pattern – the meaning – of the early experience that was consistent over time. There are many ways to express hostility or seductive behavior, and boys later seen with their sons or even daughters, don't do exactly the same things that were done to them, but when they had been treated with hostility or treated seductively and so forth, they in some way were viewed as treating their children in a similar way. Again, we emphasize that those doing the rating had no knowledge of the earlier measures.

It is not possible to remember in a literal, conscious way how one was treated as a toddler. That is one reason we selected this age for study. No one can from memory describe their treatment when they were 2 years old. Yet somehow the meanings of such early experiences are internalized and carried forward without consciousness. In our study we were able to show that the continuity observed was not due to similarities in intelligence, social class, parenting experiences in later childhood, or other possible explanations. Still, there it is. Our interpretation is that having one's own child facing the issues of toddlerhood reactivated these non-conscious emotional memories, leading to recreation of the original pattern of care – all without awareness. This is the power of meaning. We will elaborate on these themes in Chapter 10 when we discuss how meaning is carried across generations.

How parents react to toddlers' expressions of contrariness, defiance, and negativity is certainly important for the emerging sense of self and the child's evolving world view. Parental restraint and control are crucial for helping the toddler establish personal and interpersonal boundaries and finding the balance between self-expression and self-control. A belief that self-control is possible is essential for actually establishing self-control in subsequent years. Paradoxically, such self-control also makes possible spontaneity and self-expression.

Moments of great meaning also derive from reactions to a toddler's expressions of exuberance. Two- and 3-year-olds can be completely delighted with their discoveries and creations. For example, one 3-year-old set out to draw a person on a piece of paper. Drawing skills are generally quite limited at this age, and his were too. He essentially drew an ill-defined shape with two vertical, parallel lines and two somewhat large triangles attached to each side. He looked at this and suddenly exclaimed, "It's a bee!" He was both delighted and proud. His parent's spontaneous response was, "That's a great bee!" and his delight was shared. More than a century ago philosopher and psychologist James Mark Baldwin pointed out that such sharing of excitement over a child's creations are a bedrock for positive self-esteem. Many since have talked about "mirroring," "attunement," and "responsiveness" as crucial for the development of a healthy self. Equally, it would be a serious blow to the child had the parent responded, "That's no bee, and you were supposed to be drawing a person."

The Way Development Works

The meaning that each individual seeks and finds – their world view – is partly conditioned by their prior experiences. Many toddlers accept and utilize parental guidance because it has already been established that the parent is dependable and trustworthy. The child now actively seeks to maintain the collaborative relationship. Others have negative expectations and therefore are less prone to comply.

These expectations of course are open to change. World views are consolidated across all of childhood and youth and into adulthood. Bowlby's (1973) attachment theory never suggested unchangeability. It did suggest, however, that change becomes more difficult the longer a pathway has been followed. Supportive caregiving during the toddler period, including clear guidance, firm limits, and emotional nourishing, can promote positive expectations regarding the availability of others and self-efficacy. Clear and firm limits are another way in which the sense of reality is affirmed, beyond the boost given by earlier responding to the infant's intentions. Such limits say that there is a reality. There is reality *out here*. It can be understood. You can grasp it. This can happen even when care was not supportive in the first year, although it may be more difficult. Such change has been documented and is quite common in the early years.

Some parents, most often because of changes in their own lives, are better able to support toddlers than was the case with their infants. They may now be able to provide a more stable framework for the child to begin discovering what things mean and what it means to be them.

However, it often does not work this way. Toddlers who bring to the table negative expectations about self and about caregivers do so because caregivers have had difficulty being reliable and consistent. Such toddlers can behave in very trying ways and would be more difficult for any parent to handle. Now they need even more than usual consistency and reliability; yet this appears to be precisely what has been difficult for their parents. A deepening of negative expectations may well result, and these too will be taken forward. We begin to see a process where children are becoming more powerful forces in their own development. This will only increase in subsequent years.

PART II
The Growth of Meaning

CHAPTER 6

The Preschooler
The Emergence of the Person

It is no exaggeration to say that out of the history of social experiences a unique and coherent organization of attitudes, expectations, emotions, and behavior emerges during the preschool years. This organization is what we mean by the person or the self. The organizing core of this emerging self is a unique experience of reality, a personal meaning system.

This organized self of course did not emerge all of a sudden and did not come from nowhere. Nonetheless, a new level of organization in the child apart from caregivers is present during the preschool years. Preschoolers' understanding of the world and their place in it is expanding rapidly. They know their place in the family and they have preferred playmates they look forward to seeing. Whereas the toddler has an *awareness* of the self, as witnessed by mirror self-recognition studies, the preschooler has begun to *know* the self. They know some of the characteristics that make them who they are. They can describe themselves. For example, one may say, "I'm a girl. I have red hair. I have four toy ponies. And I can run fast." In brief, they have some understanding of the way they are structured, what it means to be them.

Parents and other caregivers play a dominant role in encouraging and supporting a new level of self-management by the child and shepherding into being this more emotionally regulated, coherent person. In the earliest years we have emphasized the parent's role in providing a base of security. Indeed, the sense of safety (or not), the deep feeling of connection with others, and the belief that the social world is reliably responsive to my needs and actions will remain a core of the emerging person. But parents and other caregivers do much more than this. They support the child's curiosity and achievements and even arrange the experiences that help the child's social world expand. They provide limits and guidance, promoting the child's self-management by continuing to provide boundaries when the child needs them. They hold up standards for the child and, when the child misbehaves, they hold him or her accountable.

Caregivers thus encourage the child's exploration and imagination and delight in their achievements, while still conveying that there is a reality that must be addressed. They help the child begin to have a sense of right and wrong that will flower in subsequent years. Work by Marian Radke-Yarrow (Radke-Yarrow & Zahn-Waxler, 1984) showed that children do not behave in prosocial ways because parents admonish them to do so or scold them for treating others wrongly. Rather, children become empathic by parents nurturing them and modeling empathic treatment of others, as well as by clearly stating the consequences of hurtful behavior and how the other child may feel. They explain to the child the principles and expectations regarding kindness. They take infractions seriously, helping the child understand what is proper and what is not. This is a foundation for morality, even before the child can fully understand the principles.

Questions of Meaning

As at every age, our primary questions about children during this period are at the level of meaning. How does each child see the world? It is, of course, possible to make behavioral predictions without this; for example, to predict which children will be more aggressive in the preschool classroom, which children will be more dependent on teachers, or which will be socially disengaged. Attachment history, for example, is related to each of these. But to understand *why* children behave as they do, it is important to understand how they see the social world and themselves in it. What does it mean to them when another child turns down a bid for interaction? What does it mean when a teacher prohibits a behavior? What does it mean when another child walks by and bumps the tower they have been building? Was it an accident? What would the teacher do if I complained?

We were able to bring 40 of the children from our longitudinal study into two classes at the Institute of Child Development Laboratory Preschool for intensive study. One day at the school, children were gathering for circle time, but some kept getting up and going to the drinking fountain, laughing and chattering. The head teacher told them all to come sit. Still, three remained. The teacher again said, "Ok, you have to come sit now." Finally, there was just one girl left. An aid came and took her by the hand, and went with her to the group, saying, "Brenda you need to come when we tell you." For several minutes she sat as if in a trance. Then she shouted, "Look at me!" and began gouging at her face forcefully.

It was a shocking sight. What did this mild discipline mean to her? What worldview would account for this very unusual behavior?

Consider these other examples: Vera told a teacher that she had a dream wherein the teacher threw her against a wall. Upon being reassured this would not happen, Vera asked the teacher why she *wouldn't do that?* For her this required explanation. That same day another child came running into the classroom, frenetically rushing from place to place knocking things down and shouting over and over, "Betty cut my hair and I don't want to talk about it!" (Which certainly meant to all of us that he did want to talk about it. But why did he do it this way?) In a play-pair session, one child sneered at and demeaned and rejected each overture made by his partner ("That's stupid." "Who needs it?"). Nonetheless, the partner continued to try to placate him and made bid after bid. None of this can be well understood without going to the level of meaning. Why did these children ask for help and think of their teachers as they did? Why did they interact with their play partners the way they did?

We will shed some light on these examples in this chapter and discuss them further in other parts of the book. First, we will overview the developmental tasks of the preschool child, the nature of the preschooler's mind, the way meaning making changes during this period, and how earlier meanings influence thought and behavior. This is all germane to understanding how children continue to create meaning in their social worlds.

The World of the Preschooler

Advances that occur during the preschool years have major implications for the development and organization of meaning. As happens with outer behavior, the child's inner world becomes more coherent; that is, there is a more coordinated set of expectations and understandings about the self and the social world. There is also the beginning of a process of consolidation and stabilization of meaning. Expectations that are brought forward influence experiences that are sought or avoided, as well as the interpretation of events and behavior that is expressed. Acquired expectations even shape the reactions of others; that is, children's beliefs lead them to behave in ways that evoke particular reactions from others. In this way expectations are frequently confirmed, leading to a deepening of established patterns. One sees the first organized networks of meaning.

It is typically in the preschool years that worldviews are extended to the broader social world. Even prior to the preschool years, many children of course are in a variety of out-of-home settings involving other adults and children. But in the pre-school, children encounter more structured social settings, more peer interactions, and more group activities. Interacting with new adults, and especially with peers, provides new bases for meaning making. Adults can respond in ways that confirm or alter expectations regarding available support. Other children can confirm or disconfirm one's view of the self as a worthy partner.

With peers, children participate in a new level of joint meaning making not previously available. Two children together can create a level of imagination and play that neither partner could do alone. They may spark each other's creativity. For example, two girls were constructing a playhouse from an odd array of materials that were available. One suggested using a board for the "door." The other girl, noticing a small slot in this board said, "Yeah, and this can be the hole where they put in the mail." Back and forth they went, each one's suggestions inspiring the other. To be sure, conflicts arose, but these too provided opportunities for new meanings about relationships.

While the meaning making of the preschool child is more complex than in earlier years, it is also the case that the way children find meaning is accessible to us in new ways, largely because they can *tell* us how they see the world. During infancy, we could see the child's expectations regarding its social world only indirectly by looking at actions. The infant that explored freely in the caregiver's presence, that could be easily reassured in the face of mild stress, who directly sought emotional contact when distressed and who was then quickly settled, could be *inferred* to have positive expectations regarding this caregiver. That inference is required to make sense of these observations. We can also infer expectations of the preschooler by examining actions but, in addition, the gifts of language and representation allow us another view of meaning making. We can see the symbolism in their play and we can get their responses to story stems and other verbal problems; that is, we can let them tell us what they make of these events, based on their particular understanding and the way they see the world working. We can begin to see the world through their eyes.

The Preschooler's Mind: Advances and Limitations

A researcher shows a 4-year-old two glasses that are filled exactly the same. Then she pours the water from one of them into a glass that is taller but less wide. She asks the child which has more? The child says there is more in the tall, narrow glass.

The Preschooler: The Emergence of the Person

As Robert Cooper frequently described, the preschooler's mind is characterized both by advances and by limitations (see Sroufe et al., 1992). Changes in meaning making are related to developmental changes in the way the mind of the preschooler works. Of particular note are advances in curiosity and causal reasoning, as well as advances in symbolic capacity, memory, and representational skills.

Preschoolers are extraordinarily inquisitive and, as Erik Erikson (1963) suggests, these active explorations create a first sense of *purpose* for the child. Like the newborn scanning the dark room for something to see, the unremitting desire to understand the world around them reflects the preschooler's inherent motive to find meaning. One of the most frequent words of 3- and 4-year-olds is "why?" They seem to be constantly asking that question about how things work and why they are the way they are. And it seems that every answer we parents give as to why something is as it is leads only to another why question. This is very important business, for it rapidly improves the child's understanding of the world.

Preschoolers are also great observers and active learners. They now know that events have causes, that one thing leads to another. They can understand consequences of their own behavior and many of the ways that their actions lead to results. They are curious about causal sequences in their world, and they have learned to use their acute perception to draw conclusions. All of these are great advances.

However, there remain a number of limitations in their thinking. They often fail to look at multiple aspects of a problem and may overweight one aspect or another. Thus, in the example given, the child astutely notices the change in height of the water in the narrower glass but ignores the width. It sure does look like more water in the taller glass, and that clear appearance leads to an inaccurate conclusion.

Preschoolers at times also attribute too great a role to their own perception and viewpoint in attributing causes, at the expense of logic. For example, show them a Ping-Pong ball and ask what color it is. "White," of course. Now have them look at the ball through a piece of blue plastic. "Blue," they say. Well, OK, it does look blue. But now ask, what color will it look to me standing on the other side? They again say "blue" though it is white to me, a mistake no 8-year-old would make. They know of course that I could not see it if it was totally covered. And they know that for me to see something they want me to see I must look at it. They are not without role-taking skills, and they are beginning to understand differences in viewpoint. But this situation with the blue ball is difficult because they would have to override *their* immediate experience. They would also have to think about and coordinate two pieces of information at once, something hard for them to do. That is another reason why they think there is more water in the taller glass though this logically cannot be true.

This combination of cognitive strengths and limitations points to particular vulnerabilities of preschool children. Having only a beginning understanding of another's point of view makes interacting with peers challenging, especially given that peers have the same struggles. Moreover, since they interpret things in such personal causal ways, they are prone to think that bad things happen because of something *they* did. Divorce, loss, or abuse could all be their fault. After all, there *is* a correlation between these experiences and their feelings. They do feel bad so that must be the reason it happened. Further, as we will discuss in this chapter, their advanced memory skills allow them to remember things they have done that *were* bad. Unless helped, they may distort the meaning of negative experiences and incorporate such meanings into their self-concepts.

Language also provides new issues, as well as a new way of learning and finding meaning. In addition to their direct experience, preschoolers can understand what they are *told* is the case. Given the power and authority of caregivers, children of this age have little choice but to believe what they are told. When they are told reality is one way and their direct experience informs them it is another, a distorted meaning system can result, as John Bowlby emphasized. A particular example of this would be the child that is told they are "lucky to be treated so well" when they are in fact rejected or emotionally deprived. There is no way to harmonize these two portrayals of reality.

We had occasional examples in our studies of extreme cases of distortion of a child's sense of reality through language. One very unstable mother routinely told her child that he was feeling something or doing something that he was not. She told him he was hungry when he had just eaten, that he needed to go to the bathroom when he didn't, and that something was upsetting to him when it was not (or the opposite). He became the most disturbed preschooler we saw.

Finally, changes in memory capacities are also critical in meaning making. Memory skills of preschoolers are prodigious. When preschool children and college students are shown a 20-minute animated film and tested later (without being told they were going to be tested), preschoolers remember as much of the film as the sophomores. Only if they are told in advance that they will be tested do the adults out-perform the children, because only older children and adults have strategies for using memory, like rehearsing or immediately summarizing the material, and they understand the value of having such strategies. Preschoolers don't yet know to do this. The point is that preschoolers do have excellent memories, partly because of enhanced verbal and other symbolic abilities. They can now *consciously* remember much of what happens to them, as well as things they merely witnessed or heard said.

Moreover, preschoolers can, and inevitably do, abstract and generalize from experience, creating scripts of salient situations; that is, they combine the gist of many similar event sequences. Then, because of the nature of the mind, they see new events in terms of what they have previously experienced. These scripts apply to common occurrences such as going to a restaurant or a birthday party (first you play games, then you eat cake, then there are presents, . . .). Scripts also apply to the self with others; that is, young children make generalizations from their experience of how interactions are likely to go with a new playmate or with a teacher. So what the preschooler takes forward are not the details of every event but the cumulative meaning of the events.

Like toddlers, preschoolers have expectations based on early patterns of care that are in the mind but out of awareness. However, preschoolers also have expectations based on what they explicitly remember and deliberately bring forward. They have specific as well as generalized expectations. *Thus, in a new way they bring forward past meanings and apply them to new settings and relationships.*

Preschoolers generalize from their present experience and also from their prior, preverbal experience. Having found their world to be routinely responsive they now expect teachers and peers to be responsive to their overtures. In contrast, when children expect rejection based on earlier experience, they may fail to seek out teachers when in need and avoid or be aggressive toward other children. The child in the opening scenario of Chapter 1, who went off by himself after his overture to dance was turned down, had such a history of rejection. The tragedy in this pattern of adaptation is that behaving this way will make it more likely that such children will fail to find support and responsiveness again, experiences that can now be in conscious memory. Their expectations become more entrenched. Worldviews become more generalized.

Over time, of course, positive new relationship experiences can alter expectations; different memories can be formed. However, this is difficult because of the ways different children create, interpret, and react to new experiences based upon their pasts. In many ways each child, because of expectations brought forward, enters a different preschool. If one fails to go to a teacher when disappointed or upset, one cannot discover that they will respond positively. Beyond this, even positive responses can be confusing or misread, depending on the child's history, as in the case of the child requiring an explanation of why her teacher would not hurl her against a wall.

Accessing the Preschooler's Mind

> Researcher (with picture): This child was playing in the woods one day. Then he looked around and didn't know where he was. He tried to find the path, but he was lost. What do you think will happen?
>
> Child: His mom or dad will come and find him. They'll take him home and give him cookies.

Given a general understanding of the capacities of the preschool child, we next seek to understand the inner world of their minds. The varied worldviews of preschool children can be seen in both their social behavior and by assessing their thoughts and attitudes toward themselves and others.

Detailed observation of child reactions to another in distress at our preschool has allowed us to document variation in behavior of children that clearly reflects differing worldviews, especially with regard to vulnerability. Only children with early histories of rejection and emotional unavailability show what we call anti-empathic responses. When one child complained of a stomachache, one of these early-rejected children poked her right in the spot she said was hurting. Others at times did verbal taunting, saying things like, "What's the matter? Are you just a cry-baby?" Other children with histories of inadequate care become distressed or confused or act like the pain was their own when witnessing a distressed child. In contrast, children with histories of responsive, supportive care, and continued guidance at this age in fact tended to be empathic, looking concerned and commonly doing something to help, like getting a teacher. All of the children recognized the distress of the other child. This is a common cognitive achievement at this age. The point is that the recognition of distress leads to different emotional reactions and has different meaning to different children. Those who themselves have had histories of empathic care understand that this is the way relationships work. When one is in need, another supports. The others too brought forward their understandings. For some, when someone is vulnerable, the other does something hurtful; for others, when someone is distressed it is very anxiety provoking, because they expect chaos and unpredictability will ensue.

The Preschooler: The Emergence of the Person

Differing worldviews are also revealed in the nature of bids and responses to other children and in behavior with teachers. For those fortunate children with histories of support, it follows naturally to consistently approach others with confidence and enthusiasm. Their bids are inviting and therefore usually not turned down. When they are turned down, the child simply moves on to another partner (as in the example of the second child in the opening to this book) or to another activity. These children believe relationships are valuable and that they are worthy play partners. Thus, they expect other children to respond positively to them. The bids of some other children are hesitant and lackluster or aggressive and otherwise off-putting. Their responses to the bids of potential partners are likewise ineffective, off-target, negative, or even hostile. Again, such behavior shows what they think of themselves and what they expect from relationships, as we will elaborate in Chapter 15.

Behavior with teachers also reveals how different children see the world. Some children are very dependent on teachers, although this may be shown in different ways. Some children chronically hover by teachers, seeking care or passively waiting for help to be engaged. Others are more indirect in various ways. They may act out to receive control and discipline, like the child that ran around the classroom shouting that he didn't want to "talk about it." Still others indirectly seek contact in more subtle ways. One child, for example, would enter the classroom and begin a series of oblique approaches to a teacher. Like a sailboat tacking into the wind, he would go from one place to another, always becoming closer but never on a direct line. Finally, when he arrived quite near to her, he would completely turn backward and lean against her. What these children had in common is that they all wound up having a great deal of contact with teachers (at the expense of contact with peers), almost always sitting next to a teacher or on a teacher's lap when the group gathered in a circle. This is in stark contrast to children with supportive histories who are primarily engaged with peers, often sitting next to a favorite playmate in circle time. Again we would note that all of these children are doing their best to get what they need from this new world, but for some it is difficult.

For some of the highly dependent children, the meaning is that they can only feel sufficiently safe when in contact with the teacher, an interpretation supported by their high scores on anxiety. For others, it perhaps reflected an unmet yearning for contact that was difficult to express. All of these children scored low on measures of self-esteem. None felt capable of taking on the challenges of peer interaction, and they were generally scored as being very low on "flexible self-management," what Jeanne and Jack Block (1980) called "ego-resilience."

It is also possible to see the workings of the minds of preschoolers by looking at their symbolic play, or by presenting them with problem scenarios or story stems and asking them questions to reveal how they see the world. Their symbolic capacities allow them to grasp the meaning of these problems or stories, and their memories allow them to keep the story in mind while they formulate a response. The combination of their histories and their current circumstances yields their particular interpretations.

In one approach, problem situations are described (for example, two children want to play with the same toy) and the child is asked what the solution might be. Many, of course, come up with amicable solutions (scripts such as taking turns or playing together). Some have difficulty seeing a solution, and others, especially those with histories of rejection and avoidant attachment, portray what are called "force solutions" (one child might just take it away or push the other child away). Thus, the same scenario can have quite different meaning to different children. Some believe conflicts can be solved; others not so much.

Another very commonly used approach is to provide the child with story stems and ask them about the outcome. For example, a child becomes lost, is distressed, or experiences a minor injury. Not surprisingly, many of the procedures used by researchers have involved separation themes, given that safety is a cornerstone of the child's meaning system. The most common response to such stories by children with supportive histories is that the parents will come and find them or come and fix the problem, as in the opening example for this section. Sadly, the stories of children with histories of uncertain care or rejection frequently do not entail successful resolution. For example, the lost child may "just cry," stay lost, or experience other bad consequences.

In another approach, researchers Gerhard Suess and Klaus Grossmann showed children a short series of cartoon drawings (Suess et al., 1992). In the first picture a child was shown building a block tower. In the second frame, another child walks by. The final picture shows a toppled tower. Five-year-old children were asked to explain what happened. Those with secure histories typically said something like, "This kid must have *accidentally* bumped the tower and knocked it over. He'll probably help build it up again." Those with histories of avoidant attachment significantly more often said that the second child had knocked the tower down *on purpose*. Note that there is no information in the drawings suggesting why the tower was down. The second drawing only shows a child walking by. It shows no contact with the block tower. All children this age attribute a reason for the fallen tower. That is notable developmental achievement of the preschool period. But the history of the individual children supplied the particular meaning. In ambiguous situations, already by age 5, some children tend to see intent as hostile, while others see it as benign or benevolent.

Symbolic play is ubiquitous among 5-year-olds, and it is often rich with meaning. Play is a major tool preschoolers have for attempting to master their worlds. There are things that cannot be done easily in reality, such as keeping adults from fighting or even coping with everyday worries. But many things can be reworked in play. This is why, for example, children being toilet trained often change the dolly's diaper and scold them for being wet. They become in charge and the punishment goes elsewhere.

One noteworthy finding in our study of play concerned conflict themes. These were common in the play of all children, but there were important differences in what happened *after* the conflict was introduced. For some, the conflict never resolved, either spinning from one problem to the next or being left dangling. Those with histories of supportive care and secure attachment much more frequently brought conflicts to a successful resolution in their play. (For example: "Oh no! Our boat is sinking! We're in the water. There's another boat! Let's swim! They put down a ladder for us. We made it!"). Thus, for some children, the inevitable difficulties and conflicts encountered in life don't mean disaster. Even if you can't cope with it yourself, people, especially loved ones, can be counted on to take care of it. For others, problems and conflicts mean something very different.

Deepening Meanings as the Person Emerges

A teacher has been reading a story to a few children gathered at her feet. When she finishes, she corrals Tony, taking him by the hand to find a new activity and staying with him until he is engaged. This takes some time, as he flits from one thing to another. Meanwhile, another of the children from the story group, Myra, had set off purposefully toward a group of children by a playhouse. She smoothly joins with them in the play.

Entering the world of preschool is an exciting time for all children, but how this degree of stimulation is experienced is an individual matter. If all goes well, children come to the preschool believing that the world is safe and that they are worthy of care and effective in getting the care they need. They also have a sense that their feelings are acceptable and can be adequately contained and, in general, that they can control and manage themselves. They feel a deep sense of connection with others and that relationships are valuable. They know deeply that they can count on support if their own capacities are exceeded. When problems arise, they can be solved, if not by themselves then with help. All of this is a legacy from their relationships in the earliest years.

Because meaning is taken forward in the form of attitudes and expectations, each child experiences the world of preschool differently. When we look through the eyes of some, we see a rich social world full of opportunity. The behavior of the two children just described can be explained by their very different internalized beliefs about their own inner resources. Myra expects to be able to guide herself and smoothly join another group. In her early life, Myra counted almost solely on her caregivers as resources. Now she had positive expectations about her own abilities. Later that day she was seen to cope with a quite frustrating circumstance. The children were cutting playdoh cookies with various shaped cutters. As she was reaching for one that would complete the pattern of shapes she was carefully constructing, another child picked it up first. We watched a look of disappointment on her face, but then she sighed and shifted to decorating the ones she had previously made. With great pleasure she showed a teacher one finished product. Such containment and regulation were once in the hands of her mother. They were now part of the well-regulated person she had become. All of this is because of the meanings she brought forward from her earlier social experience.

The behavior and meaning system of each child becomes more patterned and coherent by the age of 5 years. Myra, like other children with a history of positive support, can be described as filled with curiosity, well regulated, agentic, competent with peers and empathic, and also as having positive expectations for herself and others – an inner belief in both her own resources and the value and support of relationships with others. This all fits together.

For some children, of course, things are more difficult. Although they seem to want to be involved in the social world, they may need ample support to stay engaged, as did Tony, and/or become quickly frustrated when encountering a problem or obstacle, in a way that was fairly common among toddlers. Because of a history of chaotic, inconsistent and/or haphazard care, some are easily over-stimulated, easily frustrated, anxious or impulsive, ineffective in interacting with peers, and highly needing of supervision and support. They do not believe they can cope. Challenges mean hazards. Still, this type of child is not off-putting of teachers or alienating of other children. The little boy who flew into the classroom, shouting and knocking things over received lots of support from teachers, immature as he was. He "wore his heart on his sleeve," and such openness about his needs attracted our teachers to him. As different as this pattern is from that shown by Myra, it is nonetheless a coherent organization of behavior and inner world.

Other children may tend to be isolated or aggressive and even mean. They don't reach out to others and are often rejected by them. They are emotionally guarded and rigid. Even at the tender age of 5 years, they seem to be shutting out others and shutting down. These are also the indirectly dependent children. This profile can be seen as an effort at self-protection, and it all fits together. While a number of patterns can be described, it is generally the case that each child by the age of 5 years has a coherent organization of behavior and expectations.

Differences in flexible self-regulation and the variations in views of themselves and relationships can have durable consequences because of how they color interactions with others. Those with positive social expectations approach and respond to other children with more positive affect and enthusiasm. They engage in activities with spirit and competence. They can engage in the labored give-and-take of interactions with peers with persistence. They neither bully others nor are prone to being bullied. With teachers their behavior is age-appropriate and effective. By this we mean that they can rely on teachers when their own capacities are surpassed; most of the time, however, they are engaged with peers, busily learning skills that will last a lifetime.

We noted that, on the first day of our school, children with histories of positive support adopted an attitude of attentive exploration. They had little problem with their parent's departure. They checked out the various areas of the playroom and the various materials available. They responded to the teachers' warm greetings and they watched them interact with other children. Likewise, they were curious about the other children, responding to overtures and interacting some. But mostly they were checking things out. It was in the next days and weeks that they became more actively involved with peers, selecting preferred play partners and smoothly functioning in groups. Likewise, warm and effective relationships with teachers evolved. This was a world in which they felt safe and able to manage.

Other children saw this environment as frightening or overwhelming. Not only did they have difficulty separating from parents, they were hesitant and inhibited in engaging this new environment. Some children, of course, are merely slow to warm up and, over time, become engaged but for others this remained the pattern throughout the term. They hovered by teachers, stayed on the periphery of the peer group, and were hesitant to engage in new activities. They required lots of nurturance and reassurance.

Still another group of children showed a paradoxical bravado on the first day. They rushed toward social engagement with nearly everyone. One child went up to numerous children and adults, saying "Hi, I'm Ronald." While one might at first think such a child was simply very confident or temperamentally bold, in fact these were the children that ultimately were the most socially isolated, as well as showing the indirect over-dependency on teachers described earlier (as in the case of the child who approached teachers like a sailboat tacking in the wind). Likewise, in our follow-up studies at later years, these children had a lack of close friendships. In the preschool they appeared to us to be defended against their apprehension, some degree of which would be normal in this situation and conveyed a lack of comprehension regarding how relationships are formed and grow.

Worldviews are not simply brought forward from the past; they interact with new experiences and are elaborated. We saw this most clearly in our study of play pairs. The children in our preschool were each seen with the same partner for 15 or 20 play sessions in a room well-equipped with various props. The pairs were created so that every combination of attachment history was equally represented for both boys and girls. In that way these video recorded sessions revealed what would happen when children with the same or different worldviews faced the task of building a relationship.

When both children had histories of secure attachment, ratings by independent observers revealed that these pairs evolved the "deepest" relationships, based on the elaborateness and quality of the coordinated play themes developed and the degree of emotional sharing (Pancake, 1988). They were able to generate complex play themes that were often carried across sessions, becoming ever more involved. There was, of course, occasional conflict, as was true in virtually all play pairs. But conflicts were resolved, at times leading to even more creativity. We never saw bullying in these pairs.

In contrast, for pairs with both children having had anxious attachments, the play was generally not very elaborated and sometimes quite primitive. There was little coordination of play themes. So-called parallel play is common in preschoolers who do not know each other, but with these pairs it tended to persist over weeks. Moreover, if even one of the children had a history of avoidant attachment, bullying was frequent. (This typically took the form of verbal insults or derogation, given that a researcher was always present to stop physical aggression). Bullying happened every time the partner of an avoidant child had a history of resistant attachment. In the face of a vulnerable, immature partner, children with a history of rejection when they were vulnerable now exploit the other. The vulnerable partner, whose feelings of self-worth and competence have not been supported, does not stand up for him- or herself. When the pairs were two children with avoidant histories, whoever was vulnerable would be exploited. In one pair this alternated based on who seemed to be having a better week (Troy & Sroufe, 1987).

Perhaps most interesting was what happened in mixed pairs of one child with a secure history and one child with an anxious history. The child with a secure history was never seen to bully his or her partner. In fact, when paired with a child having had a history of anxious/resistant attachment, they were often nurturant and supporting. These children value relationships and seek to be engaged to the highest degree possible. So they provided the scaffolding for play, reminiscent of what they had experienced in their relationships with their parents. This is how they "know" relationships to be. This enabled their less able partners to play at a much higher level than they could alone. In different ways this was a positive experience for both partners.

When the pairing was a mix of avoidant and secure histories, there was neither much collaborative playing, nor was there bullying. It takes two to tango. Relationships are always a product of two histories. With a non-collaborative partner, the child with a secure history has no choice but to play alone. This is what we often saw. But there was no bullying. Our take on this is that the child with a secure history neither portrays vulnerability nor would accept bullying. It was a standoff, somewhat like ships passing in the night.

We were rightfully concerned regarding the futures of both those who bullied and those preschoolers who were vulnerable to bullying. We were worried about the bullies both because aggression begins to become a stable characteristic at this age and because of the alienation from others that this pattern represents. Our research shows that alienation is the link between insensitive parenting and later conduct problems. On the other hand, recent research has shown that those who are bullied in an ongoing way are vulnerable to chronic loneliness in later years (Mathews et al., 2022).

Likewise, the history-based attitudes and behaviors of children at times elicited confirming responses by teachers. Detailed analyses of teacher–child interactions showed that teachers treated some children – most often those with secure histories – as being capable and responsive. Others were treated as immature and needy and still others as needing control and discipline. The teacher reactions varied to a large extent based upon what we (but not they) knew about the children's histories. For example, raters looked at a large number of instances in which a child violated some classroom rule. What did they see in teacher reactions? Some children were simply reminded of the rule or received a response like, "Come on, Darren, you-can-do-better-than-that." In other words, they were held to a high standard of behavior and could be counted on to be responsive to a simple, clear reminder. This also showed up in the teacher's expectations of compliance. When they asked one of these children with secure histories to do something, they would turn and go on, knowing that of course the child would behave as asked. Other children required constant reminders and shepherding, as illustrated by the contrast between Myra and Tony in the preceding section. For some children, teachers would allow minor rule infractions, obviously believing allowances needed to be made for these immature children. And directives would be followed with more monitoring and directives until the child did what was needed. Sometimes teachers were pulled into doing too much for some children. Other children received strong control and discipline. Such reactions built upon and reinforced previous patterns of supportive, neglecting, chaotic, or rejecting care.

Thus, the new meanings found in this new environment often recapitulated past experience. Those who were able to embrace this new world had their beliefs in themselves and in relationships deepened. Those who were hesitant and doubtful, hovering by teachers, often had too few experiences of success with peers, deepening their doubts and handicapping them with regard to the more challenging peer world to come. Those with histories of rejection and emotional distance all too often created further such experiences. This is the nature of development. One creates, frames, and interprets new experiences in light of past experiences, often consolidating the previously established patterns.

From the outside, it certainly makes sense to say that a personality has formed by 5 years of age. Such a statement is justified both by the greater coherence in the organization of various characteristics of the individual and by the greater stability and stronger predictive power of individual variations from this time forward. Prior to this period, strong predictions to later functioning only come from assessing caregiving relationships. There is little that we can measure *in the child* in the first 2 years of life that predicts powerfully to later outcomes; yet variations in preschool behavior and adaptation often do. The famous "marshmallow" delay-of-gratification study of Walter Mischel, as well as numerous other studies, including our own, have demonstrated that, by about age 5 years, things we can measure in the child, even without the parent present, can predict functioning decades into the future (Mischel et al., 1989). As Louis Sander (1975) described so well, an organized personality has emerged from what began as an organized relationship matrix.

Change of course can happen. When children can be helped to have experiences that disconfirm their previous expectations, they can begin to see themselves and relationships in a different way. Then they can go forward with a better chance to exploit coming opportunities for growth. We saw our teachers help numerous children and we saw some benefit from therapy. And we saw all of the children working hard to adapt to the challenges of the preschool. Still, developmental systems are powerful, and this understanding makes clear the great importance of the early years.

The Way Development Works

We have made the case that basic expectations regarding the world as reliable, and the self as worthy of care and effective in getting needs met, are taken forward from infancy. These expectations support the toddler's movement toward autonomy and more ready acceptance of parental guidance. The toddler can then take forward both basic feelings of security and worth, as well as the belief that they can control themselves and be effective in solving problems. Now, as preschoolers, such meanings are consolidated and deepened as the social world is expanded and the child becomes more truly able to rely on his or her own resources, as well as evolving new ways to draw upon others.

All of this supports the emergence of a flexible, curious, self-managed, engaged, and socially competent child (Bernier et al., 2012; Sroufe et al., 2005). Such a child will acquire a great deal from the preschool experience to take forward. This is the way development works. Each phase provides the platform for successful adaptation (or not) in the next, with each phase building upon the others. Meanings that are brought forward impact meaning that is found in new social situations.

All children interpret experiences in particular ways, based on their own histories of social experience. Expecting to be rebuffed, some children don't seek social contacts. Ambiguous or neutral reactions of others may be interpreted to mean dislike, rejection, or hostility. Even positive, warm expressions from others can be misinterpreted or found to be confusing. This is what accounted for one child's dream of her beloved teacher throwing her against the wall. Her teacher had been consistently warm and nurturing with her but, because of her malevolent history, she continued to expect rejection. As we will discuss in Chapter 13, children at times engage in self-punitive behavior following discipline. In this way they are perhaps making such events meaningful in a way they can understand.

For all children, the development of individual meaning systems and their beginning consolidation in the preschool years are of basic importance because of their impact on motivation and behavior. A foundation concerning what experiences they seek and how they may react to later social encounters has been established.

CHAPTER 7

Middle Childhood
Me and My Friends

> After a game everybody shares the pizza, except maybe one guy will get an extra piece if he hit a home run.
>
> We don't like him because he cheats.
>
> She will tell me things that she wouldn't tell anyone else.
>
> The counselors assigned us to tents, but our friends snuck into each other's tents, and then we were all in there together.

During middle childhood, the ways that children seek and find meaning in their experience are vastly different from the way meaning was sought by infants, toddlers, or even preschool children. They are seeking to know and understand quite different things and they are situating themselves in very different contexts. At the same time, the four themes or principles that have guided meaning making from the beginning are still in play.

Seeking meaning is simply inherent in human development. No one has to reward children for being engaged with peers. The urge to be connected to others continues but shifts to the peer group in middle childhood. Peer relationships are inherently attractive. No one, certainly no adult, needs to tell them that this is the age when they should form deep, loyal friendships. They are inherently motivated to do this. The rules governing the norms of the peer group are not written down and require no formal instruction. It is rather stunning that this rule system is recreated across generations by the peer group itself.

Likewise, within this new context, meaning making continues to be an active process. Observing children at play, it is actually astounding how actively involved they are. They can be with peers for hours on end, endlessly creating joint projects, negotiating disputes, and establishing rules of conduct. Rarely do they want to stop, so serious is this enterprise. In past decades, one could hear parents up and down the block in working-class neighborhoods yelling for their child, "It's time to come for dinner." Today, the child might receive a text, but it is still parents that want them to stop playing.

The transactional relation between meaning and experience, our third principle, clearly applies to middle childhood. The expectations, self-beliefs and attitudes – referred to here as the worldview –formed at each age partly shape the way situations are engaged and responded to in the next period. If their expectations regarding relationships led them to repeated failures during the preschool years, then they are even more doubtful in middle childhood. So their task is more difficult in middle childhood when forming close, loyal friendships is a key developmental issue. At the same time, of course, successes in peer relationships, if achieved, can alter social expectations at a later age.

Finally, meaning remains largely social, as it has been from the beginning. Now, however, the social network is greatly extended. Teachers, coaches, youth directors, and other adults outside the family play an increased role. Most notably, peer relationships also become more central. More genuine friendships are formed, and these are coordinated with participating in the larger peer group. Part of the meaning being found is one's place in this larger network. Meaning is always derived from social relationships, but never before have peers rivaled parents for defining the self in relation to others. Relationships with equals are crucial for the ultimate meaning of closeness. Major questions that receive answers by the child in this period are what kind of friend am I? and what can I expect from those I call friend?

As we will describe in this chapter, the child's world greatly expands during the elementary school years. Still, the parents' role in the development of the child's meaning system remains important, though perhaps in more subtle ways than previously. Research from our study has shown that maintaining a structured household, with for example regular times for a family meal, are important for child well-being and even predict effective parenting in the next generation (Morris, 1980). Such times also make possible discussion of important social and political topics and their ethical implications. Other research shows that parental "monitoring" – the parent knowing about and attending to the child's activities – is also a crucial support at this time and on into adolescence (Brendgen et al., 2001; Pettit et al., 1999). Both providing structure and monitoring of the child convey parental caring and provide a base of stability during this time of change. Another way parents provide a secure base for the child is by being available to be a sounding board when the child brings to them issues with school or with peers. Helping the child to explore issues of fairness and equity that they are actively engaging at this age is of critical importance to their moral development.

Major Developments in Middle Childhood

The statements at the opening of this chapter were all made by 10- and 11-year-olds when asked questions about friendships and their experiences with others at one of our summer camps. They illustrate some of the major tasks as well as themes of meaning making in late middle childhood. Core values such as fairness, equity, reciprocity, and loyalty are to be acquired during this period. Establishing such values is crucial as children transition from an era when trust and vulnerability were an issue between child and parent to the more equal relationships they will have throughout the rest of life. They are developing an understanding of morality; how one should behave in certain circumstances and what consequences might follow when violations occur. Parental attitudes about appropriate behavior factor into this process. If a child steals a candy bar from the corner store, how the parent responds is important. Faith-based communities may also be a source of structure. How one behaves toward others may be taught in the home using religious precepts.

Middle childhood is also the age during which children develop a sense of the group and their place in it – a sense of "we" or us, as reflected in the final statement in the opening. Based on their histories, some children bring an initial meaning system that equips them well for mastering these tasks. For others they are quite challenging.

Accomplishing these monumental tasks spurs notable cognitive advances in middle childhood while, of course, at the same time, cognitive development supports the advances in social relationships. Not only does memory improve, but also children become better at organizing information and thinking logically. Don't expect to trick them by pouring water from a short, wide glass into a tall, narrow one. They know the amount can't change. It's logical. And they know that a ping pong ball would still look white to you, despite the blue filter. The filter does not and cannot change the basic nature of the ball. Of great interest to us, they now judge actions in a much more sophisticated manner, considering intentions and not just outcomes. Someone who bumps into someone accidentally is much less culpable than someone who does so deliberately. A premium is put on the meaning of the actions, and children in middle childhood understand that the same action can mean different things.

All of these examples also reveal the fact that children in the elementary years can take into account multiple meanings; that is, can consider more than one piece of information. Because this is a newly developing capacity (at the "zone of proximal development" as Vygotsky (1978) would say), it explains why riddles are so fascinating and amusing to children of this age. They get the double meanings. (What is brown, has a head and a tail but no legs? A penny. What has a bank but no money? A river.)

All of these cognitive advances, and the experiences related to exercising them, lead to an understanding of causality well in advance of that of the preschooler. Their view is more objective, and this leaves them much less vulnerable to blaming themselves for all of the negative experiences they have. Such a vulnerability, of course, never leaves any of us entirely and remains a strong tendency for some, depending on history.

In middle childhood, the child is also expected to achieve real-world competence, whether that is developing skill in hunting and gathering, success in school, or physical or artistic aptitude. For boys this competence is often shown in larger group activities, such as sports or clubs. Whatever the activity, each strives to do their best. Girl groups are often smaller and more intimate and involve more talking and sharing. In one of our camps, for example, a small group of girls created macramé bracelets together, bringing and sharing materials and talking excitedly while they worked. They actually sold their finished products. All of this is critical to the child's view of the self as competent in the social world.

Differences are apparent in children's capacities to embrace new challenges and in their expectations regarding success. When success accrues, confidence builds and expectations become more positive (Dweck, 2017). Some children face these tasks undergirded by a solid foundation. They have evolved a sense of effectiveness because their early social environment responded to their efforts, and they are curious and eager to learn because their histories promoted early exploration. A challenging task looks like an opportunity, not another door to failure. Clear differences in how children think of themselves, their parents and their peers can be readily documented.

Of great consequence, the sense of self itself becomes more consolidated and integrated. Children have a better understanding of the various features that characterize them as a particular person, and now they see themselves in terms of psychological as well as physical characteristics. They may describe themselves as "kind" and "friendly," as well as having brown hair. Others too are described in psychological terms. Myra described a friend she had recently made in the following way: "She's funny and she's kind, and she cares about you." When the researcher asked how she knew that she cared about her, Myra said, "Well, if you're upset about something, you can just tell she cares, by the way she acts." The self is now a psychological self, not just a physical self.

Moreover, all of these features of the self fit together into an overall framework. Self-confidence and lack of self-confidence become much more internalized. Children interpret and respond to many situations much more autonomously. These achievements are common to all children. Our interest is more in differences in these self-constructions and, especially, how the child feels about the self that they now see – what it *means* to them to be them.

In middle childhood, the world of peers of course becomes prominent and, while they provide structure, teachers generally are not caregivers to the extent they were during the preschool years. As important as parents have been and continue to be, peers now come to play an increasing role in children's self-evaluations and in their views of themselves in social relationships. This is the age at which children actively compare themselves with others. They no longer find it sufficient to simply say, "I can run fast," as they might have in kindergarten but, rather, they might say, "I can run faster than anyone else in my class except for Roger." Such social comparisons play a major role in the child's expanding understanding of what it means to be "me."

Not only do children spend much more time away from parents and in the company of peers, peer relationships themselves become much more complex. During middle childhood children commonly form one special relationship and a few close relationships. These true friendships are characterized by loyalty and stability. One is true to one's friend, sticks up for them, and counts on them. Friendships are also understood to be hierarchical. One has one or two best friends but other friends as well. And these other friends have their own best friends. Children understand this.

Critically important meanings derive from the relationship challenges in middle childhood. For example, Kera and Becky had become friends during the first weeks of one of our summer day camps. In time, Becky had also become friends with Aimee, who was one of the girls that rode in the same van with her to and from the camp. Kera noticed this and found it distressing. The way these young girls handled this could be a lesson for all of us adults. We happened to video record a dramatic interchange in which Kera directly expressed her concern to Becky. "I thought *we* were best friends." This was said with some emotion. Becky responded that they were best friends but that she also liked Aimee. Kera was reassured, and by the end of the camp these three girls were all friends and shared many things together. They were a core part of the macramé group described. These were powerful experiences; we think in part made possible by the secure histories of each of these three girls but also providing foundational meanings for their futures.

At the same time as children are forming close, loyal friendships, they must also find their place in the larger peer group, learning and adhering to its norms. Well beyond the case in the preschool years, children begin seeing themselves as part of a group. The words "we" and "us" find a prominent place in the vocabulary. For example, one girl described a conflict in her camp in the following way: "The boys had built a fort, and they wouldn't let *us* girls go in." Another girl told about how she and her friends had decided to let another girl be part of the macramé group. These girls understood that their group had boundaries. Children not only learn how to function in a group, they learn what it means to be part of a group – to identify themselves with a group.

Children clearly judge each other in terms of peer norms. Those who don't follow the rules of the game, who don't play fair, or who don't subscribe to the value of equity, are disliked or even rejected from the group. Likewise, there are extensive norms – prescriptions and proscriptions – concerning interactions across genders in middle childhood. These rules and norms governing behavior can be quite complex. In public settings, such as our camps, it is generally not acceptable for a child of one gender to interact with a group of the other gender. If they do, they are likely to be teased. But there are a series of exceptions or extenuating circumstances. You may interact if required by an adult (for example, a counselor says, "John, go get the lemonade from the girls' table and bring it back."). You may interact if it was inadvertent; that is, perhaps you arrived at the drinking fountain at the same time as did a member of the other gender. If there is no interaction, this is acceptable. You may interact if you have a partner and boundaries are maintained; that is, two boys and two girls may interact as long as each gender pair stays as a unit. If someone does per chance interact with someone of the other gender, this is excusable if it is followed by disavowal (perhaps a hurled insult). The list goes on. The social world is complex in middle childhood; yet decade after decade such rules are learned without adult instruction.

Children who do not adhere to these norms regarding when it is and is not acceptable to interact with members of the other gender are called out and often even disliked. One girl in one of our camps, in explaining her negative evaluation of a widely-disliked girl said, "She's fast," meaning sexually forward and too interested in the boys. She did not have our vocabulary but made it clear by a little swing of the hips what she meant.

Children at this age are often characterized as being somewhat rigid or absolutistic regarding rules and norms. Rules *must* be followed. While this is true, it must be pointed out, that such "conformity" is a crucial step in moral development (Loevinger, 1976). It is a move forward to believe that one behaves properly because it is the agreed upon thing to do rather than just to avoid punishment, as is true for younger children. Children work very hard on the whys and wherefores of rules, and parents can support these efforts. By taking the child's concerns seriously when they wonder why they are disciplined when "he started it" or in other ways see something as unfair, they help them begin to develop a code of morals. The sanctity of rules provides a stable platform for internalizing one's culture and feeling grounded in the social world. In this way it paves the way for more mature and relativistic moral thinking and behaving later. One must first learn why rules are important to ultimately understand that, at times, they must be nested within broader ethical principles.

Our summer camps at age 10 provided our first opportunity to observe systematically how children functioned in groups. In addition to observation in unconstrained settings, we also set up group tasks or challenges. This allowed us to explore how past meanings are brought to the group setting and the new meanings that can be taken forward from group activities. These tasks involved constructed groups of four boys or four girls.

The challenge tasks were similar to those used in "upward bound" programs, such as using a rope to swing across a "water" hazard. This involved having the most able person jump for the rope that was originally some distance away and swing across, then throw it back. From then on it involved cooperation to get everyone across. It was timed, and if anyone got "wet" you all had to start over. The most interesting task was the "skis" task. The "skis" were actually two long boards with four pairs of straps. The children had to coordinate and work together to walk on those boards to the end of a path, turn around and come back. Again, a premium was put on time. This is an extraordinarily challenging task.

Notice the complexity of the social capacities involved in these tasks. Foremost, to be successful the groups must function in a well-organized and cooperative manner. They must be a team; all are needed. They must have leadership as well as collaboration. They must hang in there through difficulties, encouraging and helping each other, especially those that may be struggling. They must believe they can master the task and be willing to work hard. We thought this was an ideal situation for evaluating how meaning systems were taken forward.

The groups were set up such that all four children in each group either had histories of secure attachment or anxious attachment. The expectation was that the developmental pathway initiated by secure attachment, associated as it is with entrained emotional regulation, a sense of connection and empathy with others, and experiences of engagement, sustained interaction, and conflict resolution with other young children, would set up some of these groups quite well for success.

This was precisely what we found. For example, in the "skis" task, the groups with secure histories showed eagerness and enthusiasm, finding this difficult task attractive rather than foreboding. They smoothly organized their positions, usually with an obvious leader in the front, and perhaps someone in the rear calling out signals ("left, right, left right," etc.). Often, they had their hands on each other's shoulders to promote unity, balance, and coordination. There were of course occasional glitches at first (this is hard), but soon they would achieve coordination and off they went. They looked like a single unit, as they hustled down the path, made the turn (also very hard) and came hustling back. In some cases they asked if they could do it again to decrease their time, reminding us of the secure 2-year-old children in our tool problem study who wanted to put the prize back to solve the problem again. These preadolescent children actually had a good time, as they eagerly went from one task to the next.

This is not how it went for those with anxious histories, especially the boys. As was summarized previously (Sroufe, 2020), they had great difficulty with all of the challenge tasks. They were generally disorganized and uncoordinated and struggled to come up with a plan. From the outset they tended toward bickering and distracting themselves. Once they got going, working as a group was difficult. One would start before the others were ready. Or two or three of them might get going, but they would all fall down because they didn't have another child on board. After successive failures, frustration led to criticism of each other, scapegoating, pushing each other, and at times devolving into chaos. This was an understandable outcome to a task that rested on skills they were weak in. Failure seemed guaranteed from the outset and failure happened. These individuals didn't really expect to do well. They lacked the necessary confidence that comes from previous positive experience. When put together, their negative expectations, their combined negative meaning systems, were indeed handicapping.

It becomes clear what help would be needed to enable these children to succeed in the task. An adult providing suggestions and guiding them toward the necessary synchronized movement would aid in completing the task. Moreover, succeeding in a group activity of this sort may well lead to the gratification inherent in such a success and, ultimately, to altered expectations.

In middle childhood, children not only need to form close, loyal friendships and function effectively in groups. Most complex of all, children need to coordinate friendships and group functioning; that is, maintain the special relationship even while participating in the group. They need to be able to function smoothly in groups with or without their friend and to retain special feelings for their friend even when their friend is engaged with others. This is no easy task.

Observation confirms great variation in how well all of these challenges of middle childhood peer relationships are met, and research shows that those having histories of responsive early care and positive preschool experiences more readily meet them. Thus, some children bring to middle childhood a sense of connection with others, a valuing of relationships, feelings of being worthy, and positive expectations concerning durability of relationships. Such attitudes impact the quality of their friendships. They expect to be liked and are liked. Other children do not expect to be liked, have low expectations regarding relationships, feel easily slighted, and may retreat in the face of the inevitable difficulties that arise, or largely avoid close relationships. An argument with a friend, someone else talking to your friend, and a friend preferring another activity all have different meanings to children with different histories and different current circumstances. Likewise, for some, finding a place in the larger group is relatively easy, and participating in the group, even their friend being on the other team, is not a threat to their close relationship. For example, if two best friends were selected onto different softball teams anyone watching would have no difficulty seeing their connection, perhaps through friendly banter when one gets a hit.

As our camp observations showed, others have difficulty with this coordination, and some avoid group activities altogether. Thus, they may become disorganized when in groups or play in isolation or exclusively with a single companion. When the friend is absent, they appear lost and often simply just play alone. Of course, the capacity to play alone on occasions is a positive thing. But here the focus is on children who at times give up on trying to fit in and to have friendships. Their isolation is lonely. It is no wonder that a single friend becomes so important to someone who has not developed the social skills at a level of their peers.

Peer experiences in middle childhood play an important and perhaps unique role in paving the way for the intimate relationships of adolescence and adulthood. After all, these relationships are among equals and thus in ways distinctive from the asymmetrical relations between parents and children. Here is where the view of oneself as an equal partner is forged, as is the capacity for negotiating conflicts (see Chapter 14). Therefore, middle childhood is another crucial link regarding what it means to be a self with another, to be a social partner, and to be close. Detailed study shows that the combination of close relationships with parents in the earliest years of childhood *and* positive relationships with peers in the school years together best predict the capacity for close, trusting relationships in adulthood.

The Inner World: Representations of Self, Family, and Peers

In middle childhood new venues become available for probing the child's worldview; that is, what they expect from peers as well as family members, and how they see their place in these social worlds. Beyond looking at play and other behavior, as was largely the case in prior years, now we can rely on the child to generate stories, create narratives, and respond to questions to a much greater degree.

One approach used by attachment researchers is the family drawing. Long before youngsters can put their feelings and thoughts into words, they can express both conscious and unconscious attitudes, wishes, and concerns in drawings. Such drawings were used for many years by child clinicians, but there is now a new way to validate them, as pioneered by Mary Main. Scoring schemes can be checked against what is known about attachment history, refined, and then checked again with a new sample. A certain degree of validity has been established, and a few rather robust principles have emerged. While the drawing indicators presented here do not separately allow us to reach definite conclusions regarding a child's history or current outlook, in combination they let us glimpse what "family" means to each child and how they see themselves in that family.

Most notable in the drawings of 8-year-olds with histories of secure attachment is a sense of connection and vitality (Fury et al., 1997). All family members are present, grounded, and in proper proportion, with proper placement and spacing of figures. The self is shown as well proportioned, complete, and individuated. The figures are shown as engaged, perhaps with hands or arms joined. The drawings are affectively positive, often colorful, and there is an obvious feeling of life. Children who in fact had histories of secure attachment made the clear majority of drawings classed by independent raters as meeting some combination of these criteria in our study. Only a small minority of children with anxious attachment histories produced such drawings, although there were many variations in the drawings produced.

The drawings of those children with anxious resistant attachment histories were especially characterized by some combination of very small figures (especially the self), figures separated by barriers, crowded figures and exaggeration of soft body parts. Overall, they projected an image of undue vulnerability, immaturity, and timidity. For many of these children, the experience of inconsistent or chaotic early care, wherein they were required to be vigilant regarding threat and to make continual efforts to gain comfort or attention, has led to a view of a world where challenges are large and they are small. A lack of confidence was palpable. What was portrayed in these drawings was reminiscent of the lack of agency in problem-solving that many of them showed at age 3 years and their hovering dependency on teachers and ineptness in peer relationships in the preschool years.

In contrast, the drawings of those with histories of avoidant attachment often had a quality of stiffness, lack of individuation, and, especially, lack of connection – aloneness even when with others. One very specific sign that distinguished them was figures having arms downward and pinned against the body. Being in their family does not mean closeness and connection. Affect was generally neutral or negative in these drawings, and sometimes the drawings were made using only black, though the same array of colors was available to all children. At times there was a feeling of emptiness. Both these children and those with anxious/resistant attachment histories sometimes drew incomplete figures, with missing body parts. Lack of positive affect and isolation is also what characterized the peer behavior of the group of children with avoidant histories in the preschool and in our summer camps at age 10. Difficulty connecting, alienation, and isolation are often major themes in their development.

It is important to note that the drawing variations described here are not due to differences in IQ, which we directly assessed. Likewise, it should be noted that all of the children in this Minnesota study were born into poverty. Therefore, social class is also not a likely explanation of the variations in drawing we found.

There was another group of drawings that were very unusual or odd or portrayed confusion, with starts and stops, and things crossed out or erased. Figures may have floated in the air or had distorted faces. At times there were ominous, dark images or threatening aspects. One 8-year-old child, for example, placed himself and his brother inside a tall dark tower with barred windows. Another figure was skillfully depicted as being under the ground. When asked to label the figures he said that this was his mother. His mother was very much alive and healthy at the time, though a few years later, as a preteen, he did assault her with a weapon. It meant something very scary to be in his family. Almost only children with histories of disorganized attachment made such unusual or ominous drawings. Research by others (see Chapter 10) has shown that these are the children who as infants in fact had frightening parents. The world is seen as a very threatening place to them. We will elaborate on the origins and fate of such a meaning system in Chapter 13.

When the children we studied were 11-years-old we used an array of representational techniques that capitalized on their ample language skills. We had them rapidly produce completions to sentence stems, tell stories to standard clinical picture material, discuss a moral fable, and provide interview responses regarding their own friendships and friendships in general. As before, we wanted to probe their expectations regarding themselves and others, especially parents and peers. Once again, these measures, especially in combination, revealed great variations in how these pre-adolescent children saw themselves and social relationships; that is, the meanings they were abstracting from their current and past experience.

In the sentence completion task, critical items followed warm-up items that produced routinized answers; for example, "I like to eat . . . ." (to which most of the children quickly said, "pizza"). After such easy items, almost all children subsequently responded freely and without hesitation to filler and key items. Those of special interest were items about family such as, "My mother . . ."; My family treats me . . ."; "My mother never . . ."; "My mother is happy when . . ."; and "I go to my mother when . . ." There were also items about peers; for example, "Most kids like to . . ."; Boys (girls) are . . ."; and "Other kids always . . ." Finally, some items more directly tapped thoughts about the self: "It makes me sad when . . ."; I wish I was . . ."; "When I am in a group I . . ."

For the stories the children were shown four different pictures, previously used widely by clinicians. From the Michigan Pictures, we used the card showing two nonsmiling children face-to-face, and the card showing four children playing with another child off to the side. The depicted children were girls or boys in accord with the gender of the child we were probing. From the Thematic Apperception Test we used the "slumped figure" and the blank card. The latter is always used to see what the child comes up with when nothing is suggested.

The moral fable was a tale about a porcupine and a group of mice. It was winter and the mice had found a cave for shelter. The porcupine came along and asked if he could stay there too. The mice agreed, but soon it wasn't working out. It was crowded and the porcupine's quills were a problem. The child was asked to explain the problem and to say how it should be resolved. After they gave their first solution, they were asked how else the problem might be solved. This procedure clearly evokes moral issues surrounding fairness and equity.

Finally, the friendship interview probed the child's idea about the nature of friendships. We asked about friends they had, what made the friendship special, how important is it to have a friend, and how one goes about developing a friendship. We were especially interested in their ideas about what could make a friendship end and whether conflicts, in particular, would end a friendship.

There were huge variations in responses to all of these procedures. In the sentence completions, responses ranged from "My mother "*always helps me with my problems*" to "*yells at me*" or "*is upset with me*," and from "Other kids always "*are fun to be with*" to "*pick on me*" or "*are stupid.*" Some children clearly portrayed a picture that their caregiver would be responsive when they were sad or had a problem and portrayed other children as liking them and being fun to be with. They had no doubts about their worth as a partner. Other children projected a lack of support from their parents and expected to be teased, picked on or rejected by peers. Some projected a sense of isolation.

With the cards, the slumped figure was interpreted as "*sleeping and having a nice dream*" or, in contrast, as depressed or dead. The card with two children suggested to some that they were fighting, to others that they were talking about something interesting. Responses to the group of children playing were especially rich. Note that the reason the one child is standing on the side is completely ambiguous in the picture. Nonetheless, many children said that the group would invite the child standing on the outside to play (and perhaps that then they would all be friends). Others said that they would not invite him to play (or even had kicked him out in the first place) and he or she would go home sad or mad. For many children there were conflict themes introduced in one card or another. Some children routinely brought such conflicts to successful resolution, but, as with the play of preschoolers, some children had great difficulty doing that in their stories. Bad endings prevailed. Alternatively, things would approach resolution, then take a bad turn again, back and forth, conveying an inner ambivalence. Some children saw threat or violence in all of the cards, including the blank card. Often this would suddenly intrude in the midst of an otherwise benign story.

Some children saw amicable solutions to the dilemma of the porcupine and the mice. They might divide the cave, enlarge it, create separate spaces, search for a larger place for all of them, or help the porcupine find another place to live. These responses underscore the advance in moral reasoning common at this age. Some even said, "so that they could go on being friends." And yet, there was nothing in the story presented about them being friends in the first place. This idea came from the meaning systems stored in their minds. Such a common interpretation made by children with secure histories derived from their inner views about relationships. Of course the parties have as an important goal maintaining the relationship! Other children suggested more conflict laden outcomes, for example that one party or the other would have to go (e.g., "it was the mice's place first") or they would, pardon the pun, just be "stuck" with the situation. Afterall, in the moral world of middle childhood, "a deal is a deal" and must be honored. Some again saw violence as likely, saying that the porcupine is bigger and tougher so the mice will be kicked out. Such "force solutions" were reminiscent of what some children had seen as ways to solve problems in our assessments at 4 years of age, though at this later age they were more graphic and at times elaborated. It is of note that all of the children wrestled with the moral implications of this situation. Even children with less supportive histories took up the challenge to respond.

The children also had very different views about how friendships worked based on our interviews, especially about their durability and robustness. For some children, despite intelligence comparable to the others, friendships were mystifying. For others they were seen as fragile and difficult to sustain. But, for many children, friendships were seen as vital and strong and they had clear ideas about how to build friendships. They were confident about their friendships because of this understanding. In response to the question about whether having an argument would cause a friendship to end, some saw that it would certainly end the friendship, but many said it would not. One 11-year old with a secure attachment history, for example, thought for a bit, then said: "No, I think actually you would be even better friends, because you would understand each other better." This conveys both an understanding of the depth of true friendships as well as their robustness.

As was the case with the drawings, it would be inadvisable to infer early history, or even the child's meaning system from any of the individual findings here. Rather than even relying on just one of these four procedures, our approach was to look for the coherent themes that arose across all of them (Carlson et al., 2004). While this was challenging, independent raters were in fact able to do this. As it turned out, there was, in fact, a notable degree of coherence regarding views of self and relationships portrayed. For those with histories of secure attachment and supportive care, the self was portrayed as valued and liked by both parents and peers. Relationships were seen as engaging and fun and as a place where they belonged. If problems arose, they could be worked out through their own efforts and through cooperation with others. Such resolutions were not only expected, they were valued. These children had a clear understanding of how relationships work, and they valued closeness and reciprocity in relationships. As an example, one child first talked about how she knew she and another child were very best friends, not just because "she is friendly and she's nice" but because "she will tell me secrets that she wouldn't tell anyone else." She went on to say similar things about another friend but added that she might say things to Karin (her best friend) that she wouldn't say to her. In other words she understood the hierarchical organization of the relationship network. This is remarkable for a 10-year-old child. It reflects a strong motivation to understand the meaning of social relationships and one's place in peer society.

The four procedures yielded a quite different and yet coherent picture of the inner world of other children. Some children clearly saw themselves as alone in an alienating world, with little closeness with others and little support when they were needy. Even by this age some of them denigrated others ("they're stupid") or pushed them away, perhaps even suggesting that relationships were of little value. Such a theme will emerge further when we later discuss the Adult Attachment Interview in Chapter 10. These children in fact elicited the most negative evaluations by the other children in our camp exit interviews. They were viewed as aggressive or as not fitting in.

Another group of children found relationships to be difficult, frustrating, and beyond their capacities, even though they did try to have them. These children were doubtful about getting their needs met at home or when with peers. They worried about being teased or picked on. For many, the world of peers was intimidating. Other children did not view these "worriers" as mean, but neither were they preferred as playmates.

The Consolidation of World Views

These differences in worldviews were forecast by the cumulative history of the children. The sense of connection or lack thereof has roots from all the way back to infancy. The belief in one's effectiveness and capacity for self-control goes back to the toddler and the preschool periods. The preschool period is also where one develops a first connection to the peer group and the capacities to engage and sustain interactions. We found that children who struggled with peer engagement in the preschool era often did so because of a historical lack of support. Now in middle childhood the social deficits brought forward from the prior period make peer relationships even more challenging. The tendency to give up on relationships becomes stronger, and ineptness with peers stands out even more. This is the way development often works.

By age 10 or 11 years, children have deep and distinctive views regarding relationships and how they should function. This is a basic system of morality, and meaning both creates it and evolves from it. As we have seen, some children see relationships as robust, readily withstanding conflict. When a disagreement or argument arises, they do not find it unduly threatening. After all, in their experience relationships are durable and each person is committed to maintaining the relationship. In fact, as the emotionally precocious child described earlier stated, conflicts are a normal part of relationships and a path to deeper understanding and even trust. We know we can weather this and, when we do, we will be even stronger and more resistant to dissolution.

For others, conflict, argument, and even mere disagreement are threatening; they *mean* the relationship is in jeopardy (and perhaps is even likely to end). As we learned later in our study of adult couples (Sroufe et al., 2005), those that were well functioning certainly had conflicts, like all couples do. When we explicitly asked them to discuss a conflict in their relationship (money problems, in-law problems, etc.) they certainly could disagree and things could even become a bit heated. However, they much more likely came to a satisfactory resolution than did the less stable partners. And, when we moved them on to another task, they could let the conflict go and work effectively together. Other couples kept bringing issues back up and could not regain a collaborative stance.

These different views on relationships are developmental constructions. Whether relationship conflict is threatening or relatively benign is a meaning system created age by age. Basic beliefs in the value of closeness, the capacity to trust, and the self as worthy are founded in infant attachment relationships. But that is not all there is to it. As noted in Chapter 6, preschoolers fortified with this set of expectations more actively and positively engage the other children. Because of this and the support for exploration and emotion regulation they received in the earliest years, they are also able to sustain interactions with others despite the inevitable difficulties that arise. Thus, they gain further experience with relationships being durable. They learn that conflicts can be resolved and they learn about how to do that. So, when they form the close friendships that characterize middle childhood, they have all that going for them too. All too often, those that had anxious attachments in infancy – whose belief in the responsiveness of others and confidence in themselves was compromised –are precisely the children who find interactions with other preschoolers difficult to maintain and experience frustration and failure. Conflict does lead to failure, over and over. This comes to be what they will expect and what will make sense to them.

Change and Continuity in the Search for Meaning

Development, of course, is also a product of current circumstances. For some children home life becomes more stable and supportive and, as it does, the self-confidence of the child improves. We documented that, when depressive symptoms in parents waned, child functioning, including expectations regarding self and others, improved. Teachers, coaches, or mentors can also be a source of support, as can grandparents, aunts, uncles, and other adults in the child's life. In our study we confirmed the value of such relationships.

Since competence is so valued in middle childhood, the child who develops a special talent or skill – a facility with sports, a sense of humor, an aptitude for crafts or games – acquires admiration in the group and this too can promote self-esteem. New experiences and new ways of responding, if they are achieved, can alter one's expectations and core beliefs; that is, new experiences can transform meaning. Development of talents and supportive teachers and others can lead to positive feedback and greater self-confidence. Supportive peers and adults can improve children's expectations concerning themselves and others. Likewise, decline in support or overwhelming challenges can erode previously established positive beliefs. One's sense of place in the world is a complex interplay of past history and current circumstances. The child who has difficulty navigating friendship may find positive feedback by developing a competency.

It goes both ways: expectations frame behavior, and new experiences and new competencies can change expectations. We clearly saw this dynamic as we followed children over time (Carlson et al., 2004). Still, new experiences did not erase or over-write past history; rather, they seemed to provide a new chapter. Children who had corrective experiences following negative beginnings remained more vulnerable to subsequent stresses and challenges than children with consistently supportive experiences. One could often see the shadows of their past history even when they were functioning well. The lucky ones who had experienced good developmental support found pleasure in developing social competence. Those who were not fully prepared for the social challenges of middle childhood should be applauded for their continued efforts.

Likewise, those with positive histories who encountered setbacks (and the consequent altering of their expectations for self and relationships) remained more likely to take advantage of new opportunities and rebound in subsequent periods. We will elaborate on these themes when we discuss change and resilience in Chapter 11.

CHAPTER 8

Adolescence
Finding Personal Meaning

> He's really quiet but I think that's because he's been having hard times. When you get to know him, he's really nice. He's very thoughtful.
>
> Kasondra kind of likes Adrian and he kinda likes her, but he can't do nothin', 'cause Darcia – she's Adrian's cousin – She's friends with Adrian's girlfriend, Tanya, and he knows she would tell her.
>
> I know she was upset with me, but she doesn't understand that I have to be part of the group (of black girls). I have to show them that I'm one of them.
>
> You see, we're like a family, and coach he's like our father.
>
> He's kinda obnoxious and immature but he's one of us, so we accept him.

It is almost not possible to overstate the momentous developmental changes that occur in adolescence. Beyond the hormonal and other physical changes, with their attendant consequences for self-concept and emotional experience, there are qualitative leaps in thinking ability. In reaction to a wave of intense experiences, the adolescent brain is developing rapidly, more than any time since the toddler period. And this spurt is similar in that it involves both increased dendritic elaboration and pruning and sculpting of the brain. Teens have the reasoning capacity of adults and, in time, further experiences will lead to more full integration of the brain and more complex understanding of relationships. But the brain is not fully matured. During the teen years certain control functions are still not fully developed.

Since the minds of teens are not yet fully developed, this can at times lead to both inner turmoil and outer conflict. All the issues they have negotiated before must be negotiated again, though now in new ways and in new arenas. Issues of trust and vulnerability come to the fore in relations with age mates and new regimes must be established with parents as they move toward the status of equals. All of these changes and challenges result in experiences that can be very intense. The mood swings, feelings of loneliness and even depression, but also the idealism and exuberance associated with this era all follow.

The interrelated changes in all aspects of adolescent development have clear significance for meaning making and personal meaning. Previously unimaginable meanings arise, as the person looks beyond the surface behavior of self and others to underlying feelings and motives. Entire networks of social relationships can be examined. Situations can be considered in terms of hypothetical possibilities as well as in terms of what is.

All of the statements at the beginning of this chapter were made by 15- and 16-year-olds in the Minnesota study. These examples illustrate the capacity to consider deeper meanings of behavior, to infer the motives of others, and to grasp the complexity of relationships. For example, being a quiet person can happen for different reasons; it can mean different things. The boy being described is Mikel, the case we presented in Chapter 2. Other teens could still see his inner positive core, though he was going through a difficult time.

As in the second example, motives can be both complex and conflicting. A person can want one thing but not at the expense of another. One teen can know this not only about themselves but about another teen. Look at the complexity of this second statement! This is incredibly nuanced thinking. In a new way, the person can look at things from the outside, consider both their own and another's point of view, and can even see different viewpoints simultaneously. The same situation can have different meanings for each of you.

The two teenagers referred to in the third example, one white and one mixed race, had been very close friends during the summer camp 5 years previously. The white girl had come eager to carry on the friendship and both girls were indeed happy to see each other. But the ethnically diverse camp posed particular challenges for the mixed-race girl, and she felt it necessary to consolidate her black identity by being part of the group of African-American girls. She realized that this was difficult for her friend to understand. It is noteworthy that these young women, both with histories of positive support, did have a chance to talk this all through before the camp reunion ended and reestablish harmony. Both of these teens were able to achieve a level of role taking well beyond anything possible in earlier life. Without doubt important new meanings were achieved.

The fourth example shows an advance in analogical thinking. In explaining how his basketball team had such great success, this teen was able to convey the importance of emotional closeness of team members and coach by using the analogy of family. This young man had lost his father in early childhood, obviously a hugely meaningful experience, which perhaps was in important ways reworked through his relationship with his coach.

In the final statement, a teen describes a troubled and truly disruptive boy who nonetheless was "one of us." It is easy to slip by the profundity of the development portrayed in this remark. It reflects a huge advance beyond the sense of "we" in middle childhood. "We" then referred to a group of friends or perhaps one's family. But now it is much more inclusive, including those outside of your circle and even those one may not like. It is a major step toward feeling a part of a broad community, humanity at large, or all of life. It is a culmination of a path of belonging that began in the attachment relationship in infancy and continued to the first connection with peers in the preschool years and the deeper friendships of middle childhood. All of this was documented to be true in the young woman making this statement. At the core of her network of meanings is a valuing of relationships and a belief in their worth. The youth she was describing had little of this sense of being a part of the group, and he continually revealed his alienation through his disruptive behavior; still others accepted him at least to some extent.

Many adolescents achieve all of the cognitive tools that adults have; yet, there is more growth to come. Adults, as experience accumulates, can take a longer view and have a greatly expanded notion of possible viewpoints. They can realize that there may be other complex alternatives to the one our second child proposed; that, however intricate the structure we assemble, it can be wrong (at any point); and that two such complex, alternative structures can both be true in a way. Wisdom takes time to develop, but we could not do any of this without the steps taken in adolescence.

The Expanding Mind of the Adolescent

Two prominent, emerging capacities in adolescence are new levels of reflection and abstract thinking. In fact, Piaget referred to the central advance in adolescence as the ability for "reflective abstraction." By this he meant the capacity to step outside of one's situation and to look back at it — to see it from the outside. This is part of a whole network of new capacities, such as the ability to see multiple possibilities, including not just those that are but those that might be or could be. One's family can be compared not only to other families but also to what a family *could* be like. Multiple possible futures can be entertained. One can expand thinking beyond concrete reality to hypothetical possibilities and to abstract concepts such as justice and the unconscious. There is a new meta-cognitive capacity; that is, the ability to think about thought itself.

The ability to move beyond concrete thinking for many adolescents leads to advances in morality and to a surging idealism. The solid core of morality based on working to understand why rules are what they are paves the way for now what can be described as "principled" morality. They come to understand that right and wrong are not always simple; that sometimes a rule must be broken because of a higher ideal. Moreover, morality is not simply a list of prohibitions. To be truly moral one must be committed to justice and to a greater good. They see things in the world that need to be changed, and they may feel both a responsibility and the power to work toward these changes. Such moral growth certainly does not end in adolescence, but it often surges there.

The cognitive advances in adolescence can, of course, lead to very different socioemotional outcomes. Years ago, Kenneth Keniston, in his two landmark books, *Young Radicals* (1968) and *The Uncommitted* (1966), graphically described distinctive stances regarding connection with the community in adolescents perceiving the limitations of society. Based on his extensive interviews, he found that, among those protesting the social conditions of the 1960s there were two quite disparate groups. Those he called "radicals" were actually idealistic and believed strongly that through action the world could be made a better place. They were motivated to build a more just, harmonious, and connected society. The "uncommitted," on the other hand, seeing the same ills, were more cynical and pessimistic. They saw no path toward a better society and no point in working toward it. His interviews also suggested good reasons for the way these contrasting stances came to be, with the degree of support from parents being the key. It would be for later developmental research to confirm such ideas.

Teenagers also come to understand the complexities of the inner world of the mind. Just as another may be seen to have mixed feelings, so too might you. People, including you, might not even be aware of true motives. One may do things without knowing the reason. You can understand that you behave in different ways with different people and in different circumstances, sometimes with conscious understanding and sometimes not.

Robert Selman explored some of the complexity of adolescent thought about the inner workings of the mind using a story about someone whose beloved dog, "Pepper," had died, and others were trying to decide whether they should give him a puppy. Teens realized the nuances involved. For example, one said: "He might at some level feel that it would be unloyal [sic] to Pepper to just go out and replace the dog. He may feel guilty about it. So he says he doesn't want the dog. (Interviewer: Is he aware of this?) Probably not. He both wants a new dog and yet he doesn't think it's right" (Selman, 1980, p. 106).

Finally, adolescents have a notable capacity to extrapolate from the past and project into the future. Not only *can* they think about the future in insightful ways; they *do* think about the future in ways that were not at all common in earlier childhood. They can imagine different futures for themselves, and they can examine their lives in terms of those imagined futures. At times this can lead to strong feelings, even bordering on crisis.

One 15-year-old we studied summarized some of the challenges posed by all of these emerging capacities by relating the following: "I just have all these feelings and things inside ... the feelings are so strong, and my parents don't understand. They won't let me do anything. I'm afraid that by the time I'm old enough to do the things I need to do – by the time they'll let me – I won't have the feelings anymore." We know that she may well still have the feelings, but she could not know that at the time. Teens can feel things very intensely.

One reason for potential emotional crisis is that adolescents have a new understanding of their complete uniqueness. They know that no one is exactly the same as them or can really fully know their experience. Thus, as they rework all of the previous issues of trust, autonomy, and so forth, all in new and/or changing relationships, they may have a sense of managing all of the accompanying emotions by themselves. At some level they know no one else can really do it for them.

Implications for Self and Relationships

A major target of the adolescent's emerging reflective capacities is the self. Such reflection is critical for forming a personal identity, for actually knowing who one is. It can lead to an integration of disparate features of the self and also for the first time the understanding of one's complete uniqueness. As several teens in interviews stated, "There is no one exactly like me." Younger children describe themselves more in terms of how they are like their peers.

Of course, the power of this capacity is also such that it may reveal what at first appear to be inconsistencies. You can recognize that you behave differently in different situations, that you are concealing genuine feelings, and that you at times pretend to be ways you are not feeling, perhaps in order to protect yourself or to impress others. In time, inconsistencies can often be reconciled with a more complex understanding of social nuances. Of course there are things you share with friends and not parents. Of course you are most revealing only with those you trust. Sometimes concealment is prudent. On the other hand, for some, as we will discuss in Chapter 12, deep self-reflection is too scary and inconsistencies grow into dissociative tendencies.

At every age, our understanding of who we are is inextricably connected with our social relationships. This is never truer than in adolescence. And at each age relationship networks become more complex, reaching a new apex in the teenage years. For the first time one has what are rightfully called intimate relationships, based upon mutual trust and vulnerability. Just as you know you think about others, you also realize that they can think about you, and you can think about them thinking about you. Teens have a greater understanding of what true friendship means. Deeper, and at times lasting, friendships may be formed. Sexual intimacy often first occurs. The network of same-gender and cross-gender friendships and same and mixed gender groups, as well as non-binary or transitioning friends, is extraordinarily complex. The new capacity to see the broader picture and specific features simultaneously allows you to see your place and the place of others in the group.

Our adolescent assessments, and especially the data from our teen camps, demonstrated that those with histories of secure attachment, other kinds of parental support, and earlier competence with peers, took with them an advantage in engaging these complex tasks of adolescence. A central part of personal meaning is the perception of one's place in the social world. In adolescence there are close friendships within and between genders, as well as intimate relationships. So individual relationships must be coordinated with the larger group of same-gender friends and the mixed-gender group or "crowd."

A "crowd" is an organization of couples and individuals that is distinguished by the regularity of interaction among these members. Such a crowd formed in each of our camps and was readily recognized by the counselors and observers. It was striking to us how well the teenagers in our camps could describe the network of relationships in each camp. Most knew who were in couples and even who wanted to be with someone but were not. Those who were in the "crowd" knew who all the members of the crowd were and they knew who was not. As was the case for the teen that described the "obnoxious" boy as one of us, they also had a sense of group identity. So they might well know that they were part of a couple, part of the "crowd," and part of the larger group. Other children had some knowledge of group structure, even though they were not full participants for a variety of long-standing or contemporaneous reasons. One did not have to be part of the crowd to be functioning well. But occasionally, a teen completely lacked understanding of the group structure and had little sense of their place in it. They really didn't know what it meant to fit into a group. This was usually consistent with a history of lack of early support and lack of competence with peers in the school years.

In middle childhood children learn to function in groups and negotiate conflicts with friends. Adolescents take this a step further by learning to negotiate in groups. In our teen camps we set up what is called a "revealed differences" task in the following way. The teens were told to decide among themselves how a portion of the money for the camp was to be spent, but certain rules had to be followed. They had to agree on an activity that involved the whole group (such as a recreational activity for everyone). The first step was to discuss this in a group of four members (all boys or all girls). They had to come to an agreed upon decision, and then elect a spokesperson to take their input to the next level (eight boys or girls). Each small group had made a decision that they now put forward (thus the "revealed differences" title). Negotiations get a little tougher. A new decision is made, and again a spokesperson is elected, either one of the original ones or a different person. Finally the eight boys and eight girls come together to hash out their differences and come to a conclusion in each camp.

The sessions were video recorded so that ratings could be made of leadership, involvement, self-confidence, and overall social competence, all with high reliability. These ratings correlated remarkably well with independent counselor ratings of social competence and self-confidence. They showed clearly that those with histories of positive support were higher in all regards. Across our 3 camps of 16 teens each, there were 18 spokesperson elections. Almost all of these were young people who had histories of secure attachment. Some of the qualitative findings were even more impressive, as when everyone would always turn to one particular boy when a suggestion was made. A small nod of his head would be enough for the matter to be decided. "This was not because he was the largest or most aggressive, but because of the authority he wielded by dint of his confidence and centrality" (Sroufe, 2020, p. 141). (This was the boy who made the analogy about a family when talking about his team and their coach at the beginning of this chapter.)

This procedure demonstrated in a dramatic way the different meaning systems brought forward by different young people. Some, of course, saw this very complex arena as quite threatening. They had neither the skills nor the confidence to join in and express themselves freely. Two characteristic reactions we saw were disengagement and disruptiveness. For example, one teen, who had purposefully set his mattress on fire immediately upon arriving at the camp, constantly blurted out irrelevant ideas in faulty attempts to be humorous. He wound up being shut down and ignored. As in our preschool studies, both disengagement and disruptiveness undercut important learning that could have taken place. For these disruptive individuals, incapacitating meaning systems were reinforced.

On the other hand, some of the teens obviously saw this situation as interesting and engaging. They participated effectively and enthusiastically. There was a task to be done and they were up to it. They put forth constructive ideas confidently because they felt that their opinions were valuable. They were oriented toward collaboration, a legacy of their early-formed sense of connection with others. They were able to assert their opinions but still listen to others, much as they also did with our parent–child discussions at age 13 (discussed in the following section). They were able to be vulnerable and freely express themselves. They were comfortable in this setting. This situation reveals again the cumulative nature of development. It drew upon attitudes and skills being developed from the earliest months of life, including the capacity for emotion regulation, engagement with peers, and the ability to negotiate conflicts. Disagreements are not catastrophic. They do not mean things will soon deteriorate. For them also, these previously formed meaning systems were supported and elaborated. A true integration of all of this is a boon to identity formation.

Profound changes in thinking about and understanding one's family also often occur in adolescence. Really for the first time you can realize how you have been influenced by family experiences and even *how things might have been different*. Your family can be contrasted with other families and other hypothetical ways of being. This can lead to increased family conflict but it can also represent an important opportunity for growth and change. With the new "reflective abstraction" capacities, there is the possibility of knowing that one was not to blame for past mistreatment and also to develop understanding of why parents behaved as they did.

This capacity to think about why people – you, your friends, your parents – are as they are can lead to great transformation of the meaning of experience.

Finding Meaning in "Autonomy with Connection"

Every adolescent faces two major, interrelated tasks. The first is to forge some kind of stable, coherent identity. The second is to assume responsibility for their behavior and their future; in other words to face adulthood.

Adolescence has been long understood as the developmental period in which individuals establish a network of personal meanings, including their place in the social world. Erik Erikson (1963) famously described the task of this period as forming a *personal identity*, the alternative to which is "role confusion." Establishing one's identity is a challenging task, perhaps especially so in modern times. Not only do a myriad of potential life courses lie in front of modern teens, but they encounter a great diversity of cultural, ethnic, and gender definitions in which to define a unique place. A sense of personal identity is established through exploration of one's values and ideals; that is, by developing a coherent sense of what is meaningful to you – what it means to be you. One's past meanings are reexamined in light of current meanings and with a view to the future. All of this is critical because it provides a framework and a guide for how you behave and how you appraise your behavior.

Adolescence is also referred to as the age of emancipation. Even though ideally connection with one's parents is clearly maintained, a dramatically greater degree of independence is achieved. Many current scholars describe this as "autonomy with connection." This becomes perhaps the most complex challenge of adolescence. Parents play a critical role in promoting this autonomy with connection, as do peers, but the young person now has an awareness that the future is under his or her own control. Plans and goals for the future are part of defining oneself. We looked at this emancipation task in two ways during the teenage years, through a laboratory assessment at age 13 and an interview at age 19.

Relationships with Parents at the Transition to Adolescence

The lab assessment at age 13 was the last time we observed parents and youth together. The tasks we used were drawn from Jeanne and Jack Block (1980) at Berkeley and were explicitly aimed at the autonomy/connection issue. Each task was designed so that the teen had particular expertise or would be in control. For example, one task was to come up with a "campaign" to reduce tobacco use among young people. In another task the parent was blindfolded, and the teen had to guide them in putting together objects (taken from a standard IQ test). Another was to come up with an agreed upon plan for a vacation together. It can be seen that, in some of these, the two were equal partners, in some the child had special expertise, and, in at least one, roles were reversed. In the block assembly, for example, the task only worked well if the parent could let the child be in charge. This was exceptionally difficult for some parents and for some teens. Some parents would not relinquish control and would continue trying to tell the teen what direction to give them or would try doing it without the teen's help, a complete impossibility. Some teens became passive; others frustrated and upset. Such difficulties relinquishing control were subsequently associated with independently assessed behavior problems of the teen. We will discuss the boundary issues that arose in this situation in Chapter 10.

This assessment was of special interest to us because it reflected the intersection of transforming meaning systems. It is no longer the case, as it was in infancy, of the child developing in a meaning system rather solely constructed by the parent. The teen now brings a constructed meaning system, one that is rapidly expanding and changing. Moreover, even during middle childhood the child accepts the authority of the parents' viewpoint, even when resisting that authority. But, with adolescence, the child begins to be able to question that authority, forming viewpoints that are autonomous and at times at odds with those of the parents. The teen comes to rely more on his or her own experience and own understanding. The parent is taxed to respond to this evolving situation, perhaps confronting anew issues in their own system of meanings. They have to be able to accept a great deal of change. How difficult this is will be influenced by their own histories and current supports.

How well this goes is crucial for the child's identity development – what it means to be them. As when guidance provided by parents in the 2-year tool problems gave the child the message that *they* could do it, parent acceptance of the teen's new authority tells them now that they can and are taking this step toward autonomy. They can trust in their own viewpoint and their own capacities or, in contrary cases, that they are not ready to leave childhood. This is a critical organizing meaning.

These assessments also let us glimpse an important way in which culture and situation influence meaning. Our scales were developed using video recordings from a Berkeley sample that included a number of recent Asian immigrants. A few of these teens were quite controlling of their parents, a finding that is usually associated with a traumatic history. Yet, in this group this was not associated with trauma nor with other teen problems. Instead, upon closer examination, it was found to be only in families where the parents knew little English and the child took charge, helping the parent to negotiate the tasks successfully. In some cases, it was clear that the parent instructed the child to do so. These teens were seen as socially competent in other assessments.

Conceptualizing One's Future

Later, when young people in the Minnesota study were 19 years old, we gave them wide-ranging interviews covering family relationships, friendships, school and/or work, and their goals for the future. In short, we wanted to see how they were negotiating the challenges laid out in this chapter. This work revealed that teens with supportive histories were able to maintain close connections with their families, even while they were expanding their social networks and orienting themselves toward a more autonomous future.

One of the major goals in this interview work was to determine if they had some plan for their future. Was this plan realistic? Was the plan meaningful to them? Were they committed to it? Were they taking meaningful steps to carry it out? The plans, of course, were quite diverse, and, of course may well have changed later. There were many different ideas about how to achieve the goals in question. Still, it was quite possible to appraise the clarity of vision and strength of commitment. For example, one might have a vague plan about becoming a teacher, but had dropped out of high school, had no plan for getting a GED (graduate equivalent degree), knew nothing about the local community colleges, and was currently unemployed, having lost a series of jobs because of not showing up for work. All of this would yield a very low scale score. In contrast, another might have the same plan, but they had gotten the GED, had determined the procedure for enrolment in a local community college, had the application materials and knew the deadlines, had studied up on courses, and had been saving money by working two jobs so work hours could be cut when the school term began. Therefore, despite the similarity in goal, this would lead to a very high rating.

Another young man had an idea about starting his own "splat ball" facility (where contestants try to shoot others with paint guns). While this was not a dream the researchers likely shared, nonetheless this young man's level of planning, spadework, and preparation made it realistic. He had been employed at such a facility for some time, working his way up to manager. He knew everything about the business and talked about it with great enthusiasm. He also got a top rating.

This measure of clarity and vision was predictable from the individuals' developmental histories beginning in the earliest years, including infant attachment, and it forecast adaptation at later ages as well. Finding meaning in one's current life and seeing meaning in the future are powerful things.

Opportunities and Vulnerabilities

Adolescence can be a very challenging period. Another anecdote from the Minnesota study can illustrate why this is so. We had filmed these children many times at every age, first with parental permission and later with permission of the young person as well. They never had any issue with this ... until the camps at age 15. Now they wanted to negotiate some rules and boundaries; especially they wanted places and times they could be without cameras. As one young woman explained it, "You see when we were 10, we weren't that aware of things. Now we're aware of everything." Such new awareness changes everything, including the meaning of being filmed. Teenagers have greater awareness of their inner feelings and greater awareness of discrepancies between these inner feelings and outer behavior. Since they can see this in others, they know others can see it in them. All of this leads to an increase in feelings of vulnerability. This in turn underlies the increase in emotional difficulties many teens have. However, the new awareness of feelings and the new sense of vulnerability do not have the same meaning to all teenagers. Some are able to fully engage the opportunities for growth despite feelings of vulnerability.

We were able to assess this "capacity for vulnerability" by seeing the teens we studied in emotionally challenging situations during our weekend camps (for example, trust exercises and a camp dance). Some could not participate or participated in a guarded way (shrinking back or acting up). Counselors with no knowledge of individual history rated each teen across the entire array of challenging camp experiences. It was found that those with histories of secure attachment in infancy had a greater capacity to tolerate the feelings of vulnerability and to fully participate.

It is striking that infant attachment security predicts even more strongly the capacity for close relationships in the teen years than it did in middle childhood, although it had been notable at that time as well. Usually predictions are stronger the shorter the time span traversed; yet here were these predictions to a later time. We believe that this is because issues of trust arise in a way in adolescence that is beyond what is called for in middle childhood. And trust is the core of early attachment. The central meaning of secure attachment concerns the feeling of safety in the relationship. It is this meaning that is carried forward to the teen years and beyond.

The team building trust exercises were quite revealing with regard to the inner meaning systems of the teens. For example, in one exercise, a partner is blindfolded and the teen's task is to be a guide through a walking course. Many of the teens, of course, were very supportive of their partners, recognizing the vulnerability the partner would experience. They did a good job understanding the task from the other's point of view. They led them steadily and surely, not rushing them and encouraging them when needed, much as some parents did in our 2-year tool problems task. Reminiscent of our preschool empathy studies, others behaved in quite unhelpful and, at times, exploitative ways. They might, for example, lead the partner into a tree, thinking that was humorous. One teen had found a small snake, and thought it was quite fun to put it into his blindfolded partner's hand. It clearly frightened her. Others were not mean but were simply inept at offering help. We had seen such patterns before in the ways some parents treated their children in our early childhood problem-solving tasks. And we had seen it in the behavior of the children in our preschool. The numbers of children behaving in these ways was small, but consistently they had been children with histories of anxious attachment and unsupportive parenting.

As we saw repeatedly in our studies, what was carried forward from prior developmental periods was not so much particular ways of behaving but previously acquired meanings. A striking example concerns mixed-gender relationships. As we described in Chapter 7, in middle childhood there are actually peer-enforced rules governing interacting with members of the other gender. In public settings boys hang out with boys and girls with girls. Interactions with the other gender must not explicitly reveal interest and one can only go into a zone occupied by the other gender if accompanied by a partner or if compelled by an adult, or it is accidental (for example, the chance encounter at a drinking fountain). Gender boundaries are strictly maintained. Most children abide by these "rules." And our study showed that it was those who maintained such boundaries in middle childhood that were most effective in mixed-gender relationships in adolescence. Also, it was those who formed close, loyal friendships with someone of the same gender in middle childhood who became close with someone of the opposite gender in adolescence. Experience in a loyal friendship instilled the value of close peer connections, and the meaning of these experiences provided the foundation for subsequent intimacy. As always, it is meaning that is carried forward.

On the whole, those with histories of secure attachment seemed better able to weather the challenges of adolescence. They were more likely to have effective relationships and less likely to have serious emotional problems or engage in antisocial behavior than were those with histories of anxious attachment. But development is complex, and these are generalizations from group data. Some teens with secure histories certainly struggle. As Terrie Moffitt (1993) has pointed out, adolescence is a particularly vulnerable time for getting caught in "snares," such as abuse of alcohol and other drugs or teenage pregnancy. Secure attachment history is no guarantee of eluding these. Some with histories of secure attachment of course have life-long problems, and some with histories of anxious attachment later thrive. As we will discuss in later chapters, such changes in meaning systems are themselves often understandable in light of changing experience.

PART III

The Organized and Organizing Nature of Meaning

CHAPTER 9

Meaning as the Currency of Development

The problem of finding continuity in individual development plagued developmental psychology for decades. The search began with efforts to find stability at the level of specific behaviors or constant manifestations of dimensions such as dependency, aggressiveness, and so forth. Such efforts were doomed to failure for many reasons, not the least of which was that such behaviors or dimensions are expressed so differently at different ages and their expression means something so different at different ages. All infants are dependent and being highly attentive to an adult as an infant means something vastly different than constantly hovering near a teacher in kindergarten. Likewise, no young infant can be truly aggressive, because they really do not have the cognitive capacity for deliberately hurtful behavior. Vigorousness of nursing is never going to predict aggression.

In fact, nothing that you can measure outside of the context of primary relationships in infancy can predict much of anything within the broad span of normal infants. Observational measures of temperament in the first months of life are notoriously unstable. Moreover, the behavior and competence of children changes so dramatically over time that finding individual continuity in the manifestation of specific behaviors is hopeless.

The solution to this problem was in a shift to the level of meaning. For example, infant attachment relationships are commonly stable, even though the specific behaviors through which quality of attachment is shown change in fundamental ways. Frequency of looking at the parent, smiling, and seeking contact show almost no stability across infancy, but the organization of attachment behaviors reveals the same pattern; the same meaning (see Chapter 4). Similarly, toddler friendships cannot be predictive of the loyal friendships in middle childhood, whatever superficial similarities there appear to be. These are qualitatively different peer relationships. The capacity for such loyal friendships *is* strongly predicted by the quality of infant attachment to parents; yet, on the surface, these relationships could not be more different. The relationship between peers is symmetrical and reciprocal among equals. The other is a dependency/ nurturer relationship, involving none of the joint problem-solving components of later childhood relationships. Still, a core of emotional connection and investment and a confidence in the availability of the other is maintained, and it is at that level that stability becomes manifest.

Even when one wants to measure the same thing over time, a focus on meaning is the answer. For example, we measured parent/child boundary problems both when the children were aged 3 and 13 years. There was a significant degree of correspondence in ratings made at these two ages by independent raters who had no knowledge of the other scores. But it was not identical behavior that was the source of continuity. At 3 years of age, problems with boundary maintenance were revealed solely in parental behavior (abdicating responsibility, teasing, flirting, or giggling with the child, etc.), because there can be no indicators at this age of a child violating boundaries. They can't literally engage in parenting or partnering, however much parents may thrust them toward those roles. But, at 13 years of age, many do show signs of parentification in their behavior. We saw children being unduly solicitous of parents and explicitly taking care of them. For example, one precocious boy noting a slight shiver by his mother asked if she was cold, then offered to go to the car to get a coat for her. The pattern of his behavior revealed a similar boundary issue to that revealed by the mother a decade earlier. It was not the same behavior over time that revealed continuity; rather, it was behavior with similar meaning. So it is in case after case; continuity is at the level of the meaning of behavior.

Demonstrating continuity in personality over long periods of time has likewise been a challenge. At one point in psychology, it was even argued that there was no such thing as personality because people behaved differently in different situations, as well as over time. Decades ago, Jack Block pointed out that the solution to this problem was to recognize the coherence of the personality, not look for stable particular behaviors. Of course, behavior changes, as it must both in different circumstances and across time. Behaving exactly the same way regardless of shifting circumstances would be bizarre. The stable personality differences lie in the degree to which behavior is flexibly adjusted to fit the particular circumstance, as the work of Jeanne and Jack Block showed (1980). Such flexibility was clearly related to attachment history in our observational studies. Continuity lies in the patterning and organization of behavior. And the thread that weaves this pattern is meaning. While frequency of specific behaviors changes across contexts, individual organizations (*patterns*) of behavior across varied contexts do indeed show stability (Fleeson, 2001).

In our work, it was the adaptability to the changing array of issues that was coherent across development. It was parental support for regulation that best predicted self-regulation later, not the infant's temperament. And it was this parental support for regulation that predicted the capacity to sustain interactions with peers in preschool, not some measure of how well infants interacted with other infants. There is a behavioral component here, of course. The early training in regulation provided a foundation and a prototype for staying organized and persisting in interactions with peers. But acquired meanings are equally critical. Some children prioritize social connections more, believe they will be rewarding, and expect that they can weather interactive difficulties that arise. Others do not.

Another example of continuity at the level of meaning is the link between gender-boundary maintenance in middle childhood and effectiveness in negotiating cross-gender relationships in adolescence. As discussed in Chapter 8, it was those who focused on building loyal, same-gender friendships in middle childhood, and who followed the norms established by the group, who were later most readily able to move to the complexities of the adolescent social world. They weren't really practicing dating in middle childhood. They were practicing closeness, loyalty, and precursors to vulnerability. Therefore, the challenges of adolescent commitment and intimacy meant something different to them than it did to those without this experience. Those who violated these boundaries struggled more in dealing with the opposite gender or in being intimate and vulnerable with others.

A final example from our project concerned the observed capacity of adult couples to resolve conflicts, a well-established marker of effective relationships. In these assessments, topics for discussion were selected based on issues that the couple said were especially challenging for them (finances, relationships with in-laws, etc.), so conflict routinely occurred. The amount of conflict per se, however, was not a good marker of relationship quality. What was more critical was whether couples could reach some kind of accord, how readily could they move on when switched to another task, and whether they kept bringing up issues from the conflict task and kept sniping at each other.

The strongest predictor of this conflict–resolution ability was effectiveness in peer relationships in middle childhood. One obvious interpretation of this is that middle childhood is an important arena for practicing conflict resolution, particularly because peers – as the term implies – are "equals." These skills are then carried forward. However, it is also important to look at this from the level of meaning. In middle childhood, some children come to believe that conflicts *can* be resolved and even that conflicts are a normal part of relationships. Maintaining relationships involves working on and resolving conflicts. As the precocious child in our study said, your relationship with a friend might well be stronger following a conflict because "then you would understand each other better." As adults then, these individuals are not so threatened by conflict and *expect* that conflicts can be resolved. Others with different histories will be quite threatened and either perhaps close-up or emotionally withdraw at the first sign of conflict or, alternatively, remain helplessly embroiled in conflict in an unending way. What conflict means to each of us plays a large part in how we deal with it.

What Is Taken Forward

Meaning is the carrier of development. It is what is taken forward from one developmental period to the next. This is dramatically true in the first 2 or 3 years of life when event memory is so poorly developed and procedural memory is dominant. One cannot remember instances of turning to parents, but the cumulated meaning of countless exchanges of apprehension and reassurance, distress and comforting, and sharing of discovery are taken forward as feelings of safety, deep expectations that support is available, joy in exploration, and belief in one's effectiveness in the world.

Likewise, one cannot remember instances of limit setting or guidance that occurred in the toddler period, punishment that was capricious or harsh, what happened when you became out of control or expressed intense feelings. But the meaning of the patterning of experience surrounding the expressions of impulses and feelings will endure. Whether we are prone to shame, can be proud of our accomplishments, or feel that we can or cannot control ourselves owes a lot to these experiences that are not consciously remembered.

You might well consciously remember some events from your preschool years and even some of your kindergarten playmates. You may have some memories of a preschool teacher. But you do not remember (and did not even have it as a conscious goal at the time) the learning you did about how to sustain interactions with other children. Yet again, your procedural memory was operating full force. You learned about whether this was something you could master. Your sense of yourself as a competent playmate was fostered or not.

In Chapter 6 we described how the universal human characteristics of pattern recognition and abstraction impact the memory of the preschool child. Many details of specific, salient events can be retained in memory for a time, but without continued rehearsal such details of individual events will fade. What is retained long-term is an abstraction, assembled from parts of various related experiences. For events that unfold over time these are referred to as "scripts." In the end, what is retained are the most meaningful aspects of experience, so that the memory is not cluttered with innumerable specific details. Such script construction not only applies to common, everyday events, but to social interactions between the self and others (Waters & Waters, 2006; in press). Such scripts are taken forward even as new scripts may be formed and old scripts modified. In brief, what work on scripts confirms is that meaning of experience is carried forward. It is said that each time we remember an event from long ago, it is a *different* memory, because the meaning will be different because a different brain – a different person – is remembering it. This is what is meant by memory being constructive.

Most people remember a great deal from middle childhood and from adolescence. (This is why a security question in many financial accounts is the name of your best friend from childhood. Almost all of us know this particular person's name, and few other people would.) You likely remember specific activities and even some events, such as a specific birthday party, a trip, some accident, or something that happened to your friend or your friend's family. We now know, of course, that, because memory is constructive, parts of events get merged into other events, along with things that did not exactly happen. What is real and true is the meaning of these things. What certainly gets taken forward is the affection you felt for your friend and perhaps what you felt when for some reason you drifted apart or the friendship ended. The nature of these friendships – how they worked and whether they were mutual, balanced, and gratifying – is what is taken forward to adult relationships, much more than any specific event.

Scripts from earlier in life guide individual behavior in adulthood. This has been made quite clear in studies of people in psychotherapy. Thus, individuals may re-enact rules and roles learned in childhood or respond to therapists in ways that characterize their early salient relationships. Such "transference" is viewed as commonplace. This is not because of actual similarities in the behavioral form of these relationships, which generally are quite different from other adult relationships, but because of the similarity in meaning for the person. It is the emotional aspects of past relationships that are brought to therapy, though hopefully in a new way.

Sylvan Tomkins (1962) was an early proponent of script theory and also played a large role in bringing the study of emotion back into psychology. Thus, for him, emotionally toned scripts regarding the self were at the core of personality. For Tomkins, scripts entailed "the individual's rules for predicting, interpreting, responding to, and controlling experiences governed by a 'family' of related scenes." These were acquired during the years of childhood and youth. He introduced the concept of "nuclear scenes," emotionally salient events that frame subsequent thinking and behavior; that is, they set the pattern for the meaning of future relationship episodes. Coherence in behavior over time then will be seen in relational patterns reflecting the abstracted "scenes" of each of us. In one small therapy study of individuals who had previously been in therapy decades before, blind judges were able to match individual cases well beyond chance based upon the pattern of relating across the two therapists. The people had no doubt changed in many ways across this period, and measures of particular behaviors would likely have been impotent to uncover continuity, but at the level of the core issues in the person's life – the organization of their system of meaning – there was stability.

Lester Luborsky pursued a line of work similar to script theory, and he emphasized the importance of meaning to demonstrate the stability of functioning over time in the context of psychotherapy narrative records (see, for example, Luborsky & Crits-Christoph, 1998). Luborsky developed a measure tapping "Core Conflictual Relationship Themes." Core ingredients of a theme are the person's wishes, needs, or intentions toward the other person, as well as observed responses by each partner. It was the presence of these themes, such as openness to others, resistance of authority, and so forth, that was shown to be persistent across numerous therapy sessions.

Likewise, attending to meaning will reveal the coherence of parenting behavior, as well as it does child behavior. For example, consider the pitfall in simply counting number of smiles as an indication of parental warmth. Smiles can mean so many different things, from joy to anxiety and even disdain. Consider the difference between a shared smile with head nodding and an exclamation of "good girl" versus a smile with an eye roll, head toss and a sigh, which can convey complete exasperation as well as hostility. Frequency of smiling by a parent *per se* will not be an accurate reflection of parental warmth and likely will not even be stable. And, as we discussed when we talked about seductive behavior with toddlers, there is a vast difference between hugging a child who needs comforting (or in sharing the child's accomplishment) and asking a child for a hug to reassure yourself or as a way of manipulating him or her.

The Way Adaptation Works

There is a coherence and organization to the way individual adaptation works. As Freud was reported to have written in a letter to John Dewey (Rosen, 1978), from the very beginning the mind cannot separate itself from its experience. It builds step-by-step upon that.

Jane Loevinger (1976), in her book on ego development, summarized the work of developmental and psychoanalytic thinkers such as Piaget, James Mark Baldwin, Alfred Adler, and Harry Stack Sullivan on the problem of why the organization of the individual personality tends to be self-perpetuating or, to use her word, "stable." She states that the ego (or self) "remains stable because the operations by which the person perceives his environment effectively admit only those data that can be comprehended already, hence are compatible with the current ego structure" (p. 310). Experiences that are incompatible must be ignored or distorted or assimilated "to conform to prior expectations." Parts of the objective situation simply do not (Piaget) or cannot (Adler) exist for the person. There is what Sullivan called "selective inattention" and Bowlby called "defensive exclusion of information." All of this is closely related to the emphasis in this book on the idea that the meaning of a given situation for an individual is a product of that person's history of experience. We see the world in terms of what we have experienced, and we act upon the world such that our current experience is congruent with that.

Thus, one of the primary reasons that early experience and the meanings derived from it persist is the basic nature of adaptation. In the beginning, infants necessarily adapt to the circumstances that surround them. When a baby experiences inconsistent, hit-or-miss care, it makes sense to hover by the parent, express distress at the smallest threat, and, of course, such infants have difficulty settling. As toddlers, not surprisingly, these children are easily frustrated, show limited persistence, and are unusually prone to tantrums. What they then need is even more consistent support and limits than most toddlers. But consistency is precisely what is difficult for their caregivers. In fact, their now difficult way of being will likely elicit more frustration, upset, and inconsistency from their caregivers. A cascade is underway. Their own dysregulation will become worse. They will be ill prepared for preschool and quite likely will then have upsetting experiences there. Things get worse and worse, not because the problems of infancy could not be overcome, but because patterns of adaptation tend to have a self-perpetuating quality.

Likewise, the infant that learns to withhold expressions of tender needs from a rejecting, unavailable parent does so for understandable reasons.

It forestalls further rejection. Still, this can lead them to withhold feelings from preschool teachers as well and to alienate other children. Not being able to directly bring their needs to others, they need others to come to them. But they do not behave in ways that make this easy to see. They act self-sufficient and disinterested in contact. All of this can lead to further isolation.

Early adaptations are the core of beginning meaning systems, that is, expectations about self and others. These meaning systems are then taken forward to new experiences, influencing how they are approached, how they are interpreted, and the reactions of new people involved. When, for example, new situations are routinely viewed as threatening, they are more likely avoided. If others are viewed as likely to be unavailable to help, this further leads to avoidance or other rigid strategies of coping. If, as another example, situations are viewed as difficult or overwhelming, and the self is viewed as weak, children may be unduly reliant on others. Moreover, others will tend to react in ways that are congruent with the child's expectations. Children who are aloof, uninvolved, or aggressive are shunned by other children and are difficult for adults to like. Children who are easily overwhelmed don't make good playmates and may seek too much contact and nurturance from adults. This is at the expense of engaging peers and leads to less peer competence at subsequent ages.

So it is that children, acting in terms of expectations derived from their lived experience, behave in ways that elicit reactions from others that confirm their prior beliefs. Maladaptation is simply engaging the world in ways that continue to interfere with receiving corrective feedback regarding negative expectations.

Generally, teachers and counselors understand that different children make different meanings in different situations, and their responses to them are helpful. Their empathy derives from understanding. When a child acts like he has a chip on his shoulder, they understand that this is because that "chip" was derived from experience. And they try to react in ways that would disconfirm his negative expectations about what to expect from people, for example, by not rejecting him emotionally even when limiting his behavior.

Sometimes, of course, teachers and others do things that are not helpful, perhaps because of their own meaning systems. For example, it is likely that children who for punishment are isolated in "time out" are the very children who have been rejected. An alternative would be to have an aide stay with (not play with) the child when he or she needs to be separated from the group. Thus, the child is not rewarded for misbehavior, but neither is his or her model of unworthiness and alienation confirmed. The aid may merely say something like, "I will just sit with you until you are ready to go back to the others." In this way, perhaps, a meaning system can gradually be altered.

A quite different case is the child that elicits over-involvement from teachers. We saw this happen especially with boys with histories of boundary violations (seductive behavior) from their mothers. One child was constantly on teachers' laps and had little contact with other children. One day he became quite curious about the activity of a small group of boys who were building a structure using large blocks. He began to approach them, and we were excited to be capturing on film his first serious peer contact. Suddenly, a teacher swooped in, picked him up and said, "Hi, Manny, let's go read a story." This was not what he needed at that time and ran the risk further confirming his view that he was unable to engage with peers.

This is not to point fingers at this teacher. As we discussed in Chapter 6, systems of adaptation are powerful, and children behave in ways that lead to repetition of what they have previously experienced. This coy child was very attractive to adult women. Our belief is that, with a modest amount of training, teachers could be taught to recognize that a child making you feel warm and cuddly is a reaction that calls for examination, just as much as does a child that makes you feel angry. When we are armed with an understanding of how adaptation works, we will be more effective in our interventions.

CHAPTER 10

The Role of Meaning in Intergenerational Transmission Effects

Psychologists are keenly interested in questions regarding intergenerational transmission of behavioral patterns and of parenting. Does what you experience in early childhood potentially have durable effects all through your life? If so, does what you experienced, as a child, influence your parenting and, therefore, your own child's experience? If so, how is this possible? What exactly is carried forward from one generation to the next? The belief in such effects has a history back to ancient times. A focus on meaning has allowed empirical demonstrations to be carried out. It turns out that it is not specific behaviors learned in social relationships that are taken forward but the meanings derived from these social experiences. Such meanings may be expressed in different ways.

Continuity of Parenting across Generations

Family systems theorists have long argued that patterns of parenting are transmitted across generations (e.g., Boszormenyi-Nagy & Spark, 1973). Relationship systems are "conservative" and self-perpetuating. The more they change, the more they are the same, because the meaning is conserved. We learn to parent by being parented.

One of our first looks at this came from the study of seductive parental behavior. Recall that, by "seductive," we refer to parental behavior that uses sensuality to control or manipulate a child or otherwise draws the child into an inappropriate semi-spousal role. One example was a mother, who in response to a toddler's failure to comply with a directive, called to him in a plaintive voice and asked for a kiss. Then after the kiss and a caress of the child's bottom said, "Now, put that away for mamma." Other parents were observed to engage in sensual kissing with the toddler, fondle the toddler's genitals, or promise sensual affection if the child would comply. In this sample of mostly single mothers, living in high stress, such behavior was seen with 18 percent of the boys and only 2 percent of the girls.

A number of explanations could be offered for these observations. Certainly, socioeconomic factors would be involved. If these mothers had more social support and less stress, this behavior would be reduced. Similar economic situations can make behavior more similar. But it isn't just this. One of the strongest predictors of such behavior was the mother's report of having been sexually exploited by her father, stepfather, or other male family member. (Understanding such links is one reason to be cautious about blaming parents when they mistreat their children. They have histories too.) These reports of early abuse history were obtained independently from interviews carried out before this part of the study. It is noteworthy that it is the meaning of these experiences that was carried forward. These mothers, of course, did not engage in the behaviors that the men visited upon them when they were children, but quite different, culturally specified female behavior.

When first reported, some suggested that this was all just parental nurturance; that is, that these parents were just warm and cuddly. However, the seductive behavior correlated not with measures of warmth, but with independently scored measures of hostility and lack of emotional support given to the child.

Moreover, a simple genetic interpretation also falls short, and we were able to show why. We asked a number of clinicians to speculate how mothers who treated their boys seductively would treat their daughters. Would they treat them seductively too? There was consensus among the clinicians that, rather, they would treat them with hostility and disdain. This was based on family systems thinking. If, in a given family, a father is sexually exploiting his daughter, he is not able to meet his needs with his wife (or she with him), and the mother is not protecting her daughter or is even rejecting of her. Otherwise, the behavior of the father would not be allowed. The meaning system internalized by the little girl in such a family is that adults meet their needs with children, that this is done on a gender basis, and that as a girl I am unworthy. Thus, they treat their daughters negatively because they have learned this is how mothers treat daughters and because their daughters are reflections of their own inner feelings about themselves. As Ivan Boszormenyi-Nagy and Geraldine Spark say in their marvelous book, *Invisible Loyalties* (1973), the conservative, balanced nature of the family system is preserved. Meaning is retained.

This was a complicated but testable hypothesis, and we strongly confirmed these predictions. In fact, our observations of how mothers who are seductive with sons treat daughters led us to emphasize a specific feature of rejection; namely, derision. They tended to be hostile in a particularly demeaning way toward their daughters *as girls*; for example, saying, "Well, it took you long enough to do that. What are you, just a stupid little girl?" We would point out that both this derisive pattern and the seductive parenting pattern, different as they are, both have one thing in common – both entail a violation of appropriate parent–child boundaries. In both cases there is an abdication of the supportive parental role, and parents are addressing their own emotional needs to their children. The broader, boundary violation concept became a key in subsequent study because it can be manifest in a variety of ways toward both boys and girls.

We concluded that these mothers were not just manifesting a general seductiveness trait. It is not that some women are born with a seductiveness gene. In fact, the women who behaved seductively with their firstborn did not necessarily treat even a second-born son seductively. (The family clinicians would say that this role was already occupied.) They were instead recapitulating an entire organization of meaning derived from their childhood experience. Even in looking at the seductive behavior with sons we were tapping into the larger organization of meaning.

A study with Vervet monkeys by Lynn Fairbanks (1989) decades ago also shows how parenting experience may be carried forward without relying on simple genetic interpretations and, of course, without any potential bias from verbal report. She looked at the amount of physical contact each infant was given by its mother. She found that this predicted strongly how much these second-generation mothers would subsequently hold their own babies. Since these monkeys produce multiple offspring and are often still having babies when some of their offspring mature and have babies of their own, she could rule out several alternatives. For example, she could see if an offspring mothered her baby as her own mother was now raising another one (an interpretation based on modeling). Or she could look at the average amount of contact the original mother gave all of her offspring (the best estimate of a genetic measure of contact giving). Neither of these things predicted as strongly as the degree of contact directly experienced by each baby. Even monkeys do as they have experienced, without the need for us to infer conscious memory.

It was not possible to do this exact same study with humans, but we could come close by following a sizeable group of infants for the next 40 years. How would the children whose parents treated them seductively, derisively, or with support and nurturance treat their own children when they became parents? We were able to carry out the same laboratory assessments at 2 years of age in both generations with boys and girls (and mothers or fathers). Part of this assessment involved the series of tool problems of increasing difficulty, described in Chapter 5. The toddlers were certain to require parental support and guidance to solve them.

Two years is an age well before there is substantial verbal memory. These children thus could not "remember" in the dictionary sense, or what is formally termed "declarative memory," how they had been treated when they were 2 years old. Yet we found, remarkably, that there was a degree of predictability across this substantial span of time (Kovan et al., 2009). Supportive emotional presence by one's parent predicted the capacity to be emotionally supportive of one's own child two or three decades later. Likewise, hostility and generational boundary violation showed continuity across time. (In this study, we statistically controlled for later child experiences, parent education, and life stress among other things.) Therefore, the procedural learning based on countless affective exchanges with caregivers in early life is carried forward across time. This was one of the first studies of its kind based on direct observation in both generations, without relying on retrospective reporting.

Importantly, it was once again the case that continuity was at the level of meaning. Scores on measurement scales across generations were similar but *specific* behaviors could be radically different. One little boy's mother showed sneers and other signs of disgust at his difficulties, shrugged her shoulders and looked away when he asked for help, and in other ways conveyed her hostile feelings. Years later, with his own son, he laughed at the boy's failures, teased him about his inadequacies, and even said things like, "You can't even do it. I'm smarter than you." These were behaviors we had not seen from his mother toward him, but the meaning and consequences for self-esteem are similar.

It is equally the case that emotional support and positive feelings toward a child can be shown in many ways. It is not the case that things like frequency of statements made by parents during the tool problems showed continuity across generations. A parent who did not speak much may have shown a great deal of support by her physical presence, drawing nearer to the child when the problem became difficult and giving smiles of encouragement and a shared hug when the problem was solved. That child as an adult may well have supported their own toddler, but this might have involved lots of verbal encouragement ("good boy, you're getting it, that's right"), and a celebratory "Way to go" and high fives when the problem was solved. In each case the child would *feel* supported and something important about the nature of self and relationships would be learned. Consistency and coherence are found at the level of meaning.

How much a mother verbalized to her child, how many times she approached and so forth did not predict frequency of the same behaviors in the next generation. But if your mother had been emotionally supportive of you, you were more likely to be emotionally supportive of your child, even though your way of expressing this support may have been quite different. Such continuity applied even in the case of our new fathers who tended to have a style quite different from that of Minnesota mothers. The meaning of the disparate behaviors is what remained the same.

Interviews with adults (see The Adult Attachment Interview section) reveal great variations in the ways that love and support were expressed to them by their parents. One parent may be remembered as very demonstrative, giving frequent hugs and physical nurturance when one was ill. A specific memory might be: "When I was little my mom always would come in and hug me good night." As long as these behaviors were responsive to the child, they certainly would convey love (and to the child a sense of being loveable). Memories for another child or the same child with another parent might be quite distinctive and still have the same meaning. "My Dad wasn't very expressive of physical or even verbal affection, but he was always there for me. He worked very hard, but he never missed my games even though that meant he would have to go back to work later. And I did hear him sometimes talking to his friends about how proud he was of me and what a good son I was. Later, when I would come home from college, he always jumped up and came to shake my hand and tell me he was glad I was home. So I knew he loved me ... always knew it." This hypothetical child, as an adult, may show his love in a way that is distinctive from either of his parents, or more like one than the other. But it seems likely that he will be able to show love.

Continuity of Attachment Relationships across Generations

Some of the most exciting research findings have to do with continuity in attachment relationships across generations. This work actually began with efforts to determine whether a parent's way of thinking about attachment relationships could predict a subsequent infant's attachment quality (e.g., Main et al., 1985). This was followed by efforts to show that infant attachment could predict parent attachment ideation and even infant attachment in the next generation. This second problem is much more challenging because decades pass between the two assessments. Beyond these questions regarding stability over time, we now also have some understanding of the process by which continuity is achieved when indeed it is. One key in this work has been the Adult Attachment Interview.

The Adult Attachment Interview

The Adult Attachment Interview (AAI), created by Mary Main and colleagues (Main & Goldwyn, 1998), followed in the Ainsworth tradition by having meaning at its core. In fact, *the explicit goal was to determine what attachment relationships mean to the person*. The interview seeks to utilize the same type of pattern recognition approach that Ainsworth used, this time based on narrative accounts of the person's attachment history.

At the beginning of the interview, interviewees are invited to provide a general overview of their early lives. They are then asked to provide five adjectives or phrases that describe their relationship with a major attachment figure. Next, they are asked to provide examples from *as far back as they can remember*, from about ages 5 to 12, that exemplify these adjectives. For example, if the person had said it was a "loving" relationship, the interviewer would say, "Can you give me an example of something you remember that shows how the relationship was loving?" Multiple examples are sought for each adjective, and this whole process is repeated with other attachment figures (referred to in our study as "people who raised you").

Other parts of the interview ask about what would happen when the person was injured or ill, about how they were disciplined and whether discipline was ever harsh. Were they abused? Finally, there were questions about losses. Who was lost? What was the interviewee's reaction? Did they go to the funeral? What was that experience like?

While there is attention to the reported experiences in the interview, and scales for these, the main focus is on *how* the person talks about their attachment history; that is, his or her "state of mind" regarding attachment. There is no score for the number of positive adjectives for example, though it is of interest because people who have processed their attachment history often have some balance in their depiction of parents. Rather, the focus is on the quality of the examples provided to support the adjectives. For example, being beaten to make someone behave better is not good support for "Loving." Whatever the balance of positive and negative adjectives, it is important that the examples be cogent. It is also relevant that there is clarity and some precision to the descriptions. The overall goal (and the major scales) has to do with the coherence of the narrative. For example, in addition to shaky examples for "loving," also saying later,

"I didn't go to my mother when a dog bit me because I knew she would be mad," is incongruous. It is contrary to the idea of loving. It reduces the coherence of the account.

The Adult Attachment Interview is quite arousing for most people. It is an unusual topic to be discussing with a researcher, and it often stirs up many memories. For some, of course, it is an interesting and rewarding experience, perhaps even leading to fresh, new thoughts. For others it can be quite threatening, awakening or reawakening thoughts that are upsetting or things they do not want to know. There are many different reactions, but Main grouped them to be consonant with the three major categories in the Ainsworth system.

The major group of interviews is categorized as "autonomous," equivalent to Ainsworth's secure pattern. They are called autonomous because the individual is free and open in thinking about and processing his or her attachment history. The interviews of these people are quite coherent. Their descriptions fit the adjectives. If their adjectives are positive, they have good support for that. There are minimal inconsistencies in the things that are said. These interviewees are collaborative with the interviewer, being concise but adequately clear and descriptive. They may even correct themselves or further clarify to make sure the meaning got across. Even if they describe difficulties with their parents, their accounts are balanced, and they show some understanding of the parents' situations. They have made peace with negative experiences. They have been processed and integrated. Whether they describe largely positive or negative histories, they clearly value attachment relationships.

These characterizations are quite compatible with Loevinger's (1976) descriptions of the autonomous level of ego development. Such individuals can tolerate uncertainty, can acknowledge and deal with conflict, and can "unite and integrate ideas that appear as incompatible alternatives" to others (p. 23).

Another group of individuals in some way keep themselves distant from feelings about relationships. They are called "dismissing" because either they claim to be unable to remember childhood attachment experiences, present an unduly glossy yet unsubstantiated picture, or describe negative experiences but claim that they had no impact on them, much like Miguel, whom we described in Chapter 2, when he said that his mother's death had no effect on him. Sometimes attachment experiences are just seen as unimportant. As one young man said about the infrequency of getting together with his family: "We just don't see the point." The interviews of these cases are not collaborative, because the person seems to not want to delve into it. They may come up with few adjectives. They may make terse statements about having nothing further to say. The interviews may be quite short. Obviously, this group is analogous to the infant group referred to by Ainsworth as "avoidant."

A third group is called "preoccupied" and is parallel to Ainsworth's anxious/resistant infant pattern. These individuals are generally quite willing to talk, but their discourse is frequently rambling and drifts off target. The interviews are often quite long. Often, several adjectives are negative but, rather than talking about them in a processed way, the people get caught up in reliving them. Some members of this general category become clearly angry when talking and may try to get the interviewer to join them in their outrage. For them, the past is present. They have never let go. Others seem to get lost in the interview, with numerous irrelevancies or sentences that trail off into nothingness.

These, of course, are generalizations that condense a great deal of individual variation. Nonetheless, as Marinus Van IJzendoorn (1995) and others have reported, research has shown that the various states of mind captured in these interviews predict the subsequent attachment relationships of infants. It is especially clear that those who are autonomous, even when they described their histories as having negative components, are more likely to have infants that are secure with them than those in the other two groups. There is also a clear link between dismissing and subsequent infant avoidance. Note that this link is at the level of meaning. It is what attachment experiences have meant to the person that is being assessed, not their actual attachment history, which in most studies was not directly assessed, and thus can only be assumed to be captured.

A final category derived from the AAI, that is somewhat independent of the other three categories, is called "Unresolved with regard to loss or abuse." Many interviewees report losses, and some report abuse. Among those reporting such experiences, some can do so in a coherent and understandable way. Again, they show openness and a sense that they have made some peace with the experience. Regarding serious losses, they have gone through a grieving process and have come to some acceptance of the loss. They can speak clearly about it. With abuse, they address it with frankness and without becoming thoroughly pulled back into the experience. They do not deny that it was painful, nor do they feel responsible for it. They may have forgiven the person; at the least the experience does not still have a hold on them. These speakers are called "Resolved."

Others become confused in talking about loss, for example; perhaps contradicting themselves by saying they have never been to a funeral and later talking about the funeral of a loved one; confuse the self and the deceased (mixing pronouns I and he or she); talk about the deceased in the present tense as though they are still alive; or focus on quite peripheral or irrelevant details (for example, the color of the curtains at the funeral). With abuse, they may again contradict themselves (saying they never had such experiences, then speak about some specific times when they were clearly harshly treated). They may have recall so vivid that it is as though it happened yesterday when it was years before. They may speak of it with an ominous quality ("I can still see the gigantic belt swinging back and forth.") There are many ways that a lack of resolution can be shown. As with infant attachment assessment, it requires training to master this procedure; yet it is learnable and makes great sense.

Given some of the experiences described, it may not be surprising that resolution has eluded some of these individuals. Nonetheless, lack of resolution of loss or trauma has significance for functioning in the world and for parenting. This measure is a strong predictor of disorganized attachment in the infants of these individuals. It has other implications that will be discussed later.

The AAI has had a great impact on clinical practice and early intervention (Slade & Holmes, 2018; Steele & Steele, 2008). Like the AAI, measures such as the parent Internal Working Model (IWM) of the Child, and others patterned like it, focus on meaning. With the AAI, one is asking what do trust and closeness mean, what does vulnerability mean, and, in short, what does attachment mean? With the IWM of the child, one is asking what does the child's vulnerability mean and what do its needs mean? What does this child mean to you? Most prominent in psychotherapy circles has been the work of Peter Fonagy (1999) on "reflective function" and "mentalization." These were ideas that Fonagy got directly from his training with Mary Main on the AAI. Reflective function refers to the ability to think about thought itself – the inner workings of the mind. At its core, mentalization refers to the capacity to see the worldview, the network of meanings of the other, and thereby join in a truly reciprocal relationship process in therapy. Likewise, successful early intervention programs, such as the Video Feedback Training program of Van IJzendoorn and colleagues (2023), the ABC program of Mary Dozier, and the Minding the Baby program of Arietta Slade, Linda Mayes, and others, were directly influenced by training with Main on the AAI and Ainsworth's ideas regarding attending to meaning. In these quite successful programs, parents are helped to understand their own distortions of meaning on route to accurately seeing the nature of the infant mind and what infant behavior means.

Before leaving this section, a comment may be made about attending to culture when administering the AAI. For example, in Mexican culture, it is common to speak about those who have died as though they are still alive, especially during the celebration known as Days of the Dead. This by itself cannot be taken as an indication of lack of resolution concerning loss. Likewise, in many Asian cultures it is taboo to speak negatively about one's father. The absence of negative comments in that context does not mean the idealization that characterizes some dismissing interviews. As always, attending to meaning is necessary.

Stability of Disorganized Infant Attachment

While demonstrating intergenerational continuity of infant attachment relationships is difficult given the years spanned, there has been moderate stability in the sense that secure infants more often have secure infants in the next generation. Moreover, one specific pattern of infant attachment has been shown to clearly predict the same quality of attachment in the next generation; namely, the disorganized pattern.

In the Ainsworth procedure some infants show a coherent pattern of balancing exploration and attachment, seeking increasing contact without ambivalence as stress increases. Others show a coherent pattern of avoiding the caregiver more strongly as stress increases. Still others seek contact but are not settled by it and may mix contact with anger. But the poverty of exploration and ongoing distress of these infants make this pattern coherent too. These patterns all make sense, even though they vary in effectiveness. One can understand why infants might behave in these ways given certain histories of experience.

However, other infants show anomalous or contradictory behavior, become disoriented or immobile, or otherwise show an inability to maintain organized behavior. Their behavior is difficult to interpret. For example, what does it mean if, when the caregiver returns, the infant approaches while keeping his or her head averted or turns around and backs toward the parent? Does this show a desire for contact (as in the secure cases) or a wish to avoid? It seems to be both at once, but that is not a coherent strategy. Or, upon mother's entry the child goes flat on the floor, face down and becomes frozen. Such a stoppage of behavior is quite anomalous for an infant. As a final example, the infant moves away from the parent while crying loudly. It again seems to be both expressing and inhibiting attachment behavior at the same time. The list of possible disorganized behaviors would be extensive. What they have in common is that they make sense only when we assume the infant is afraid of the caregiver.

Infants with frightening attachment figures are put in an impossible situation (Main & Hesse, 1990). As humans they are strongly biologically disposed to immediately go to parents when frightened. At the same time, they are biologically disposed to flee from the source of fear. When the parent *is* the source of fear, this is an unsolvable problem. These imperative goals are incompatible. They cannot flee to and away from the parent at the same time. Thus, we see the array of conflicting behaviors. Backing to the parent does in a way do both at once. Going flat on the floor or spinning in circles prioritizes neither contact seeking nor fleeing, nor does simply becoming dazed and immobile. When parents behave in abusive, frightening, or unfathomable ways, infants frequently show disorganized attachment.

Looking at all of these reactions, the Italian scholar Giovanni Liotti (1992) saw them as proto-dissociation responses. We adults sometimes split off incompatible ideas in our minds. Such a segregation of thoughts, impulses, and feelings, and failure to integrate them into a coherent whole is called "dissociation." Infants with frightening parents, he reasoned, are forced to do the same thing. They cannot integrate their organized attachment behavioral system with fear emanating from the attachment figure. They either remove part of the experience (by not attending the parent, for example) or psychologically leave the situation entirely, by becoming dazed or disoriented. Liotti's hypothesis was that, in the face of subsequent loss or trauma, these infants would be vulnerable to exercising this acquired dissociative tendency. They would also be vulnerable to many forms of psychopathology, as was subsequently found (see Chapter 12).

It is this disorganized attachment pattern that shows substantial continuity across generations. Infants classified as disorganized with greater frequency grow up to have infants who also show the disorganized pattern, based on assessments made by completely independent coders, who had no knowledge of the prior assessments. In the work at Minnesota, we ruled out neurological underpinnings of these anomalous behaviors by carrying out direct assessments of neurological status and temperament early in the first year. This partly tempers an explanation based on inherent infant characteristics. Moreover, as was the case with the findings with 2-year-olds already discussed, it was not the specific behaviors that showed continuity. The second-generation infant might well manifest disorganization in a manner quite distinctive from that of the first-generation infant. It is the meaning of experience that is carried forward, not learning of particular behaviors.

Processes in Carrying Forward Meaning

It is our assumption that there is a process in carrying forward the meanings of early preverbal experiences. It is this process that both developmental researchers and clinicians seek to understand.

The Developmental Process underlying Continuity of Infant Attachment

The continuity in disorganized attachment across generations, based on a measure at 12 months of life, is astounding. In this case we even know quite a bit about the developmental process underlying this continuity; that is, how it is that these early experiences impact development and lead second-generation parents to behave in frightening ways. Liotti's ideas about dissociation provided a key. If infants with disorganized attachment are indeed later prone to dissociation, that may be the link to the Unresolved state of mind in adulthood which then predicts disorganization in the next generation.

In Minnesota we found exactly this. Infants who had shown the disorganized attachment pattern and subsequently experienced abuse were quite likely to show dissociative symptoms when assessed as teenagers and as young adults. Disorganized attachment in infancy also specifically predicted Unresolved status on the AAI, and dissociation mediated this connection. The path clearly went from disorganized infancy to dissociation to Unresolved. Adults appear to be unresolved regarding loss or trauma precisely because they have dissociated in response to these experiences and failed to integrate them.

The only thing remaining to be shown was how then does parental unresolved status (and the associated tendency to dissociate) lead to disorganized attachment in infants of these parents. Main and Hesse (1990) proposed that such parents, especially when in dissociative states, would behave in frightening and unfathomable ways toward their infants. This is precisely what home observation studies by Deborah Jacobvitz (Jacobvitz et al., 2011) and by Carlo Schuengel and colleagues (1999) have shown. Parents who are Unresolved more frequently loom at their infants, talk in depersonalized voices, grimace, go into dazed states, and in other ways behave in a frightening manner, and such behavior does in fact predict later infant disorganized attachment. The intergenerational cycle is complete.

The Manifestation of Boundary Violations in Childhood

One implication of a process viewpoint is that we will see the effects of early boundary violation experiences, and the meanings acquired from them, at various points in childhood. Parent–child boundary violations in the toddler period, for example, might well appear as certain kinds of child boundary problems in the preschool period and middle childhood, as well as adolescence.

In this work our focus was on how various patterns of early boundary violations between parents and children showed up in representations and social behavior. In middle childhood representations, one notable theme with children who had experienced boundary violations was a kind of incoherence in their narratives, how one idea dissolved into another without anything being concluded. This was especially true in the TAT stories. There would be the beginnings of a story theme, but it would fall apart, only to be picked up on a different track, which then also devolved into another theme. In short, the narrative showed a lack of containment and thereby a lack of coherence.

This relative lack of boundaries also showed up in their behavior at multiple ages. In the preschool these were the children that elicited undue nurturance from the teachers or had great difficulty containing their impulses. In middle childhood, they were highly represented in the children who were observed to violate gender boundaries, and they at times had difficulty respecting the boundaries of others. This can be best illustrated with a case example.

During one of our summer camps, one of us had a vivid experience of the impact of boundary violations on a child's development. A child we will call ES grew up in a home almost completely devoid of boundaries. There were no boundaries between the home and the external world, with people moving in and out, sexual and drug activities of all kinds taking place, few organized routines, and general chaos. Neither were there boundaries between ES and his mother. She was physically and sexually inappropriate, and she used a diffuse and disorganized array of tactics to respond to his behavior, which was, of course, out of control. He was both impulsive and aggressive.

One day at the camp we were walking the children to a nearby playground to play some ball games. The author happened to be walking with him. Usually, when two people are together, metaphorically they each have a semi-permeable membrane around them. This allows ongoing exchange yet still preserves the integrity of the individual. This was not possible with ES. First, it was almost like he was radioactive. There was an incredible tension emanating from him that you could not help but feel. It wasn't hostility. ES liked the author. But it penetrated. It was almost overpowering. Second, as they walked, ES continually intruded into the author's space, repeatedly bumping against and crowding him to the edge of the sidewalk. Again, at no point did this feel aggressive. We are quite sure he had no awareness of what he was doing. It just felt like there was no boundary around this child. It seemed that, in parallel, the inner core of his personality was likewise disorganized. And he did have a disorganized attachment history.

The Way Development Works

The work we have just described illustrates the cumulative, step-by-step nature of development – how every beginning is an outcome and how every outcome is a beginning, as development continually builds upon itself. Another facet of this work illustrates the process underlying resilience and the fact that behavior is always the product of the entire history of the person, as will be more fully discussed in Chapter 11.

It intrigued AAI researchers that some individuals described rather negative histories yet were secure (autonomous) in their state of mind regarding attachment (so called earned secures). They were of special interest because their infants were secure as well. How could this happen? It was necessary to fight through the tendency to think that these individuals just "raised themselves by their own bootstraps," a tendency that underlies much resilience research. There was a more developmental explanation. Recall that, on the Adult Attachment Interview, the interviewee is only describing events back as far as kindergarten, or at the most the preschool period. None of us can actually remember our infancies. Since the Minnesota study had data beginning in infancy, we could shed light on this matter. It turned out that these autonomous individuals who described negative histories, had more often been secure as infants as compared to those non-autonomous individuals with negative histories, an idea that had been suggested by Mary Main herself. Apparently, one major fact in coming to grips with negative parenting experiences is having had an earlier period of security.

It is also the case that people who are in the midst of a difficult period often see even histories that were benign as more negative than do people who are currently thriving. In particular, we found that adults who were currently depressed described their childhoods in more negative terms than our childhood data suggested was in fact the case, accounting for some in this earned secure group. This is not to say that they were "distorting" the facts, only that this is the way the human mind works.

We had many examples in our longitudinal study of resilience being supported by early positive experience. Current supports also play a role, and that likely was the case with some in this "earned secure" group. Adversity can indeed be overcome, but this is much more likely with a positive foundation and current supports. Early experience and current support structure the meaning of later negative experiences in childhood. And it is what these experiences mean to the individual that guides their parenting.

CHAPTER 11

Competence, Resilience, and the Fate of Early Experience

The developmental concepts of competence and resilience are closely related, both in their definitions and in their histories in psychological research. "Resilience" really boils down to being "competent" in certain circumstances. But what is competence and how can we measure it?

Norman Garmezy, a pioneer in schizophrenia risk studies and resilience research, famously defined "competence" as "the ability to expect well" (Garmezy & Streitman, 1974). He was speaking of competence in a broad sense, not in the sense of having particular skills, such as carpentry or hitting a baseball. He was referring to being generally competent as a person. He was suggesting that competent individuals believed that if they tried hard their efforts would be successful. They somehow were able to persist in the face of adversity, could get up again after falling down, and could find some inner reserve when needed, all because they had an inner belief that they would prevail.

It seems to be an inherent characteristic of human beings to be resourceful in times of hardship, to draw upon something deep inside when it is needed. How often we hear stories of heroism following earthquakes or tornados, or during times of war. How often we hear a devastated community described as strong and resilient. "We are resilient people. We will recover and rebuild." Resourcefulness and perseverance in times of crisis are widespread. Still, it seems to be the case that there are individual variations in such coping ability and resilience. How is it that some adults are better able to reach deep inside and call upon strengths never before needed? How is it that some children succumb to the stresses and hardships in their lives more than do others? How is it that some seem to recover from periods of difficulty with ease, while other children continue to flounder?

While Garmezy's definition of competence is not fully adequate as a guide for research, it contains an important core of truth. It is closely aligned with the emphasis on meaning as central to understanding human functioning, because of the important role it attributes to individual ways of viewing obstacles and setbacks.

In our longitudinal research we found it useful to define competence as "the ability to draw upon personal and environmental resources to promote good developmental outcome" (Waters & Sroufe, 1983). As we will describe in the following paragraphs, this definition also turns out to have meaning at its core. Moreover, it provides a way to address the problem of circularity that is inherent in most general definitions of competence. Competence, as is also true of resilience, can often just be a label for some observed outcome. For example, in the face of adversity, why is someone doing well? Because they are competent. How do you know they are competent? Because they are doing well in the face of adversity. Without going further, the construct of competence is not an explanation but merely a label for something already observed. Left implied is the idea that competence is something that some children just have.

Our developmental definition allows for some cumulative validation as a way of getting beyond the circularity problem. The key is in confirming "good developmental outcome." You tentatively know you have adequately captured competence at a given age if it is related to good developmental outcome at the next. With just one such demonstration, circularity remains a problem because both competence and good developmental outcome are mutually defining. How do you know that you adequately measured competence or good developmental outcome? You can acquire validity in a program of developmental research. If you have captured competence and good developmental outcome, the outcome measure you used to define competence at one age should predict good developmental outcome at the next phase of development, and so forth. With each successful prediction, confidence in the specific measures of competence and in the general approach increase.

Meaning enters our competence work both in terms of how we think of the capacity to draw upon inner and outer resources, and how we define good developmental outcome. Drawing upon resources is again more than a matter of skills, though skills are important; it is the belief and expectation that one can do so. The preschooler who needs help with a problem and effectively seeks adult support does so, in part, because she or he believes that support is available. As we have noted throughout, the same situation can mean quite different things to different children; it can mean an unsolvable problem or an opportunity, depending on what one believes about available resources. This includes both what your experience has taught you about *your* effectiveness, as well as what it has taught you that you can expect from others.

Good developmental outcome has to do with the capacity to negotiate issues that are particularly salient during a given developmental period, issues such as forming an effective attachment, becoming engaged with the preschool peer group, or forming a loyal friendship. These salient issues always have meaning at their core.

We have previously said that forming an effective attachment relationship is the key issue in infancy. It draws upon all aspects of cognitive, social, and emotional development in the first year of life, as well as the cumulative interactive history with caregivers. An effective attachment relationship, by definition, means that the infant is confident in the responsiveness of the caregiver, with the accompanying belief that they can elicit needed responses. My caregiver will know what my signal means and they will do what I need. The outer resource, the caregiver, can be drawn upon precisely because of the inner resource – the belief that they will respond to my signal. Thus, the securely attached infant is a competent infant. This conclusion will be supported if secure attachment predicts a "good developmental outcome" in the next phase of development; namely, the toddler period.

Competence in the toddler period is defined as successfully moving toward guided self-regulation; that is, acquiring some kind of balance between expression and containment of impulses with the support of caregivers. Doing this well depends on guidance and structure by caregivers and the history of entrained emotion regulation. But it also depends on the child's acceptance of parental direction, which is based on already established expectations that the caregiver is dependable, as well as the belief that regulation and recovery following dysregulation are possible – that is, the meaning of regulation challenges. All of this is the outcome of competence as defined by effective attachment in infancy. Finding strong links between these two periods is, therefore, confirmation that attachment assessments are indeed capturing competence, though in infancy it is really the competence of the pair.

If conceptualization and measurement is adequate to this point, functioning well in these first two phases of development should predict "good developmental outcome" in the preschool years. Here two salient issues are acquiring a degree of self-management and successful entrée into the peer group. Successful self-management draws upon the guided self-regulation in the preceding period. Successful functioning in the peer group capitalizes on these regulation capacities and the positive expectations concerning self and relationships that go all the way back to infancy. The fact that both self-management and the ability to sustain interactions with peers are predicted by attachment history and by toddler experience further validates the entire framework. The competence now established by the preschool period provides the foundation for the friendships and successful group functioning in middle childhood, which, in turn, prepare the child for the complex and more intimate relationships of adolescence.

So it goes age by age until, ultimately, trusting adult relationships and effective parenting are predictable from the assessments in infancy and throughout childhood and adolescence. And it is not just specific skills acquired at the previous age that promote good developmental outcome, important as these may be; it is also the attitudes and expectations – the derived meaning from previous experience – that leads to positive functioning.

Resilience

Risk research and studies of competence rather naturally led to the rise of research on resilience. Those studying risk factors for schizophrenia, for example, at first were focused on predicting adult schizophrenia from childhood to enhance prevention and early intervention. Risk factors studied included poverty, high stress, family history of schizophrenia, and other indicators of psychopathology or family dysfunction. Each of these was supported as a modest risk factor for schizophrenia. But soon they discovered that even given some environmental or biological risk factor, most at risk children did *not* develop schizophrenia. Even when one twin developed schizophrenia, another growing up in the same home often did not. In the same manner as the military men described by Pat Barker (1991), these children became of great interest, again because of what they might tell us about prevention and about factors that are protective in the face of risk. Why didn't all the men experiencing war trauma become disturbed. More generally, it was observed that whenever researchers looked at responses to adversity, there were great variations in outcome, with some individuals struggling and exhibiting behavioral and emotional problems and others apparently doing well.

At the same time, those studying competence were uncovering the important role for expectations about the self and others. These "resilient" children, these children who prevailed in the face of adversity, seemed to have some special attitudes or beliefs that supported them. For a time, the phenomenon of resilience was described in circular and at times almost magical ways. In fact, at first such children were referred to as "invulnerable," implying that for some children it did not matter what they experienced. Some just somehow had the right stuff. At other times, it was thought that certain inherent traits, like IQ, would explain resilience.

This is still all too prevalent today. The term "resilience" is at times thrown around carelessly, often with the misleading idea that there are some special people who, simply by dent of inborn character, can meet every challenge. The term "dandelion children" has recently been used, implying that some children thrive (perhaps even do better) in horrible conditions.

It turned out that, as Ann Masten (2001) has described it, if there was magic involved, it was "ordinary magic." Like everything else, resilience is an outcome of development with a central place for meaning. Resilience is not something that some children simply have; it is constructed step-by-step, based on experience, and is always accompanied by support in the environment. No children are invulnerable. As Arnold Sameroff (2000) showed, when enough risk factors pile up, there are almost no children who thrive. All of us are dependent on support.

Also, it seems, resilience emerges when support (internal and external) outweighs risks. In the Minnesota study we found, as had others, that parents who experienced maltreatment as children more likely abused their own children. Yet, some of them did not. They "broke the cycle" of abuse (Egeland et al., 1988). Three factors were found to account for this: (1) they had an alternative caregiving figure in childhood who was nurturing; (2) they had therapy in their youth lasting more than 6 months; and (3) they (almost all of them) currently had a relationship with a supportive partner. Such relationship supports apparently over-matched the history of maltreatment, helping them to continue to "expect well."

We thought that we might know how the capacity to expect well in the face of difficulty was actually developed and maintained. First, confident expectations regarding self and other are at the core of attachment theory. If this theory is valid, then those who have a history of secure attachment should as a group more likely have such positive expectations and be more resilient than those with histories of anxious attachment. Second, beyond attachment, declining risk and ongoing support from the social environment should also be important. We were able to test this in two basic ways.

In our longitudinal studies we had very solid measures of family life stress. High stress clearly reflects adversity, and, indeed, conditions of high stress were correlated with child behavior problems in our study, age by age, as has been true in other studies as well. Our first examination of resilience was to define a large group of children who were experiencing high stress in the elementary school years (Pianta et al., 1990). Using well-established cutoff scores, we divided those with high stress into two groups, those having notable behavior problems and those who did not. This second group could, of course, be defined as "resilient," because they were doing well in the face of adversity. We reasoned that, despite high stress, this must be because there were protective factors at play for these children. In particular, our focus was on a history of support, including secure attachment. In fact, when there was secure attachment in infancy it was significantly less common for children to show clinical levels of behavior problems than if there was a history of anxious attachment, even with comparable levels of family stress.

The implication was that the history of secure attachment allowed some children to prevail even in stressful conditions. Several reasons for this could be suggested. Children with such histories are generally more able to regulate their emotions and more frequently get along well with peers and teachers. These and other developed skills for recruiting resources would certainly help. But we believe the capacity to expect well – to believe that things will be all right despite adversity – also helped them prevail.

This was even more apparent when we looked at resilience another way. Many children, of course, have periods of difficulty, including children with histories of secure attachment. Anyone can hit a bad patch. The question is, who can more readily rebound after a period of difficulty? Rebounding following such a period is a classic, dictionary way of defining resiliency. We studied this form of resilience by first defining a group of children who had consistently shown problems across three separate assessments from age 3 years to age 4½ years. We did it this way to be relatively certain that these children were struggling. Most of these children had histories of anxious attachment. Still, in our high risk/poverty sample, there were a good number who had been secure; yet their problems were comparable to the others. Without a developmental analysis, or had the study begun only at 4 years of age, there is at this point just one group of troubled children. But, considering history, we viewed them as two groups. This allowed us to now ask the key question: Who would be more likely to recover from this period of trouble? We found that, indeed, when we followed them to third grade and looked at behavior problems, those with histories of secure attachment were more likely to have remitted their problems than those with histories of anxious attachment (Sroufe et al., 1990). Note that, without the history data, their "resilience" would have been mysterious and may have been attributed to inborn characteristics. Since our study was comprehensive, we were also able to control for factors such as child IQ.

We repeated such an analysis at different periods of development and found each time that secure attachment history was predictive of recovery from periods of difficulty. For example, some children experiencing behavior problems in the elementary school years remit these problems by adolescence, even though there is substantial continuity across this age span. Again, we found that those with a history of secure attachment in infancy were more likely to recover. We also found that decreases in family stress across this period accounted for some positive change. Taken together, early history and improved circumstances accounted for virtually all the cases of resilience.

Thus, something remains a part of resilient children even during times when they are having difficulties. They have something special inside all right, but it is not just inherent, magical stuff they were born with; it is a legacy of early positive care and current support. Resilience is a developmental construction.

The Fate of Early Experience following Developmental Change

This work on resilience informed us that early experience is not erased when circumstances or quality of adaptation change. Rather, it retains a potential to influence later behavior. Individuals with early supportive parenting can recover from periods of adversity and remain more able to capitalize on new supports or new opportunities. One example of this came from our studies of depression. While those with secure attachment were a bit less vulnerable to ever developing depression, some nonetheless did. When they were depressed as adolescents, however, they were less likely to be depressed as adults than those depressed teens with histories of anxious attachment. We were able to show that this was in part because they had formed a stable partnership between adolescence and early adulthood. Interestingly, forming such a partnership did not lead to remission of depression in those individuals with a history of anxious attachment in infancy. So those with secure histories were better able to draw upon support from their new partner, we believe because of what was laid down in the early years of their lives.

With close observation, it is possible to see the residue of early positive experience even when the child is having a difficult time. For example, among the children who were functioning poorly, as judged by the teachers in our preschool, there were some who had histories of secure attachment. Were the teachers somehow able to still discern that history? After the school term had ended, we asked our teachers, who had no knowledge of the children's histories, to see if they could judge who did and did not have secure histories among those having current problems. They were highly accurate in doing this. When later interviewed, they said it was because they could still see a core of self-esteem, some spark in the child, or sometimes a kind of indignation about the current situation in their lives. They were seeing the shadows of the past in these young children.

It is of course not just positive histories that are maintained. Development works the same way in all cases. Histories of anxious attachment or early trauma are not erased either. Children with such histories often retain entrenched negative expectations and remain more vulnerable to later adversity, even when they have functioned well for a time. They are still susceptible to seeing setbacks as portentous or dire, as meaning that they will certainly slip back into old negative patterns. When challenges and setbacks have such negative meanings, negative developmental outcomes are more likely. Therefore, continued support is necessary.

A child we will call AC illustrates this process well. Her early experience was characterized by emotional unavailability, rejection, and, at times, physical abuse at the hands of her overtaxed, alcoholic, unsupported mother, as well as a chaotic homelife with a series of unstable people coming and going. She manifested an avoidant and disorganized attachment in infancy, was very disorganized and helpless as a toddler, and was immature, passive, and poorly oriented as a preschooler, almost virtually unable to interact with the other children. (For several days she was seen to climb into a baby carriage that had been brought into the classroom and remain in it for some time.)

Then, in a striking turnabout, by age 10 at our summer camp she was functioning quite well. She was graceful, socially skilled, well-liked by counselors, and quite popular with peers. There were explanations for this turn around, including extensive therapy that had happened for both AC and her mother. Nonetheless, the change was remarkable, and it filled us with questions. Graduate students would ask, has she really changed? Clearly, the answer was yes. The empirical facts did not lie. Then, is her early experience gone? This cannot be, according to our developmental theory drawn from Bowlby (1973). All of one's history is retained. Even when there is change, history should not be lost. How was one to make sense of both her history and current functioning? Was her earlier history somehow erased?

In fact, one could still see echoes of her early experience even at 10 years of age. For example, while clearly popular, in our camp interviews she continued to express doubts that the others really liked her. More compelling, and consistent with group data we have published, she again struggled in the future. As a teenage she became quite disturbed, with dissociative symptoms, thought problems, and self-abusive behavior. To understand her world view now, as an adult, one needs to know all this history, plus her experiences in her early adult years and the current supports available to her. And this is true for all of us.

Continuity, Change, and the Nature of Maladaptation

Understanding how and why early experience is preserved is a key to understanding both adaptation and maladaptation. It also helps us understand why change is so difficult and how it can nonetheless be accomplished.

A primary definition of the word "adaptation" refers to the process of an organism fitting to its environment. Organisms must accomplish some kind of fit to their environments; those that are not fitted to their environments, like a polar bear without fur, simply perish. This seeking to fit is inherent across species and is certainly characteristic of humans. All infants will necessarily adapt to the environment they find themselves in to the full extent of their capacities. Therefore, when we say that anxious attachment patterns are maladaptive, we are not referring to the infant's failure to adapt in this sense. Rather, we are referring to the developmental consequences, present and future, of the adaptation that has been made. In fact, we believe it is in the nature of infants to make the *best adaptation possible*, given their circumstances and their limited capacities as infants. When the adaptation is not functional, this is because the infant had no choice but to adapt to unsupportive circumstances in the best way they could.

It is reasonable for an infant that experiences hit-or-miss or chaotic care to become dysregulated and fretful and later to become easily threatened by minor things and preoccupied with the caregiver. In taking this stance, it may be more likely that they get the attention and protection they need from inconsistent caregivers. When caregivers aren't "hearing" well, infants necessarily speak more loudly through their behavior. It is also natural that caregivers find this fretfulness annoying, and the toddler becoming upset does not make consistency more likely. This child, then, is more likely than most to become a "difficult" toddler – easily frustrated, whiney, and demanding. It will need consistent, firm, and clear limits, *even more than most toddlers*; yet this is precisely what is difficult for this caregiver to provide, perhaps even increasingly so. Without effective guided regulation, self-regulation is put in jeopardy. This child will have few tools for engaging peers and teachers in the next phases of life, making supportive and corrective experiences less likely. Their belief that they can control and manage themselves will be compromised. This is the way maladaptation works; the limitations in the particular pattern can lead to deeper limitations because the child is ill-prepared to draw upon the very resources needed, and at times even behaves in ways that make it less likely that those resources will be available. The meaning of challenges – the negative expectations acquired at each phase – and the negative ways of behaving become more and more consolidated.

In a similar way, those with histories of avoidant attachment, in the face of rejecting care, reasonably learn to withhold expressions of tender need. In that way they avoid the painful feelings that come when they are turned away (or worse) and perhaps keep from further alienating an unresponsive caregiver. Tender needs come to be eschewed; they signify forthcoming rejection by their caregiver. These are understandable generalizations from their lived social experience. However, when these expectations are taken forward to other relationships, they are handicapping. The defiance of authority figures and disdain, antipathy, or aggression toward other children can be seen as preemptive strikes to maintain separation, all in accord with an acquired meaning system. However, these patterns of behavior preclude the very corrective experiences that could lead to more positive expectations regarding relationships. These children wind up alienating teachers and being rejected by other children. Moreover, even when they encounter supportive or otherwise positive reactions from others, the meaning of these is missed or distorted, as when Vera could not understand why her teacher would not throw her against the wall (Chapter 6). When the teacher said that this was because she loved her, she even asked her why *that* was so.

It is because of these self-perpetuating loops that patterns of maladaptation tend to become more entrenched. Anxiety, attention problems, and misbehavior lead to both academic and social failures at school that, in turn, often lead to more problems. What is labeled "oppositional-defiant" behavior in the preschool years becomes "conduct disorder" a few years later and, all too frequently, an array of serious problems in adulthood. All the problems that clinicians see, be it repeatedly being in inappropriate relationships; knowing how to be close only through fighting; struggles with addiction, isolation and depression, all can be constructively viewed as patterns of behavior acquired because, at one time, they served the person or protected the individual from some kind of psychic pain. The patterns then took on this self-perpetuating character. Meanings derived from experience are at the center of all of this.

PART IV

Meaning and Disturbance

CHAPTER 12

On the Meaningfulness of Disturbance

The idea that behavior problems and psychiatric "symptoms" have meaning has a long history. Freud, for example, took the position that the same laws apply to normal and abnormal behavior alike. It was one of his greatest insights. In this view, disturbance was meaningful. Anxiety, for example, was a warning signal to the self that some threat was present and thus functioned to forestall trauma. Other psychoanalytic theorists similarly suggested that disturbances were functional; they served the person in some way, including as protection against more extreme pathology. As Carl Jung (1990) argued, all seemingly disturbed behavior makes sense from within the mind of the person. For example, a lie makes no sense unless the truth is seen as dangerous.

Scholars of diverse perspectives have agreed with this general idea. Family therapists argued for decades that disturbance is meaningful, and that the "identified patient," the family member with the "symptoms," was actually the one making sense of the whole system; in fact, the only one calling out the disturbance in the family. Thus, what appears to be problematic or even bizarre from an outside perspective is part of the coherent organization of the individual person in the system they are in. Attachment theorist Bowlby (1988) argued that distorted views of the world are the reasonable outcomes of one's past experiences. There are reasons why each of us behave in the ways we do, even when those behaviors seem peculiar or maladaptive.

Sometimes the reasons may seem obvious, as when Lady Macbeth continually washed her hands in response to her guilt ("blood on her hands"); or the case of the woman who had an intense phobia of the dangling cloth strips at the car wash (whose mother dangled a belt at her side and swayed it back and forth as a precursor to a beating); or the bully with the abusive father. All of these make sense. Then there was the child we described running into our preschool classroom, shouting over and over that he didn't want to talk about it. It was obvious to anyone with clinical training that he was upset and asking for help and did so in the only way he was able, given his immaturity and compromised development. Sometimes, of course, the reasons for problems are quite difficult to understand, even after deep probing. Numerous complex influences are often in operation. Nonetheless, it is proposed that, if we knew enough, we could see the reasons for troubled behavior. Whether we are discussing the range of everyday problems most of us share, or extremely atypical behavior, all can make sense upon close analysis. We agree with Freud that all behavior – including disturbed behavior – is meaningful.

The newer field of developmental psychopathology, which emerged in the 1980s, takes this idea even further. A major proposition in this framework is that all behavior, normal and abnormal alike, develops according to the same principles. When one understands typical development and how it unfolds, then one can begin to see deviations more clearly. Understanding normal and atypical development are complementary enterprises. Each task bears on the other because what is abnormal is defined as deviation from normal development, and what is normal is highlighted when development goes awry. "Just as personality or the emergence of competence involves a progressive, dynamic unfolding in which prior adaptation interacts with current circumstances in an ongoing way, so too does maladaptation or disorder" (Sroufe, 1997, p. 252).

Normal and abnormal behavior develop following the same processes. The capacity for emotion regulation develops. The capacity for sustained attention develops. The capacities for empathy, closeness, and social connection develop. So too do emotion regulation *problems*, attention *problems*, and difficulties with social relationships, and they develop in exactly the same way as positive functioning. As always, development is cumulative. Disturbance, like normal functioning, develops in a cumulative manner, always building upon what was there before in a step-by-step process.

As one example, the steps involved in acquiring the capacity for emotion regulation begin in the earliest months of life. At that time, regulation is largely in the hands of caregivers, who must coordinate their stimulation and soothing to states of the infant. In the next months the infant moves from unintentional to intentional signaling of needs and desires, but still has little capacity for self-regulation. The caregiver must read both these intentional and nonintentional signals accurately and respond appropriately, building up stimulation when the infant can tolerate it and backing off when the infant needs a break. If this is done effectively, the infant gradually builds tolerance for ever-higher levels of arousal. In the toddler period the child has some beginning capacities for self-control and regulation, but these require scaffolding by attentive caregivers in terms of structure, limits, and support, because toddlers can over-arouse themselves and are easily drawn into highly arousing interactions. When all of this goes well, there are three critical achievements. The young child has been trained in arousal modulation; has had experiences of becoming highly aroused without becoming disorganized; and has learned that even if organization breaks down, it can be easily reclaimed. They have both a beginning capacity for self-control and an expectation that control is possible.

So what does it then mean when a child is frequently out of control, has difficulty remaining focused, flies off the handle, and cannot easily calm down again? It means this entrainment in regulation has been compromised, likely step-by-step. Caregivers provided stimulation not keyed to the infant, misread or failed to notice signals, continued stimulation when the child needed a break, and perhaps teased, provoked, punished, or emotionally abandoned, wittingly or unwittingly, just when the child was on the edge of disorganization.

Likewise children who are alienated from others frequently have histories of rejection; that is, they have been alienated. Children who are chronically worried that something bad might happen have repeatedly experienced bad things happening outside of their control. Just as any normal way of functioning derives its meaning from its place in the development of the person, so too does the meaning of disturbance. It derives from experience.

A Note regarding Blaming Parents

Throughout this book we have underscored the role of early social experiences in providing the foundation for adaptation, because of the cumulative nature of development and the meanings that are taken forward from early life. This chapter emphasizes the role of care, especially in early life, as we explore maladaptation and disturbance. At times, this developmental approach has been viewed as casting blame on parents. There are several reasons why we do not see blaming parents as constructive or even justified.

First, parents of course have their own histories and their own sociocultural context. The meaning systems that they bring forward are in large part derived from their own experience, as was true for their parents and their grandparents. Thus, blaming parents would lead to an almost infinite regress back through the generations all the way to Mitochondrial Eve. There is no usefulness in this. It is focusing on the role of experiences that will guide us toward helping the next generation of children, not critiquing parents.

Second, research on the context within which particular parents are operating shows that parents are embedded in circumstances just as children are embedded in families. Repeatedly, the Minnesota study showed that when parental stress decreased, child adaptation improved. As we mentioned in Chapter 4, this even applies to changes in infant attachment relationships. Children that were anxiously attached at age 12 months were often secure at 18 months when family stress decreased during that interval. Across development, as family stress declines and/or social support increases, parents do better and children do better.

Further, numerous intervention studies have shown that, as parents are helped with their own secure-base needs and distortions from their own histories, they become better parents, and security in their children is promoted (e.g., Dozier, 2019; Labella et al., 2024; Slade et al., 2023; Van IJzendoorn et al., 2023). These studies also show the importance of parents as allies in the treatment work. In all, we might say that, should one have an inclination to assign blame, the finger might well be pointed at society at large.

None of this changes the important role that early care plays in promoting serviceable meaning systems and positive adaptation. Likewise, it plays a pivotal role in the creation of distorted meaning systems and disturbed behavior. We behave the way we do largely because of what we have experienced.

Explaining Common Problems

The perspective of meaning helps explain why people behave in the ineffective ways they do, why they get in the same encumbering situations time after time, and why they exhibit tendencies that others find irritating. Many of these ways of behaving are things we all do to some degree and sometimes exhibit to a detrimental degree. But all of this is understandable. In this section we will consider three common issues – things that all of us deal with: behaving in a controlling way, idealization of others, and emotional dependency.

Over Control

Why are some people often, and all of us sometimes, over-controlling of others? We used to think about this almost categorically. Some people were controlling; they had a problem. Others were not controlling. But thinking about all of our friends, our acquaintances, and ourselves, we were hard pressed to think of very many people as not being controlling. The need to control others seemed to be widespread. The more we thought about this, the more reasonable it seemed that the motive to control one's experience would be universal, a part of human evolution. It is akin to the need for personal power or agency. We need to feel that we can impact our world. Control is at times a distortion of this need, but it often is normal. With our large brains, the ability to forecast the future, and the capacity to imagine innumerable possibilities, including threats and calamities, the business of living could be quite overwhelming. Seeking to exercise control over the environment, including perhaps especially the social environment, would be crucial for keeping anxiety within bounds. It is something we all need to do. When we become aware of the urge to control others, we can realize that we are feeling anxious or afraid of something, be that criticism, emotional withdrawal of the other, or something even more serious.

The first questions within a developmental psychopathology perspective are, how do people *usually* develop to optimize a particular characteristic, and how do things look when development is going well? Only then do we ask "how can it go wrong?" The tendency to exert some control over experience is normal. Its function is to control fear and anxiety. How then can things go awry with this normal system? As is generally the case, two possibilities appear, for it would seem that too little control over experience would be just as dysfunctional as trying to have too much.

With too little control one would simply be directed by what others want and would risk being completely buffeted about by the external world (and one would likely provide little guidance to others concerning one's needs). This limited exercise of control would likely result from being treated as a nonentity, being stripped of all sense of agency, and repeatedly experiencing powerlessness. Such individuals would likely be both passive and anxious.

On the other hand, since the function of control is to avert fear, those who are exceptionally over-controlling are so because they do not feel safe. This could be because of deep, historical reasons or because of chronic current threats or exposure to uncontrollable trauma, such as combat. A negative consequence of being over-controlling, however, is that it both requires preoccupying effort and is off-putting to others. The motive to control would be underlain by numerous fears, many of which are social. These include fear of loss or abandonment, fear of humiliation, fear of being exploited, and fear of incurring another's wrath. In accord with John Bowlby's thinking, we would argue that such fears derive from actual experiences of chronic threat and/or uncertainty in the person's experience.

Previous attachment theorists, including Mary Main, Erik Hesse, and Karlen Lyons-Ruth, have addressed the issue of control. They have suggested, partly based on empirical observation, that those with disorganized attachment in infancy will later be over-controlling. In particular, they point to efforts to control the behavior of the parent. The rationale for positing this is that the parents have been frightening or unfathomable and, thus, attempting to control their behavior is a way of coping with this potent fear. This would seem plausible. And, because of the complex trauma often involved in the histories of these children, their efforts to control will be desperate, multi-faceted, and rigid (Lieberman & van Horn, 2008). However, we think it is important to avoid concluding that *only* those with disorganized attachment will be controlling (or even be the only ones with a control problem). We believe that those with other attachment histories will also have a control motive, including those with secure histories. Moreover, those with histories of avoidant or resistant/ambivalent attachment will often have control issues that are maladaptive.

How then do we conceive of the intersection between control and attachment history? In our current view, emphasizing the organization of meaning, we give priority to the way the control motive is expressed differently depending on history. As is general in Bowlby's theory, we begin with what we view as positive, serviceable exercise of control and then consider the various ways in which this might be compromised. Those with histories of secure attachment would generally have a more flexible use of control as part of a broader set of coping strategies. Use of control would not be rigid or entrenched, largely because these individuals are less fearful. They might well (appropriately) become more controlling when genuine threats arise. But such a stance would not be habitual.

Those with histories of anxious attachment would be less flexible in their efforts to control others; yet would vary in their manner of exerting control. Those with histories of avoidant attachment more often might control others through disengagement, withholding of investment, or intimidation. Often it is as though they are saying, "You can't hurt me because I won't get close to you" or "You can't hurt me because I don't care." Those who are aggressive might be so in part to control the behavior of others. In contrast, those with histories of resistant attachment would attempt to control by being overly involved in managing every detail of social situations. They would try to "hold all the balloons in their hands at once," and strive to do everyone's part. Because of the chaos and uncertainty they experienced, they must try to control everything. As is true of maladaptation in general, there is a rigid and pervasive quality to these strategies.

Our meaning position also leads us to emphasize the great variations in what is threatening to the person and thus activates strong efforts at control. In the case of those with an avoidant or dismissive posture, interpersonal intimacy itself entails substantial threat. Others wanting to be close or even showing interest in one's inner self could be inherently threatening. Bullying, a prime example of excessive efforts to control others, was observed in our longitudinal study to only be common in those with histories of avoidant attachment (Chapter 6). But there are many less obvious ways of controlling closeness with others – of keeping emotional distance. These would include being unrevealing, presenting a false front (image management), engineering a focus on superficial matters, and responding cynically to the overtures or stated intentions of others. In contrast, for those with histories of haphazard, chaotic, or inconsistent care, social situations that are highly stimulating, or rapidly changing situations or circumstances, might be inherently anxiety provoking because of their association with breakdowns in organization. (These individuals may also become cynical, not because of alienation, but because of the repeated failure of their efforts to control and get the nurturance they seek.) Paradoxically, the reactions of these individuals tend to create even more chaos in their experience. This is a characteristic of maladaptation – the pattern of reaction perpetuates the problem.

Idealization

As with control, many of us had thought of idealization as pathological; that is, as a disturbed form of mentation in which another is attributed an unrealistic lack of flaws or as having the capacity for rescuing us from whatever problems or limitations we were encountering. Once again, however, idealization would seem to be something that everyone does to some extent. In that sense it must be "normal" and at times must even have positive functions for the person. In brief, all of us have a need for beacons – those we look up to. Perhaps we may see them as having characteristics (or even characters) we would seek to emulate, and as setting standards toward which we strive. It also might help keep alive our belief in human growth and potential. When idealization is not extreme, and is kept in balance with other coping strategies, it can be a positive force in our development. We can continue to recognize that, in reality, no one is perfect, while still having admiration for others.

There are again two basic ways that normal idealization may be distorted. Most obvious is the case of those who defensively idealize others, including parents, as a way of keeping themselves from seeing the actual facts about their treatment or as an attempt to keep alive an unrealistic fantasy of rescue (this person will save me). It would be inordinately difficult to acknowledge that those one desperately needs to be available for care and support in fact are not available. Another side of this type of idealization is the idea that, without the attention, affirmation, or praise by this other, I am a worthless person. Again, we all depend on affirmation from others, especially those we care about, but this need should not be consuming. In the Adult Attachment Interview (AAI), this type of idealization is revealed through unrealistically glowing descriptions of parents and parental care, as well as a disjuncture between verbal characterizations of a parent and descriptions of their actual behavior. (For example, "my father was very, very loving ... When he beat me that was because I needed it and he wanted me to be a good person.")

It is easy to recognize such over-idealization as a problem because of the distortion of reality involved. This is a characteristic scored in the AAI, and it is part of the dismissing state of mind. Parents with this state of mind have an increased likelihood of having infants with avoidant attachment. As Bowlby suggested, one plausible pathway to this dismissing state of mind is a childhood wherein what parents did (emotionally neglecting, harshly treating, or rejecting a child) contrasts with what they tell the child is reality ("I treat you so well"; "you are so fortunate be given such good care"; "I do these things because I love you"). It is difficult for a child to deny the validity of these statements made by caregivers, even when we can see them as contradicting the parent's behavior.

However, the other end of the idealization continuum would also seem to be problematic; that is, an inability to see the good or value in anyone. This was well depicted in Salinger's (1951) novel, *The Catcher in the Rye*. The main character, Holden Caulfield, sees everyone, especially every adult, as "phony." There is no one who merits respect. This is often a near kin of cynicism and a perpetual search to see the bad in people. Paradoxically, this would also seem to be a result of an avoidant attachment history. The solution is to not care, to embrace alienation. What happened to me was not significant; it was of no importance. One does not "see the point" of emotional closeness. This is indeed a characteristic of some other individuals who have a dismissing stance of the AAI. Because of the history of rejection and emotional neglect, this approach is also a way of protecting people from the pain of recognizing their deprivation. However, as with denial of harsh treatment itself, this comes at great cost.

It is developmentally normal for young children to idealize their parents. In psychoanalytic theory this was subsumed by the concept of identification. During the preschool years such idealization – ascribing great power, understanding and competence to parents – helps children cope with their own limited power in the world and even helps them believe their own power is stronger than it is, as Louis Breger (1974) described so well in his book, *From Instinct to Identity*. Such idealization of parents generally passes in early adolescence, often to be replaced by more realistic appraisal. But it is critical throughout development to have some people to admire, to look up to. A failure to idealize is as much of a problem as over-idealization, and it is an equally meaningful characteristic.

Dependency

Like idealization and being controlling, being dependent on others is normal, and dependency problems can also take two forms. Dependency has an obvious function in human development. Humans are the most socially connected of species and are thoroughly dependent on others for protection and care for a long period of development (Bohannon, 2023). Normatively, we never stop being dependent. Rather, expressions of dependency become transformed. In preschool age children, expressions of *emotional* dependency wane; that is, children much less often need reassurance, coaxing, and comforting to act on the world. At the same time, "instrumental dependency" increases. Children still rely on others for help with things beyond their capacity, but they seek such help in more direct ways. As development continues, the task is to increasingly evolve individual coping capacities while still staying connected with others. At one time researchers focused rather exclusively on adolescent emancipation or autonomy, a separation of youth from their parents. In time, however, it was realized that autonomy did not imply separateness, even from parents, and the modern conceptualization is "autonomy with connectedness" (Chapter 8). Normatively, we remain emotionally dependent upon others at times, even in later childhood and adulthood. Especially when we are seriously ill or have experienced a major loss, we need emotional support from others. The major change with later development is that others can also be dependent on us.

What might disrupt this typical progression and leave the individual unduly emotionally dependent, constantly seeking reassurance? Problems of over-dependency do not result because some people are born with a dependency need. We all were. Rather, it is when dependency needs were not adequately met in early life that dependency remains an issue. One definition of secure attachment is effective dependency. A major claim of Bowlby, clearly supported by research, is that even those pushed too early toward independence later will be *more* dependent. The failure to shift from emotional to instrumental dependency in the preschool years means that early dependency needs were not adequately addressed.

As with all problems, meaning plays a central role in over-dependency. When young children are not given the care they need, or when they are required to try to take on tasks which are beyond them, such as taking care of their parents or otherwise solving the family's problems, they are doomed to failure. Moreover, they may well be fated to more generally see solving problems or meeting their needs as beyond their capacity, even when objectively they are not. They are so small, and the task is so large. They have needed help they did not get. Now they feel they need to lean on others at all times. Every task looks big to them. It is not surprising that, in our study, measures of anxiety and measures of emotional dependency were closely related. When a child believes his or her coping skills are inadequate, anxiety follows, as does the chronic need to lean on others.

What about the problem of insufficient expression of dependency? Our longitudinal work allowed us to see the burying of dependency needs over time. The process was not always the same. For those with avoidant attachment histories, signs of impending alienation were apparent early. In preschool, these were the children that showed their dependency only indirectly (as in the case of the child who approached teachers through a series of oblique angles) and often not at all when the need was greatest (as when the child at the opening of this book went off by himself after being rejected by a sought-out dance partner). They also tended to be aggressive or even hostile and thus were rejected by other children and controlled by teachers. Still, in the preschool and elementary years, these children were rated as more dependent than those with secure histories. So with these children there was a gradual burying of direct expressions of dependency under a coat of cynicism and pseudo-self-sufficiency. One prototype was our participant who, after repeatedly laughing at his own son's difficulties in our 2-year tool problem situation, chided him: "What took you so long? Are you too stupid? I did that much faster when I was your age." (While he could not possibly remember this, in fact he had the same difficulties at age two, because his mother was just as critical and unhelpful.) This is a reflection of buried dependency needs. To empathize with his son, to see his struggling and need, would be to confront his own unmet needs and longing.

Viewing Childhood Disorders through the Lens of Meaning

John Bowlby (1973) took the position that the worldviews and problems of children, and of each of us, are the products of lived experiences. One of the examples he used was school phobia. While certainly some children have experiences at school, especially at later ages, that make them not wish to go, this generally is not the case with younger children. These phobias should actually be referred to as school refusal or separation fears, and it turns out that generally they are not irrational but meaningful. What Bowlby argued was that typically such children actually had been threatened with abandonment or loss. Somehow it was routinely suggested to them that their caregiver would not be there when they came home. For this reason they did not want to go.

Our work on the outcomes of early attachment experiences supported Bowlby's view on the meaningfulness of children's problematic behavior. This longitudinal work lets us know, for example, that children who are chronically anxious and worried and who hover near teachers do so because they have experienced a world that was insufficiently stable, predictable, or safe. It was also a world where, if they were alarmed, reassurance and comforting were not promptly and effectively available. They are vigilant and worried because it is required that they be so. This was the adaptation that was required for them to get some degree of responsiveness from an unresponsive environment.

In a similar way, one sometimes sees children who "have a chip on their shoulder," who are ready to strike out and behave as though it is them against the world. They alienate others, exhibit little empathy, and are often isolated. Why do they act like they have a chip on their shoulder? It is because, metaphorically speaking, a chip has been put there. They have experienced chronic early rejection and/or emotional unavailability. It has been precisely when they sought help with their tender needs that they were rebuffed. The world has been alienating, and now they are alienated.

In cases where children have been abused or otherwise encountered frightening behavior from their attachment figures, that is, from those who should be their source of protection, the situation is dire. It is an impossible dilemma. They cannot both flee from and go to the same person. The later tendency to dissociation of these individuals is understandable. Cutting off some part of the experience was one of the only solutions available. Extreme conflict behavior, distracting themselves from their need, and putting their attention to irrelevant places were available early. This pattern of adaptation was required of them in the circumstances in which they lived. For this reason it becomes a well-worn pathway. Later, segregating aspects of their experience becomes a habitual practice.

Viewing the way different children behave from the perspective of meaning leads to both richer and deeper understanding than nondevelopmental interpretations. Children with problems subsumed under the label of "conduct disorder," including aggression, provide a valuable case in point. Two things had been noted for some time regarding these children. The first was that these problems are quite stable, often even intractable. People used that to argue that this was evidence that conduct problems must be biologically based. Why else would they be so pernicious? The second observation was that aggressive children often attribute negative intent in ambiguous situations. It would be tempting, then, to conclude that aggressive children have a cognitive deficit, and that such distorted thinking is the cause of their aggression.

However, such a contemporaneous correlation tells us little about how such thinking originated. Is it just there, part of the package of being inherently aggressive? Following children through time reveals that these children have a history of being rejected and even being treated with hostility. This leads both to the tendency to be aggressive and their particular worldviews. For them, when situations were ambiguous, negative events frequently *did* in fact happen. Rather than having a mental hardware problem, they generalize from their experience as all human beings do. They develop expectations based on their histories. In the end, ambiguous situations have different meaning for them, and this accounts for the link between aggression and negative attributions (Chapter 6). And, of course, such a pattern is stable, because such a worldview interferes with getting corrective feedback from the social world. When, for example, children peremptorily strike out at others, they have no opportunity to see that the other's intentions were benign. Longitudinal studies aimed at the roots of meaning are the tonic that can protect psychology from the all too common tendency to attribute problems to inherent deficits in the child.

The Meaningfulness of Even Extreme Disturbance

On careful analysis, even the most extreme disturbances of behavior become coherent. For example, we discussed the role of dissociation in the intergenerational transmission of disorganized attachment in Chapter 10. In its extreme form, dissociation is central in Multiple Personality disorder and in Borderline disorder. But, even short of that, dissociation is a rather extreme sign of disturbance. Finding oneself somewhere and having no idea how you got there, or otherwise having large gaps in experience, very much compromises functioning. And having to segregate prominent aspects of experience creates a sense of unreality.

For example, one problem associated with dissociation is self-mutilation, for example cutting or burning one's body. In interviews of these individuals, Tuppett Yates (2004) found that such behaviors are often not suicidal gestures but rather have the motive of "feeling something." Disturbed as it is, it can be seen as a striving to retain contact with reality. In the case of disorganized infants, the precursors of dissociation they exhibit are in response to a frightening parent. They must cut off some of their experience to cope at all. As we will discuss further in Chapter 13, dissociation is more generally linked to trauma, primarily physical and sexual abuse. For all individuals, dissociation begins as a protection from psychic pain. In its origins, it is functional and, in that sense, meaningful. Of course, given the lens of meaning, there are many layers in the interpretation of self-mutilation. Especially when young children are abused, like all of us they cast about for meaning and try to make sense of this situation. It is quite unfathomable for a young child to think of parents as bad. Given their view of causality, it only makes sense that they caused this physical and/or psychic pain. Therefore, they must have deserved it. Self-injury can be the punishment they deserve. It can also be a way of mastering the situation; they now have control of the pain. When abuse has been at the hands of caregivers, there is also the meaning that they are not loveable, of no worth, and deserving of pain and mistreatment, as we suspected with the girl who gouged her face in our preschool classroom.

We believe other extreme symptoms also are functional. For example, at first glance the behaviors of children with Kanner syndrome (classic autism) seem completely baffling and purposeless. These include stereotypic behaviors, such as rocking, self-injury, and flicking the fingers in front of the face, as well as "negativism." Negativism refers to refusals to perform tasks that have previously been mastered. At certain points in learning, children may suddenly seem to do things that are wrong, even though moments ago they had done them correctly. That this was negativism, and not a sudden loss of cognitive capacity, is demonstrated by the fact that at times errors in choice tasks were well beyond chance. In fact, they sometimes make anything but the right choice. That rather clearly rules out a cognitive deficit. Why would a child do any of this? Obviously, one thing these behaviors mean is that these children have a rather extreme need to control the stimulation in the environment. All of the behaviors – rocking, finger flicking, and negativism – can be explained in this way. But a full explanation is more nuanced than this.

Uwe Stuecher, as a graduate student at Minnesota years ago, spearheaded a very detailed study of one case for his doctoral dissertation (see Sroufe et al., 1973 for a published description). A central part of this work was a project to uncover the function and meaning of Tommy's finger flicking and its relation to negativism, using behavioral and heart rate measures. Stuecher had documented that Tommy sometimes engaged in mild, low-level finger flicking when he was by himself in his room. This was in accord with one function frequently suggested; namely, self-stimulation to increase arousal. However, it had also been observed that this child seemed to increase this behavior, and do it with great intensity, when demands were placed on him or he otherwise was stressed and clearly aroused. The goal was to determine the meaning of this behavior which, like many behaviors, can have multiple meanings (Sroufe et al., 1973).

For some reason, one of the things that Tommy at times refused to do was to complete a drawing of the number 4. He would do the top of the 4 (the "L" piece) and would start drawing the downward line at the top, but when he came to the line at the bottom of the L, he would not cross the line. This was neither a conceptual problem nor a motor skill problem. He sometimes made the 4 correctly. He would always trace the number 4 and he would put pieces of felt together to make a 4, and he could draw other equally complicated numbers routinely. Crossing the bar on the four was where paradoxically he sometimes "drew the line." He could do it but he would not do it. At these times his conflict and high arousal were apparent, through tension in his muscles, strong pressure on the pencil point, and heart rate acceleration. Moreover, as he approached the crossing point with his line, intense finger flicking occurred. This finger flicking started shortly after the HR acceleration began and pushed the acceleration higher, after which it dropped precipitously. After just a few of these episodes, Tommy simply immediately drew the 4 incorrectly, without elevated HR or finger flicking. His conflict was over. Moreover, at that point he also did other things incorrectly. This behavior was exquisitely organized. The clear interpretation was that the finger flicking here was the other side of arousal modulation; namely, tension release in the face of very high arousal. The manifest negativism likewise removed the child from conflict. Thus, both negativism and his stereotypic behavior were mechanisms for coping with the high arousal that came from relinquishing control to his therapist. All of this behavior was meaningful. (Across the course of treatment, both the frequency of finger flicking and negativism diminished, and performance on tasks, including drawing the number 4, improved.) Extreme as the symptoms of classic autism are, they are nonetheless meaningful.

Likewise, critics of standard psychiatric viewpoints, such as R. D. Laing (1965), have argued that the symptoms and behaviors of even the most disturbed adult individuals are coherent and meaningful. Those afflicted with schizophrenia certainly exhibit unusual thoughts, extreme disturbances in affect, and great difficulties with social interaction. Their behavior is no doubt atypical and their suffering is real; yet, it is argued that the symptoms make sense once one can understand their history and circumstances. When only one of a pair of identical twins is diagnosed as schizophrenic, which happens more often than could possibly be the case if schizophrenia were solely a genetic disorder, evidence suggests that the diagnosed twin was the least favored. A number of studies have now shown that those with psychotic symptoms are more likely to have been abused and scapegoated as children (Varese et al., 2012). These studies emphasize the neurobiological consequences of early trauma and stress.

Without doubt, such disruptions in CNS development may well contribute to the emotion regulation problems of those diagnosed with schizophrenia, as well as the difficulties with reality contact and thinking. However, we would put more emphasis on the way these experiences shape the thoughts, emotions, and worldviews of the individuals. For example, suspiciousness regarding others and feelings of persecution are likely not without basis. All of us generalize from experience. It is expected that, when one has been tormented, harshly criticized, or otherwise mistreated, one comes to expect such treatment from others. Regardless of the degree to which the nervous system may be compromised, manifest behavior and cognition are meaningful.

The thoughts of these individuals are easily interpreted as simply peculiar until looked at more closely. As an example, we once witnessed a young psychiatry intern interacting with a patient on a hospital ward. He was an arrogant man and very inexperienced. He addressed the patients in a condescending and supercilious manner. He approached one woman and, talking to her as though she were a child, said: "How are we today?" And then he said, "Now, dearie, it's time for us to go down to the dayroom." She replied, "Oh, are we going to your house?" The next day at rounds he reported this as an example of her extreme thought disturbance. Our take was quite different. We thought that, within the limits of options open to her, given the vulnerability of her position, it was an exquisite calling out of his insincerity and phoniness. She knew quite well they were not going to his house. He missed the sarcasm entirely.

Conclusion

Putting on the lens of meaning leads the way to increased compassion for ourselves, our parents, clients, and others, whatever the degree of disturbance may be manifest. We can illustrate how the lens of meaning increases understanding of disturbance by presenting two cases.

Gary, a clinical case we studied and knew well, had the common problem among men of being unable to be emotionally present (or to even know what he was feeling). In addition, he was completely unable to express any anger at his partner. While this too is common, for him it was an extreme taboo that he did not understand. When he did feel anger, it frightened him. He saw this as related to his childhood history but did not understand how. He did report that he never observed his mother, father, or brothers express anger toward anyone in the household. Anger, in fact, seemed to be taboo in his family.

When asked what happened if he became angry as a child, he said that he tried to always do this out of earshot. He was frustrated and angry frequently but he learned to do this in private, because he was punished when it was observed. His mother would "fly at him" and treat him quite harshly. He said this was both frightening and confusing. It was confusing because his mother was characteristically a gentle and calm woman. It was frightening because she seemed to lose control, and these reactions seemed to come "out of the blue." Her flashes of anger did not make sense to him.

Our understanding of attachment, trauma, and dissociation (Chapter 13) helps make sense of all this. Gary's mother came from a physically (and possibly sexually) abusive household where her father was extremely violent toward her mother and her brothers. The climate of unpredictable violence was pervasive. From this history, Gary's mother had determined that there would be no anger in her subsequent household. Anger was seen as dangerous. Because of her particular history of trauma and possibly disorganized attachment, Gary's expressions of anger likely propelled her into a dissociated state which therefore made her behavior unfathomable to him. Within this context, his problems become understandable. Her fear of anger became his fear of anger, as a warped meaning system was taken forward across generations.

Consider also the case of "John," portrayed in the documentary film, "*John Was Trying to Contact Aliens.*" John was a man with a passion. Beginning at about age 12, he began to build equipment that allowed him to transmit audio into space. Largely self-taught, for more than 30 years John developed more and more sophisticated equipment until he was able to nightly send programming millions of miles from Earth. Essentially, he became a DJ with a station that sent a great variety of the world's music into space. His eccentricities were well known in the community, and he knew his incredible expenditure of time, effort, and money into this enterprise was unusual. Without doubt his effort to communicate with extraterrestrials could have been called a disturbance – an obsession.

Symptomatic or not, John's behavior was meaningful. John's father had left him when he was a baby. Then John was raised by his loving grandparents, because he had very little contact with his ephemeral mother, seeing her less than a handful of times. Still, he remembered her well. He described her as being a bit odd, different from everyone else, not really part of the community, and he even used the term "alien" to convey how she did not fit in, though the makers of the documentary did not at all comment on his use of this term, nor any of the causes of his preoccupation. In light of his history, is his relentless effort to find and communicate with "aliens" anything but understandable? It is notable that John was able to set aside his preoccupation in middle age when he found love and a life partner. (It should also be pointed out that the United States, in collaboration with other governments, now regularly transmits radio signals into space and has built a gigantic array to listen for signals from the beyond. Moreover, we launched a probe to go beyond our solar system. Central in its cargo is some of the world's greatest music!)

Things are not always as clear-cut as in the two cases we have presented here. We will often not have the information that makes clear the meaning of particular problems. Sometimes the problems we have or others have will seem mystifying. But they are no more mystifying than the strange behavior of John. Along with Bowlby, we believe that the strange beliefs and fears that many of us have would make sense if we had enough information. They do have meaning.

CHAPTER 13

Trauma and Meaning

Trauma is generally defined as an overwhelming event or, more commonly, an ongoing series of overwhelming events against a backdrop of a highly stimulating, chaotic, and threatening environment (called "complex trauma"). The word "overwhelming" means that it is beyond the response capacities of the brain, body, and mind. In the early years, of course, when regulatory capacities are still being formed and there is limited flexibility, the system is more easily overwhelmed. Early trauma disrupts all developing systems of the individual, from memory functioning, to emotion regulation, to representations of experience. It compromises, disrupts, and distorts normal functioning and the developmental trajectory. As Bessel van der Kolk (2005), a leading trauma expert, has said, "Chronic trauma interferes with neurobiological development and the capacity to integrate sensory, emotional and cognitive information into a cohesive whole. Developmental trauma sets the stage for unfocused responses to subsequent stress" (p. 401). Most notably it distorts the coherence and organization of usually integrated systems of functioning. It thereby has a devastating impact on the capacities for making meaning, especially when they are in early phases of development.

Trauma and Brain Development

One of the core processes of development is "differentiation." This refers to the fact that development proceeds from the global to the more specific, from general outlines to refined structures. There is not a complete little person inside the fertilized egg that simply gets bigger. At first there is just a mass of cells. Later there is a rough outline of a body with protruding buds that will become arms and legs. In time the arm buds, for example, elongate and then become jointed. Hands form and fingers lengthen. These become jointed and nails form. Given this differentiation process, one can quickly see why early insult can be so critical. When any basic form is compromised, so too is all subsequent development.

The same process that governs embryonic development of course also applies to the pre- and postnatal development of the brain. Like everything else, brain development is guided by differentiation from limited complexity to extraordinary complexity. The process is cumulative or, as Joan Stiles (2008) says, "it builds upon itself." There are three particular features of brain development in humans that make it especially vulnerable to early trauma.

The first feature is that our brains develop quite slowly in comparison to other species. The brain is quite ill-formed at birth and is constructed over many years. Necessary neurons are present at birth, but little differentiation of brain structures and systems has occurred. There is a paucity of dendritic elaboration in most areas. Full maturation of the human brain is now determined to occur only by about age 25 years, although development is more rapid in the very first years. This slow development turns out to be an adaptive advantage. The prolonged development of the human brain is what allows it to achieve such great complexity. Moreover, this complexity is achieved in interaction with our particular environments and experiences, which is what has allowed humans to thrive in so many circumstances and to have such a wide range of cognitive capacities. At the same time, however, prolonged growth means prolonged vulnerability.

The second feature is what is referred to as asymmetries in brain development; that is, different structures and systems in the brain come online at different points in time. The primitive brain stem structures that control vital functions such as breathing are present at birth. Ample mid-brain neurons are present, as are cortical neurons, but there is little interconnection between cortex and mid-brain emotional centers. Such interconnections begin to richly emerge only in the second half year of life. Moreover, the frontal cortex is the last part to fully develop. Because of this, as Robert Sapolsky (2010) says, "... that part of the brain that makes us uniquely human is the most shaped by environment and the least constrained by genetics" (p. xxiv). The development of higher brain centers is especially "experience expectant" (requiring certain environmental input for its development) and "experience dependent" (being individually crafted by individual experience).

As Allan Schore (e.g., 2003) has described in numerous books and papers, it is also the case that the two hemispheres of the brain develop at a different pace. The surge in growth of the right hemisphere, which is associated with emotion expression, emotion regulation, and the stress–response system, precedes the growth surge in the left. The right hemisphere is developing very rapidly in the very first year of life, supporting social engagement and the formation of attachment relationships. The growth surge in the left hemisphere, which is heavily involved in language and verbal memory, does not begin until late in the second year and continues thereafter. Much can be stored in the emotions and in the body before it can be stored in conscious memory. Likewise, excitatory ("sympathetic") systems develop in advance of inhibitory ("parasympathetic") systems. This all means that activation systems are well in place before the infant has much capacity for inhibition and control. Excitatory and inhibitory systems are tuned and balanced within caregiving relationships over the first 3 or 4 years of life. In the early months, therefore, regulatory capacities are quite vulnerable to disruption. All of this makes clear the risk of early trauma and the need for sensitive and responsive early care to provide the regulation the infant cannot.

The third feature of brain development, already implied, is that development is not characterized by adding neurons, like building a structure with Lego, but by the organization of increasingly complex systems. While it is now understood that neurons can be created all the way into adulthood, and interconnection of neurons occurs all along the way, infants and children have many more neurons than adults do. This "overproduction" of neurons in prenatal life allows for the pruning and sculpting of the brain in reaction to experience. What happens with development is that neurons migrate and undergo massive elaboration of their dendritic ends, allowing them to contact many other neurons, all in response to experience. This ultimately supports all of the complexity of human behavior. In addition, brain and body become exquisitely organized, including the development of a critical stress–reactivity system, known as the hypothalamic–pituitary–adrenal axis (HPA). Thus, the process of brain development is extraordinarily complex. It is remarkable how well this process typically goes, but it is certainly vulnerable to disruption.

In this context of development, it is clear and obvious how devastating trauma would be for the development of the brain systems underlying meaning. In fact, recent studies with humans show that brain systems underlying memory, sensory integration, emotion regulation, and stress reactivity are all impacted by early trauma. Child maltreatment, for example, is linked to reductions in the volume of the hippocampus (critical for memory), as well as the volume of anterior cingulate and ventromedial and dorsomedial cortices, among other things (Teicher et al., 2016). All of this is critical to how experience is organized. Teicher et al.'s review of early trauma found consistent reports of augmented amygdala response to threatening stimuli, diminished ventral striatal response to anticipation or receipt of reward, diminished connectivity between prefrontal regions and the amygdala in maltreated individuals, with profound implications for emotion and emotion regulation. When trauma occurs in the earliest years, disruption is greatest, because vital structures are immature and undergoing rapid development in interaction with experience.

Trauma and Psychological Development

The self is nothing more and nothing less than the cumulative integration of experience. Trauma disrupts integration. Therefore trauma has a devastating impact on the self when early integration is occurring.

All aspects of the development of the self or psyche – social, emotional, and representational – occur in complete parallel with brain development. They develop according to the same processes and in a coordinated manner. Development of the capacity for partnership, as well as the capacities to experience and express emotions and to form expectations for self and other, occur in the same time frame as developments in brain structures and their complex interconnections. Specific emotions such as fear (in contrast to startle), anger (in contrast to high arousal and distress), and surprise (in contrast to rapt attention) emerge only in the second-half year (Sroufe, 1996), when the amygdala and other emotion centers begin to be connected to the cortex.

Representations in the first months are not symbolic representations but rather generalized action sequences (Stern, 1985). Anticipatory expectations (and the ability to connect past experiences with present) emerge toward the end of the first year, along with specific attachment relationships, and then blossom in the second and third years.

All of this has dramatic implications for the vulnerability of infants and young children regarding trauma. As discussed in Chapter 2, whether infants have or do not have confident expectations regarding their caregivers, whether they feel secure or chronically anxious, is the product of their cumulative history of interactions. It depends on implicit or procedural memory, long before specific events can be recalled. Nonetheless, specific experiences of great intensity can disrupt the consolidation of this kind of memory. Singular events would not tend to have lasting effects but, if traumatic events are routine, chronic anxiety and lasting disturbances in the stress reactivity system would occur.

Regulating stress and fear are two of the critical achievements of psychological development, and trauma poses a great challenge to these achievements. When threat or stress is detected in the midbrain's emotional centers, this triggers the HPA axis. The hypothalamus releases corticotropin-releasing hormones and the pituitary releases adrenocorticotropic hormone. These in turn lead to release of adrenalin and cortisol. Adrenalin promotes immediate bodily reactions to stress (increased heart rate and blood flow to the skeletal muscles, as well as increased glucose for stronger muscular reactions). Thus, the body is prepared for flight or fight responses. Cortisol in the blood allows the reaction to be sustained over a period of time. All of this is normal and has been functional throughout human history. When mature and well-developed, this system functions quite well, and occasional extreme stresses can be weathered. However, when stress is chronic or trauma frequent, the system is easily compromised while it is developing. Maltreatment in young children has been demonstrated to cause a baseline increase in cortisol levels (Bruce et al., 2009). Such lingering of cortisol in the blood leaves the child chronically reacting as though stress were continuously present.

Attachment theory and various psychoanalytic theories have suggested not only that caregivers are important regulators of fear, but that separation from an attachment figure is a major source of fear. In his book on Separation, Bowlby (1973) proposed a number of evolutionarily based fears that he called "natural clues to danger." These natural clues, which function to help keep young ones safe, include being alone, darkness, and fear of strangers and unfamiliar places. The immature infant is, in fact, more vulnerable in such situations. Alicia Lieberman (e.g., 2017), following Freud, suggested that, in the first years of life, fear of loss and fear of loss of love are also prominent.

We would emphasize that what these and other writers are pointing toward is the acute alarm that is experienced by the child when there is a threat to the integrity of the self (see Breger, 1974). In the case of the young infant, the nascent self is completely interwoven with the caregiver. For this reason, separation, especially in strange and unfamiliar places, is alarming. If you have reason to doubt that the caregiver will return, this is a threat to your very survival. However, even infants, and certainly preschool children, are motivated by much more than avoiding separation. We know this because they increasingly initiate physical separation by exploring at increasing distances, and later deliberately perturb relationships with caregivers. Such expression of their curiosity allows them to determine the boundaries of their behavior and to learn, as Lou Sander (1975) has said, that relationships are durable and robust and that such perturbations can be repaired either by their efforts or those of the parent. The importance of social relationships for maintaining the integrity of the self remains across development, but motivation becomes increasingly complex.

A major point of the preceding paragraphs is that stress and fear are common to humans. Stress will happen. A whole variety of fears will be experienced. The HPA axis will be activated with some frequency. This is actually important, because that is how the system becomes tuned. We have evolved to have and tolerate these experiences. Reacting to naturally occurring dangers is in Bowlby's terms, "sensible and efficient." Stress need not and cannot be absent. Parenting need not and cannot be perfect.

At the same time, the immature self is quite vulnerable. Stress and fear, if intense or chronic, can easily overwhelm the system. Continual threats of abandonment and harsh treatment of the toddler's impulses, and other forms of trauma can profoundly disrupt development and create a chronically distorted sense of reality, as well as distortions in the stress reactivity system. When excessive cortisol secretion is sustained in early life, this can lead to neural cell death in areas that are under development and are crucial for memory and integration, such as the hippocampus (Siegel, 2003). Sensitive and responsive caregiving is critical for avoiding this. Caregivers must protect young children from undue stress and trauma, provide them with the regulation they cannot provide themselves, and guide them as they traverse the path through early fears.

Trauma and Meaning

One of the major functions of the mature brain is to regulate and integrate the flow of information (Siegel, 2020). We are constantly bombarded with sensory information coming from inside and outside of the body; with coded information in language and gestures; and with information from the brain itself, that is, memories and expectations. It has been estimated that the brain can process about 11 million bits of information every second. However, our conscious mind can only handle 40–50 of these bits (Agarwal, 2020). Much more is coming in than can be made the focus of conscious attention or be stored for later retrieval. Obviously, much of this information must be excluded from attention, while some becomes a focus. And for it to have meaning it must be organized and integrated. We don't just see various wavelengths of light; we see objects. We don't just hear sounds; we hear words. What the words mean depends on the other accompanying words and their order (the dog bit the boy versus the boy bit the dog). Beyond this, the meaning of any utterance hinges on accompanying gestures and both the present and historical context. All of this depends on integration. All of the information from the outside and the inside (aches, heart palpitations, changes in respiration) must be integrated to be processed, in order to have coherence of experience, to have whole percepts and memories. *This is what meaning is; the organized experience, not the disparate pieces of information.* That is how crucial this integrative function of the brain is. And a major impact of trauma is to disrupt integration.

Memories themselves are integrated constructions. Infants have little ability for conscious memory before the acquisition of symbolic capacity, so that early memories are assemblages of procedures and affect. Even following language acquisition, many details of experiences are often omitted, and various events may be merged into an abstracted script. When we hear or read a story, it is generally not the words we remember, but the plot and the outcome. We don't store all of the individual features of an event, but a coherent assembly. Coherent, integrated memories include coordinated percepts, thoughts, sensory information, and affect. The fact of integration explains why sometimes a smell (for example of Eucalyptus trees) can bring back a flood of associations (for one of us, a childhood home in California).

Like everything else, the capacities to regulate and integrate the flow of information develop. Newborn infants only have primitive capacities for regulating input. Their system may merely shut down, as for example when infant boys sleep very deeply following circumcision or when infants even fall asleep in the presence of repeated loud sounds. Thus, in some ways, newborns have built-in protection from intense stimulation before they have integrative capacities. Somewhat later, infants rather reflexively turn away when stimulation is too great. This will be effective in curbing arousal in the presence of responsive caregivers. However, young children are rather easily distracted and easily overwhelmed, leading them with some frequency to become completely disorganized. Responsive care not only helps young ones stay regulated and open to integration, it actually provides training in staying regulated and organized in the face of expanding amounts of stimulation. We must at first regulate the flow of information for them.

The development of these integrative capacities, and development of the central and autonomic nervous systems themselves, is quite intricate and complex. It takes at least the first 3 or 4 years for various regulatory systems to develop. This means, among other things, that young infants are hugely dependent on caregivers for regulation in the early years of life. Moreover, the regulating activities of caregivers actually tune and balance these excitatory and inhibitory capacities, ultimately leading to self-regulation by the child. This, of course, involves considerable time and investment by sensitive, responsive caregivers. As Dan Siegel (2003) has put it: "Relationship experiences have a dominant influence on the brain because the circuits responsible for social perception are the same or tightly linked to those that integrate the important functions controlling the creation of *meaning*" (p. 11, emphasis added). These functions include those that regulate emotion and the organization of memory. The overwhelming nature of trauma means precisely that the capacities for regulation and integration are swamped.

It is no surprise that early stress and trauma would be especially devastating. Integration capacities are most vulnerable to disruption when they are only beginning to come online. When such disruption is extreme, the result will be dissociation, wherein aspects of experience become segregated or split off. In his insightful book, *The Inner World of Trauma*, Donald Kalsched (1996) described such dissociation as a "severing of affect" from the body. When emotion is segregated from thought, there is a fragmented sense of reality.

Early attachment relationships are so important because developing systems are easily compromised. Supportive, responsive caregivers provide the inhibition and modulation functions that infants in the first year or two cannot provide for themselves. Caregivers offer a good deal of protection from stresses that arise and, when infants are nonetheless overtaxed, help them recover. This is why variations in the responsiveness of care have the impacts attachment research shows they do. The impact of trauma is often mitigated by caregivers. This analysis makes clear why maltreatment or other frightening behavior on the part of caregivers themselves in the early years is so devastating. There is no protection from trauma at the hands of caregivers.

Attachment, Coherence, and Trauma

There are two general feelings or senses that are fundamental to defining how we see ourselves and the world we live in; that is, the meaning we make of things. The first is whether we see the world as threatening or benign. A principal function of early attachment relationships is to regulate fear, as Mary Main, Erik Hesse, Arietta Slade, and others have made clear. When we are secure in our attachments – when our relationships have protected us from overwhelming fear – we feel safe, and this colors the meaning of everything. When we do not feel safe, and especially when attachment relationships themselves have been traumatizing, we will see ourselves as helpless and/or under attack and the world as generally threatening.

The second important sense concerns the continuity, wholeness, and coherence of our experience. Are our feelings accessible to us, and is there an alignment and harmony between our perceptions, ideations, and feelings? When we have this sense, we can see ourselves traveling in the world, and we can see others with substantial accuracy, having the capacity to view the minds of others. We can behave with authenticity. There is no need to segregate, dissociate, or sever affect in the body from its corresponding images in the mind, thus losing meaning, as Kalsched described. This crucial task of constructing and maintaining a coherent sense of self becomes quite challenging in the face of early, complex trauma. The extreme arousal and "psychological shock" of trauma leads to dissociation (Mears, 2012). And with dissociation the infant or young child can no longer efficiently process information from the external or internal environment, leading to fragmented experiences and distortions of the self (Schore, 2003).

The devastating and pernicious role of early trauma is more than speculative. In our research at the University of Minnesota we used a cumulative risk index (child maltreatment, witnessing parental violence, family disruption, high family stress, and poverty) to represent complex trauma (Appleyard et al., 2005). We found that this was strongly related to disordered behavior both in childhood and adolescence. Moreover, when such risk was present in *early* childhood, the effects were more devastating than similar risk that did not occur until middle childhood. Even when statistically taking into account traumatic circumstances in middle childhood, early child risk was still predictive, despite the intervening years. Moreover, in another part of our study, our work showed that when early trauma occurred in the context of a prior history of disorganized attachment (the pattern associated with frightening parents) this was predictive of dissociation – the tendency to split off aspects of experience – in later life; that is, to a fragmented self (Ogawa et al., 1997). Thus, beyond the consequences of inadequate care in general, complex trauma compromises the very organization of the self – the organization of meaning.

PART V

Integration and Conclusion

CHAPTER 14

Integration

The goal of this book has been to explore how people come to have the meaning systems they do and, in this chapter, we will pull together much of what we have learned. First and foremost, meaning is a developmental construction. The worldview of every person is built up step-by-step based upon the cumulative history of experiences we each have, especially experiences in social relationships. In time, we each evolve distinctive and persistent worldviews.

The English poet, Ralph Hodgson has captured the important differences in meaning systems, as poets uniquely can. Hodgson had a wonderful ability to illustrate profound truths by twisting common phrases. His most famous is, "Some things have to be believed to be seen." This captures nicely the way in which *how* we see the world colors *what* we see. It also explains the outlook of those we call resilient, who have the capacity to "expect well," even during difficult times, and can capitalize on opportunities for growth that come their way. Hodgson also once wrote that "the handwriting on the wall might be a forgery." This would seem to be an antidote to cynicism and an apt lesson for those that see threat everywhere or routinely see malicious intent in the actions of others. For all of us it is a reminder to keep our expectations positive.

Numerous psychologists, sociologists, and philosophers before us have shed light on some of the themes we have stressed in the development of individual meaning systems, especially the active nature of meaning seeking and the role of social relationships in making sense of the world. Some have even suggested that the very goal of development is the establishment of an enduring, coherent, and serviceable meaning system. This list certainly includes James Mark Baldwin, Charles Cooley, George Herbert Mead, and, more recently, Robert Kegan (1982). Each of these theorists argued that the very sense of the self is intertwined with social relationships. Kegan, for example, described seeking meaning as the activity that makes us persons, and that making sense of one's experience is a lifelong process that occurs in a continuing social-cultural embeddedness. There is no free-standing individual. Baldwin (1897) described how parental responses of exuberance to the 3-year-old's creations increased joyful reactions and provided a core of self-worth for the child. Likewise, Cooley (1909) coined the concept of the "looking glass self," making explicit the idea that the self is a product of social relationships. Cooley directly influenced Mead (1913), who said that the child evaluates his conduct as good or bad only as the parent reacts to and interprets his or her behaviors. "Until this process has been developed into the abstract process of thought, self-consciousness remains dramatic, and the self which is a fusion of the remembered actor and this accompanying chorus is somewhat loosely organized and very clearly social" (p. 378). Only later in development is there an emphasis on the meaning of the "inner speech" of the individual, or what has become known more recently as one's narrative identity or personal story (Habermas & Bluck, 2000; McAdams & Pals, 2006).

We would take these insightful positions even further. It is not just that the self develops with reference to others or requires the support of others. Rather, following the thinking of Louis Sander (1975), social relationship precedes the self. The self literally derives from, emerges from, *springs from* early relationships. The organization of the first relationship is the prototype for the organization that *becomes* the self. The core meanings around which the self is organized come from the first relationships and thereafter are expanded and altered within subsequent relationships.

All psychoanalytic theories, and psychoanalysis and other psychodynamic therapies, are concerned with meaning, for without interpretation there is no psychoanalysis. Neo-analytic, object relations, and self-theories have been explicit about the core of meaning. Christopher Bollas, for example, in *The Shadow of the Object* (2017) and other writings, made clear that what was taken forward from infancy were the meanings derived from the relationship. His idea of the "unthought known" emphasized that these understandings preceded the capacity for verbal memory. As the term ego shifted to the word self, the ego as process rather than as a thing became prominent in many psychoanalytic theories. Jane Loevinger (1976), in her book, *Ego Development*, outlines a number of theories that she refers to as "structural" and "developmental." "Most ego theories," she says, "are structural; that is, the ego is seen as striving (or as *the* striving) for self-consistency and meaning." Organization is not something the ego does, it is what the ego is. "The striving to master, to integrate, to make sense of experience is not one ego function among many but the essence of the ego" (p. 59). Alfred Adler broke with Freud over the prime motive for humans. For Freud it was drive reduction, whereas for Adler it was a striving for coherence, consistent with one's early-acquired worldview. Fingarette (1963) took this one step further, stating simply that the self *is* the search for meaning. All of these theories are inherently developmental.

Two other prominent and hugely influential examples of theorists who emphasized meaning and development are Abraham Maslow and Erik Erikson. For example, Maslow's (1954) famous hierarchy of needs had at its pinnacle "self-actualization." One of the central features of the self-actualized person was finding a coherent sense of oneself, built up over a lifetime of experiences.

In outlining his eight stages of "man," each of the issues Erikson (1963) presented had meaning at its core, from the first issues of trust vs. mistrust and autonomy vs. shame and doubt, through to industry vs. inferiority and so on. What does it mean for the developing child to basically trust others or not, to have a sense of hope or not? What does it mean for the elementary school child to have a basic sense of competence and industry? What does it mean if one's sense of place in the world is totally confused in adolescence? Development is explicitly geared toward achieving coherence and meaning. Erikson referred to his final stage in adulthood as integrity vs. despair. Either one achieves a sense of integrity or is filled with dissatisfaction. Just what is this sense of integrity? "It is the ego's accrued assurance of its proclivity for order and *meaning*" (p. 268, emphasis added). Notice the words "accrued assurance" to emphasize how a complex, yet coherent meaning system is constructed over time, in accordance with the developmental view we are espousing. All of these theories emphasize the inherent motive to seek meaning, the active and dynamic nature of this process, and its social nature.

In a sense, of course, the worldview of every person is coherent; that is, it is understandable based upon the particular history of the person. In another sense, however, some of these worldviews are incoherent in that they contain notable gaps, propositions that are strikingly inconsistent, or expectations that, while once valid, no longer make sense in later life. Thus, the child that sees pervasive hostile intent in the actions of others (as in the interpretation of the fallen block tower in Chapter 6) does so because in his or her experience ambiguous situations frequently *did* entail hostility. But such a viewpoint may no longer reflect the reality of the preschool, where teachers are nurturant and accepting and other children simply want to play. Many adults operate within a set of expectations that were understandable at some earlier time in their lives, but no longer fit current circumstances.

While some aspects of our worldviews were derived from acculturation or direct teaching, many aspects were not derived in this way. We were not directly taught to have a meaning system or even encouraged to do so. Nor did we choose to develop one. We had no choice but to do so; it is simply in the nature of the human mind to seek and find meaning. We actively engaged in this pursuit from very early in our lives, and we do so now, however handicapped we might be. In the same way that we naturally looked to the source of a sound in the early months of our lives, and as we sought to understand the meaning of the behavior of others toward us in our childhood years, we are now impelled to seek understanding of our experiences and the feelings they evoke.

Moreover, central to the world views we evolved were our primary social relationships. One salient observation in our study of preschool play pairs was the degree of creativity the children exhibited together, far beyond the complexity of what either could do alone. While this is most obviously true early in life, and while there is certainly meaning in non-social pursuits, social experiences remain at the core of our worldviews. Social relationships promote meaning making throughout life, as has often been portrayed by great novelists. In her book *The Black Tower*, for example, P. D. James (1975) describes a relationship between Chief Inspector Dalgliesh and an aging woman in a small convalescent retreat. Although they had never previously met, both knew and were very fond of a cleric who has died. Over several encounters they shared feelings and reminiscences about Father Michael. In doing so they not only grew closer to each other but also deepened their understanding about the loved one they had lost. They created meaning together beyond what either could have achieved grieving on one's own.

These were some of the themes developed throughout this book. The final theme, the theme we wish to emphasize in this penultimate chapter, is the cumulative, dynamic, and transactional nature of the development and organization of meaning. It is here where the power of a developmental viewpoint is most notable and developmental research has made its greatest contribution.

Meaning through the Lifespan

Before reviewing individual variations in meaning systems, we will first outline the general trends in meaning making that occur within each phase of development. These developmental changes are critical for understanding how distorted and nonfunctional world views can arise and their cumulative, transactional nature.

Integration

In the very first months of life the infant is not seeking meaning in what we would describe as a deliberate way. They actively engage their environments and thereby experience a variety of events and emotional states, but they do not do so with intention. Still, they are embedded in a meaning system created by their caregivers so that what are best described as affective meanings do begin. They do have countless impactful experiences.

It is in the second half year, with the flourishing of intentionality, that infants act *in order to* produce a result, be it a reaction from another, a banging sound, or some other sensory experience. A new level of understanding can result when they deliberately signal a need to a parent and get or fail to get a result. Likewise, they can now actively explore the physical world. When the year-old repeatedly drops a variety of objects from the highchair tray, they are learning not only about the object world but also about the consequences of their actions.

A leap forward happens in the toddler period. While toddlers may not yet know that they are *trying* to create meaning or to understand their place in the social world, they are much more deliberately testing the nature of reality and, especially, the workings of relationships. The emergence of self-awareness, their understanding of the other, and their understanding that their goals may be contrary to the goals of caregivers allow them to begin to understand what it means to be them. Personal boundaries and limits on behavior and expression are critical aspects of reality that begin to be grasped by age 2 years.

The preschool child is quite deliberate and purposeful in making sense of their world. This is a major step. Preschoolers are all about investigating causality. This of course shows up in their countless "why?" questions. They are asking why things are the way they are. They are not satisfied with merely observing that things happen. They need to know why they happen. These questions encompass the physical world (why do the clouds move?) and, especially, the social world ranging from "would you be my friend?" to "why wouldn't you hurt me?," as Vera asked her teacher.

A critical advance in this period is the child's understanding of their own role in causality. This promotes an expanding sense of agency, of power in the world. It is also a vulnerability, because of the tendency at this age to attribute too great a role to their own perceptions and to the results of their own actions. This can lead to a kind of inflated sense of themselves, since they fail to compare their behavior to others. Such minor grandiosity is important and functional for exploring reality, but it does leave them open to massive deflation if they are harshly criticized or otherwise not supported. Over-evaluating their role in causation can also lead to pervasive guilt. Taking this big step toward authorship is a crucial advance in meaning making, and cannot be skipped, despite the potential for accepting responsibility for negative experiences they encounter. This is especially likely to happen if they are told, or otherwise encouraged to believe, that indeed they are responsible for hardships and difficulties.

Armed with logic, the elementary-school child makes further major strides in meaning making. They know how things work. They are realistic. They see things the way they are. Such a sense of certainty, of being grounded, is another crucial step in meaning making. This can provide them the confidence needed to take on the social challenges of middle childhood and prepare them for the even greater challenges of adolescence. But such "realism" too has limitations. At this age, there is a new kind of inflexibility in thinking. Children may well conclude that this is not only the way things are but this is the way they *must* be. I am this way. You are that way. We might have different views but there is just one reality. Some views of what this fixed reality is can trap a child in a negative meaning system.

Another advance in middle childhood concerns the sense of the self, as it is now influenced by the child's explicit comparison of self with other. Practice in accurately reading social cues expands the ability to understand reality. Further, what it means to be you now includes your friends and your group. Me and my friends becomes part of one's self-definition. You see yourself as belonging to a group. One's boundaries are both expanded and better defined.

Adolescent advances in thought and understanding provide an opportunity to overcome both the logical gaps in the preschooler's thought and the insufficient flexibility of the middle-schooler. Adolescents can think about multiple meanings, including how things might be or could be, not just how things are. They can see multiple points of view and understand that another's reality may be different from their own. They can imagine a variety of ways things could be. They can look anew at what they have been led to believe is the case and see alternative possibilities. If a current situation is unacceptable, it doesn't have to stay that way. There are abstract ideals regarding morality and justice that may not correspond to the way things are. At their best, these new capacities for viewing the world can lead them to see themselves as a potential agent for change. Again, these are important achievements that are best not side-stepped. Still, they create yet a new challenge. It is of course possible to see many ways of how things could be, and maybe should be, and feel confused and overwhelmed by uncertainty or powerlessness to create the changes one clearly sees are needed.

Ideally, at each new phase of development limitations in meaning making of the preceding phase are overcome. Preschoolers explicitly and actively seek the meaning of experiences, leading to an understanding of causality far beyond that of the toddler. The elementary school child can see the world more realistically, moving somewhat beyond the vulnerability to feel responsible for negative life experiences. Then the adolescent can use the logical tools acquired previously in a more flexible way, seeing not just what is, but what might be and can be. They have a new chance to change meaning systems brought forward over the years. But they can also see what may not be possible for them, generating feelings of despair beyond those of younger children.

Individual Variations in Meaning across Development

The changes in development that occur age by age, along with the new opportunities and challenges they provide, are the backdrop for understanding the gradual development of both serviceable and problematic individual meaning systems. In Chapter 5, for example, we discussed how meanings taken forward by the toddler from infancy impact meaning making at the later time. Toddlers who experienced inconsistent or chaotic care, and were anxious and fretful as infants, are more fretful and difficult as toddlers. They don't believe in the reliability of caregivers, so they are even more difficult to reassure now. Not expecting reliable responses to their expressed needs, they now need more consistency and reliability than do most toddlers; yet this is precisely what is challenging for their caregivers to provide. So it is not so much that infancy left permanent scars on the psyche; it is rather that a pattern of engaging and interpreting the environment was initiated. It is this stance that is taken forward. The child will then present more of the very problems that the particular surrounding social environment is ill-prepared to address. The parents make one futile effort after another and often wind up throwing their hands up in resignation. So it is that in the early months of life caregivers largely create all of the situations the child experiences but, as development unfolds, the child becomes an ever more active participant in shaping his or her own experiences. This is the essence of the transactional model of development.

The difficult toddler fosters the increasingly inconsistent parental behavior that deepens the child's expectation that needs may not be met, regardless of their actions. Whatever the history of experiences, every child will take both the meanings from infancy and the toddler period into the preschool. Depending on the depth and breadth of the rejection that the child experiences, it is more or less difficult to turn this around.

Then, because of the active way in which preschoolers are seeking to understand the nature of things and the reason things happen, each child in part creates his or her own preschool experience. When the child's natural curiosity has been previously thwarted by parents, the child will be hesitant now. The child that was not guided and supported in regulation as a toddler is easily frustrated now and cannot sustain interactions with other children, therefore becoming an unfavored playmate. The child with a history of emotional rejection self-isolates now, or is aggressive toward other children, or when injured or disappointed, goes away from teachers and off by her- or himself. This can contribute to a particular meaning system, having as a core being alone even in a social world. Such children get the corrective experiences of positive feedback and nurturance that are potentially available more rarely. The low levels of trust that they brought to preschool may then be deepened.

Meaning in the Preschool Years

The way in which meanings internalized from earlier periods influence meaning making in the preschool period can be seen in a number of ways. There are many case examples – the child who went off into the corner when rejected by his potential dance partner; the child who routinely received discipline because of his aggressive behavior; the girl who dreamt that her teacher mistreated her; and the child who threw tantrums and became upset with potential play partners whenever difficulties arose. One poignant example was a child who was picked on repeatedly by his play partner in the most deprecating manner. One day when his partner was ignoring him for a time, he was heard to say, "Aren't you going to tease me today, Harold?" This was treatment he expected and, alas, that his behavior encouraged.

The internalizing and carrying forward of meaning systems can also be seen in systematic observation of the social behavior of preschool children. One can observe time spent involved with teachers, time alone, emotional expressions, and behavior such as aggression and so forth. One observation of great interest concerned the *way* the child initiated contact and responded to contact with other children. In particular, we observed that the children with histories of responsive, reliable care in the first 2 years of life dramatically more frequently coupled their initiations to others with smiles, enthusiastic voices, and other signs of positive affect than did those with histories of inconsistent care or chronic emotional rejection (Sroufe et al., 1984). Likewise, they responded to the overtures of others positively more often. Moreover, such behavior was associated with more frequent and more sustained interactions and with measures of popularity and acceptance (see also Youngblade & Belsky, 1992, for similar findings). Because of their history of support, they believed relationships were worthwhile, that they were valuable partners, and that their overtures would be welcome. They then acted toward other children within this meaning system. The result was that, in fact, they *were* more valued partners and the relationships with others were more rewarding. This is the way prior meaning systems and new experiences work together.

Those who experienced histories of chronic emotional unavailability or rejection from their parents more likely failed to approach others at all, or they did so in a lackluster manner, without smiles or enthusiasm. At other times they were aggressive in their encounters. They apparently did not expect much from others, and they fulfilled this prophecy by being neglected or actively disliked. The meaning system they brought forward was deepened and perpetuated. Again, the impact of early experience is not best conceived as a kind of scarring, but as initiating a pattern of adaptation that children then actively carry forward and is perpetuated through their manner of engaging and interpreting the environment. And for many of the children who had experienced a varied pattern of rearing, the outcome was also mixed.

One interesting sideline of our preschool study concerned the link between social competence and "attractiveness." At the time we were running our preschool, a number of psychologists had become interested in physical attractiveness and its social consequences. They showed photos of the child to get ratings of attractiveness and found that these ratings predicted social success in various ways. We added a wrinkle to this work. We had ratings done by two sets of judges. While they rated the same photos, one set of judges knew the children and one set was unfamiliar with them, as was typical in attractiveness research. Still, the task of both sets of judges was to rate physical attractiveness. The result was that the ratings of the judges that knew the children correlated with social competence more strongly than the ratings of judges who did not. We reasoned that the first set of judges could not help but see the inner child when they rated, because they knew them. Thus, it is not facial bone structure but rather the child's projected personality that is more potent. This is another product of meaning history. When children have been supported and affirmed, they radiate a potential for engagement that is attractive to others.

Meaning in Middle Childhood

The cumulative history of meanings from infancy through the preschool period is taken forward to the years of middle childhood. Some children take positive expectations with them regarding both teachers and other children from the preschool years. They expect teachers to be resources, and they expect other children to like them. They look forward to school and expect to like it. Our research confirms that this turns out to be true – all of it, including liking school. For other children, the meaning of the preschool experience and the transition to school is not so positive. As one child in therapy said during a summer session when he was asked what he thought second grade would be like: "Oh, there will be lots of problems in second grade." And for such children, one can indeed expect that there will be problems.

Early experiences of secure attachment, and parental emotional support in general, and the meanings derived from such experiences, continue to have implications (e.g., Shulman et al., 1994). Thus, direct observation in a summer camp setting showed that those with histories of secure attachment in infancy were more socially skilled than those with histories of anxious attachment, were less often socially isolated, and more often had a reciprocated friendship. Much of their time was spent with another particular child, and in sociometric interviews each named the other as friend. Camp counselors also nominated them as best friends. That relationships and closeness are possible and valued are deeply ingrained in some children. Moreover, beyond chance, those with secure histories selected other children with secure histories as their friends. This no doubt was because of their mutual openness to engagement and their emotional readiness for interaction. Then, in becoming friends, their joint capacities were combined in a synergistic way. This again is how development works. Previously acquired capacities promote new kinds of experiences that then lead to new capacities.

Certain capacities acquired by these children during the pre-school period were drawn upon to promote these close friendships. They had already learned how to sustain interactions in the face of difficulty, that disagreements and conflict could be weathered, and that there were great rewards in maintaining relationships. Friendships had already acquired value, and now they could be deepened.

Integration

From the interviews and projective assessments carried out with the children in middle childhood as part of the Minnesota study, we know that experiences from the early years are internalized and brought forward. Children with secure histories and positive engagement with preschool peers indeed project more positive expectations regarding peers in projective assessments (see Chapter 9), believing that others will like them, that relationships can be sustained, and that conflicts will work out.

Shmuel Shulman, drawing on his own research as well as the work of others, has outlined two dimensions of friendships in middle childhood and three stages in the process of friendship formation (Shulman et al., 1994). These studies reveal differences in the meaning systems of children with different histories. The first dimension Shulman discusses concerns a sense of closeness with the other, involving mutual support, affection, and the beginning of intimacy. Such closeness, and the vulnerability that attends it, require the foundation built up throughout the prior years. The second dimension concerns the level and range of activities that are shared, which includes the joint creativity in the activities of the partners. It can be seen that these two dimensions are mutually supporting. The amity between them sustains the joint activities, and the joint activities enhance the emotional sharing. Important new meanings are created for each partner.

Shulman's three stages in the formation of friendships in middle childhood are: (1) "pre-togetherness orientations" (an interest in each other that can often happen quite early in the acquaintance); (2) "connectedness" (as they spend much time in proximity and engage in a range of activities); and (3) "creative relatedness" (as they engage in very elaborate play and evolve the capacity to cope with conflicts). Children of all attachment backgrounds form friendships during this age period, although those with secure histories more often form relationships that are durable and of deeper quality. Moreover, looking at relationships across these stages reveals qualitative differences in the nature of friendships of those with different attachment histories. As Shulman's work shows, when those with avoidant attachment histories occasionally do form a friendship pair, there is a paucity of positive emotional expression, limited signs of physical affection, and a narrow range of activities. Moreover, there is an "exclusive" nature to these friendships. They play apart from the others and cannot coordinate their play with the larger group. The friendships of those with resistant attachment histories are best characterized by their lack of stability. They too lack the ability to coordinate their play with others. Different meaning systems are brought to these relationships, and vastly different meanings will be taken forward from them. To their credit, those who struggle keep trying, such is the strong, universal urge to connect to others. The efforts they make at friendship may provide a launching point for expanded social relationships in the future.

Meaning in Adolescence

As discussed in Chapter 8, this entire cumulative history is the foundation for negotiating the complexities of adolescent relationships. The most meaningful relationships in adolescence draw upon the capacities to trust, to maintain a sense of autonomy even while being deeply connected, to regulate emotions and sustain engagement in the face of challenge and interpersonal conflict, to be intimate with others through sharing deep feelings, and to coordinate friendships and intimate relationships in an ever more complex social network. The close, loyal friendships and the engagement in the peer group in the middle childhood years are the springboard for these later relationships. The shared sense of morality established in middle childhood is a guide to behavior and expectations of behavior in adolescence.

A core feature of adolescent relationships is intimacy; that is, the capacity to be vulnerable with another and to mutually share the deepest of feelings. Andrew Collins and colleagues (1997) have traced the development of this capacity though all of the ages of childhood. Not only does this capacity derive from a trusting and secure relationship with caregivers in infancy, but from all that these infant relationships initiate. This includes the sustained engagement and empathy that some preschoolers achieve and the warm, close relationships of the pre-adolescent years. As they state: "With time, satisfying friendships, and eventually romantic relationships, involve not only mutually self-disclosing behaviors but also experiences of feeling understood, validated, and cared for" (p. 70). Those with secure histories, and positive experiences with peers, have the capacity to be vulnerable that enables such true intimacy.

As was true in middle childhood, interviews with teens show that those with secure histories have the same positive expectations regarding the value of closeness and, in addition, the belief that their partners will be supportive of them. They expect that their partners will respond sensitively to their feelings. They will be emotionally available and respectful of their needs. Intimacy conveys something different to these teens with positive relationship histories than it does to those with less positive experiences.

Meaning Systems in Adulthood

Finally, the cumulative, transactional nature of development is further revealed in salient adult relationships. Not only can supportive partners transform an individual trajectory, but what individuals bring from their histories impacts the quality of the relationship. Again, it is the entire history that is involved. For example, insecure attachment in infancy predicts more hostile (and less trusting) adult relationships, but so too does lack of adequate social functioning in middle childhood. Most often, cumulative measures across time yield the strongest predictions. But there are nuances and links can be complex. The capacity for vulnerability in adolescence, well-predicted by attachment history, largely mediates the link between middle childhood and adulthood, suggesting that this capacity derives in part from middle childhood peer competence and then leads to the particular quality of adult relating.

Moreover, for certain outcomes, early attachment was the stronger predictor, while in other circumstances measures from later ages were stronger. As one example, peer competence in middle childhood was far and away the best predictor of conflict resolution in adult relationships. This is not surprising. The equal status of peers makes it precisely the place for learning the meaning of conflicts – whether they can be negotiated or not and how exactly to do such negotiation. Thus, the meaning of adult relationships and individual ways of relating draw upon the cumulated history of the person. Meaning systems are complex social creations.

In this book we have emphasized the formative, pre-adult phases of development, based on the view that mature meaning systems are created step-by-step, beginning in the earliest months and years of life. Nonetheless, we recognize that creating a world view is a life-long enterprise, with much development, even transformative development, occurring in the adult years. This goes beyond even the couple formation and transition to parenthood that we do touch on and the section on creating narrative identities discussed in the final section of this chapter. This work has mostly been done with young adults. There is less work available on Erikson's stage of development in older adults (integrity vs. despair). Clearly, meaning will be at the core of such study, because the sense of integrity arises when the meanings from prior history are brought forward and assembled into a coherent whole.

At the end of his life, Erikson and his wife introduced a ninth stage, that really is a continuation of the eighth. In a beautiful paper, Erikson (1984) described this stage at the approach of death in the following way:

> Epigenetically speaking, then, we can say that all the later age-specific developments are grounded or rooted in (and in fact dependent on) the strengths developed in infancy, childhood, and adolescence. And if the sense of autonomy "naturally" suffers grievously in old age, as the leeway of independence is constricted, there can also mature an active acceptance of appropriate limitations and a "wise" choice of involvements in vital engagements of a kind not possible earlier in life ... (p. 163)

What begins as hope in infancy, progresses through will and purpose in childhood, the fidelity of adolescence and love in adulthood, finally to wisdom and acceptance, and ultimately to faith; that is, the belief that there is meaning in the universe and meaning in life.

Mature Meaning Systems

From George Herbert Mead and Erik Erikson to contemporary scholars, many have viewed the ultimate task of development to be integrating one's life experiences, evolving a sense of wholeness and coherence. Such an integration of the past and the present has meaning as its core and often takes the form of a narrative or life story (Habermas & Bluck, 2000).

In his book on emerging adulthood, Shmuel Shulman (2024) emphasizes the protracted process of becoming an "author" of one's life. This search for adult identity capitalizes on all of the cumulated experiences of the person and then serves "as the developmental platform for personal growth and construction of meaning and purpose for the future" (p. 132). Each of us constructs and creates an "evolving story" that integrates our past experiences, our present experiences, and our anticipated future (Singer, 2004), what McAdams (2013) calls a *narrative identity*. As Shulman concludes, "through the search for meaning, and subsequently interpreting their memories, individuals can infer who they are, what their lives mean, and how they wish to navigate their lives" (2024, p. 132). From cradle to grave, it is this search for meaning that guides individual development.

CHAPTER 15

Conclusion

Obviously, development is complex. Individual meaning systems are dynamic. The Minnesota Longitudinal Study of Risk and Adaptation documented lawful change at every age. New social relationships can have great power in changing trajectories and opening up new meanings. Even some with histories of alienation and conduct problems were at times able to make new connections and see new opportunities. While those with early support more often capitalize on later opportunities, a coach, a teacher, or a life partner may be a key for anyone. Moreover, while social relationships have far and away the greatest impact on development, other experiences can play a role too. We found that, especially in middle childhood, some special skill or ability at times helped children find a better place in the social community. Many people, including the authors, have experienced great changes in worldview through therapy and counseling. What is true for all of us is that our meaning systems are coherent: they make sense in the light of our experiences.

The case of "Ricky" illustrates the many ways meaning is woven into the tapestry of development and the complexity of development itself. It is an intricate story, as most are.

Things went well enough in the first year of Ricky's life. His attachment was assessed to be secure but there were more signs of anxiety than are typical, likely due to a chaotic surrounding environment. Then things took a number of turns for the worse. While Ricky's mother clearly cared about him, she had a series of unstable relationships and her work schedule meant that Ricky was in the care of a variety of people who were often not attentive or responsive and sometimes frankly maltreating. Moreover, this was a case of clear boundary violations, as his mother engaged in seductive behavior with him and in other ways relied on him for emotional support.

By age 5, Ricky was one of the most anxious, dysregulated, and out-of-control children we saw at our laboratory preschool. In addition to the coy, adult-pleasing type, this was one of the classic patterns we saw as a legacy of seductive parenting. When a child is struggling with control issues, flirting, being amused, or touching him inappropriately can push him over the edge, and this happened with Ricky repeatedly in our assessments. Such behavior is itself provocative and stimulating – not what he needs. Ricky virtually flew around the classroom, especially when arriving at the beginning of the day. As he careened from place to place, he often referred to himself as "Batman" or "Superman." This was his child's way of fantasizing power in a world in which he felt frightened and small. He is the one we had in mind when we described the anxious pattern of seeing the world so big and self so small. The job of taking care of his mother emotionally was indeed too big for him, as it is for any young child.

Things looked a little better when we saw him at one of our summer camps at age 10. In contrast to early childhood, he was now not noticeably smaller than the other boys. He was still anxious and, in many ways, socially incompetent. He was clearly not a leader, but he was well coordinated and especially good at basketball. This gave him credibility with the other boys and was a boost to his self-esteem. However, things were not going well at home. In addition to pervasive lack of support, he was still his mother's caretaker and there was an increasing climate of violence. His mother's live-in boyfriend was physically abusive of both his mother and Ricky himself. This did not bode well for the teenage years. Our research has shown that a stable adult male presence in middle childhood is a protective factor regarding adolescent conduct problems for boys. On the other hand, men coming and going, or the presence of an unstable man, is apparently worse than no man at all (Pierce, 1999).

We learned about much of this violent background from Ricky himself when we interviewed him at age 19. This interview took place in the kitchen of his home and was notable due to the presence of a handgun on the table. He said this was necessary because some members of another gang were after him. Also notable was the degree to which he had "bulked up." He had always been on the small side but was now quite muscular. Despite his baby face, he had a tough veneer. He told us how and why this had happened. When he was 14, his mother's boyfriend had become even more abusive. He came home to hear his mother yelling and the boyfriend assaulting her. Feeling deeply responsible for his mother, Ricky rushed at the boyfriend. "What happened next," our interviewer asked. "Well, he was bigger than me so he put me down. I told myself that is the last time that will happen." That's when Ricky started working out and becoming tougher. He attributed a great deal of meaning to this culminating incident. He told us that the boyfriend rarely comes around anymore and that he was the one now afraid of Ricky.

Like most lives, Ricky's life story is a complex mixture of hardships and yet some positive features, like his attachment relationship in the first year. Alongside the toughness and bravado of his late teenage years, we could still see the scared little boy inside of him. He at times seemed quite vulnerable in our interviews – almost shy. Despite the anxiety-producing chaos of his homelife, a core feeling of being valued was still deep inside of him. The emotional connection with his mother, compromised as it was in some ways, remained as a resource. In early adulthood he formed a solid relationship and left his conduct problems behind. He had a notably tender relationship with his own toddler. In our adult interviews, his contemporary world views reflected this complex history. Despite the complexity, his meaning system was coherent.

Behaving in terms of our meaning systems impacts our lived experience throughout life. Once the lens of meaning is put on, one sees countless examples of how different worldviews impact daily experiences. Drivers of the express buses to the University of Minnesota provide an illustration. These express buses had many of the same riders – students and staff – and the same few drivers, day after day. Some of the drivers were jovial and greeted the boarding students and staff warmly each day. It did not take long before many of the riders were equally warm in greeting the driver, often also thanking them when they got off the bus. These friendly drivers daily encountered a friendly world, one which they played a large part in creating. Other drivers were glum, largely silent, or even crabby. Some riders still said "good morning" to them and perhaps said thank you when they left, but the effusiveness was not there. Many riders said nothing to these drivers and often did not even look at them. So for these drivers, the daily experience was without much joy. They created an unfriendly world, no doubt confirming longstanding views. As William James said about the price of pessimism in his famous lecture on suicide: "Your mistrust of life has removed whatever worth your own enduring existence might have given to it; and now, throughout the whole sphere of possible influence of that existence, the mistrust has proved itself to have had divining power."

Or consider the refreshing case of the 90-year-old man that we heard going over his quarterly health report in his assisted living facility. This man was nearly blind and very hard of hearing. In addition, he had very serious heart problems, along with a variety of other conditions. When he came to the final item on the questionnaire that asked him to rate his overall health, he turned to us and said: "I would say excellent, wouldn't you?" And you know, considering his attitude, we had to agree with him. He also told us that the staff at the home were remarkable. He said everyone treated him so well and were always happy to visit with him. This was no wonder when you saw how he greeted each staff member with a cheerful smile and warm words. Looking back over his entire life, this man described his experiences in very positive terms. In addition to being a farmer he had sold insurance in his rural community. In his day, farming was grueling work, and most of us would not think that selling insurance was a very positive occupation. Yet he was proud of what he knew about farming and said about selling insurance that it was a marvelous job, because it allowed him to meet so many wonderful people. He said he could not have had a better life.

We know nothing about the attachment histories of this elderly man or any of the bus drivers, or what combination of early and later experiences led to their worldviews. But, based on the cumulated developmental research that is now available, we do conclude that the systems of meaning described are the coherent outcomes of their histories.

Personal Meaning

As you read this book, you very likely found yourself reviewing your own history, wondering about your pattern of attachment and other aspects of your experience. It is like when anyone takes a class in abnormal psychology. With each chapter you find yourself thinking, "Oh, I have that." Then you turn to the next disorder and think that fits you even better. One of us thought we fit categories that are not even used today, like psychasthenia (essentially a neurotic) and probably should be glad there was no ADHD category when he was in school. For children, the major diagnosis used to be "adjustment reaction to childhood," and we may have both had that! It is natural to do this kind of projection – to see parts of ourselves in these descriptions. It is a reflection of that pesky universal motive to seek and find meaning.

It really does make sense to see ourselves in multiple ways. Those DSM "categories" of disorder really are not categorical. They are not pure, distinguishable types. People don't fit neatly into one category. What is called "co-morbidity" is universal; that is, people given one diagnosis routinely fit another. For example, half of children given a diagnosis of ADHD also qualify for a conduct disorder diagnosis, and half fit the anxiety profile. Many children fit all three categories. (Moreover, our research showed that problems waxed and waned with changes in stress and supports.) Co-morbidity is not unique to childhood problems. In adulthood, anxiety and depression are so co-morbid that some have argued the two categories should be merged. We are all a collection of different problems and strengths. So it is reasonable to see ourselves in diverse category descriptions, because most of us have a bit of this and a bit of that.

Likewise, experienced attachment researchers know that avoidant, resistant, and secure are not pure types either. These categories have served attachment research well, because they obviously capture much that is going on. Still, we know that these are not rigid categories. Attachment patterns are multi-dimensional, and all coders observe many cases that seem to fall between the categories or seem to be blends of more than one. Beyond this, attachment patterns sometimes change over time, even with the same parent whose own situation may change. Infants often show a different pattern of attachment from one parent to the other. Therefore, it is not surprising that many people see aspects of themselves in more than one of the categorical descriptions. For personal growth, this is probably the best way to look at it.

Histories of experience are often complex and nuanced, and so too are the networks of meaning each of us construct. Still, attachment research, and the study of the development of meaning more generally, is a helpful guide for understanding how and why we see the world in the way that we do. However complicated the picture, it is also hopeful to know that our meaning systems are lawful constructions derived from our histories of experience.

In the End

We began this book with some of the thoughts of Emily Esfahani Smith regarding the power of meaning. It is fitting to come back to her work in the end. Smith (2017) concluded that there are four keys to a meaningful life. The very first of these she called "belonging," "the basic sense of connection with other individuals and the broader community." We all need to feel like we belong. Such a connection is what Bowlby referred to decades ago as "we-ness" and later as emotional bonds and attachment. It is also closely related to Erikson's idea of basic trust. It is the core of any meaning system. In complete accord with work on adult attachment relationships (e.g., Crowell, 2021), Smith goes on to say that there are two reasons why people feel they belong: first, they are in relationships with others based on mutual care: "each person feels loved and valued by the other." In attachment terms, we would say each partner can provide secure base support for the other.

The other reason she provides for the feeling of belonging is that such people have frequent pleasant interactions with other people, much like the happy bus driver described in the previous section. Connections with others as the core of a meaningful life has been emphasized by poets, such as Percy Bysshe Shelley, and by spiritual leaders like the Dali Lama, who taught that the key to a "joyful" life was compassion for others. It is also supported by the longest study of happiness ever carried out, the Harvard Study of Adult Development (e.g., Waldinger & Schultz, 2016). Their most robust finding was that warm relationships within the family and with others was related to later physical health, as well as to midlife emotion-regulatory styles and late-life security in intimate relationships. Nothing was more important.

The second key to a meaningful life Smith called "purpose," which refers to a goal-directed life filled with meaning. She suggests that, when we have long-term goals in life that reflect our values and serve the greater good, we tend to imbue our activities with more meaning. As one example, Smith describes a college graduate whose job was to clean the droppings out of animal stalls at the Detroit Zoo. While this is not a job many of us would want to do, this woman described it as her dream job. From childhood, she had always wanted to work with animals and help their lives be better. Like our farmer/insurance salesman, she found great meaning in her life's work.

The third key is referred to as "storytelling"; that is, drawing particularly relevant experiences into a coherent life narrative. "Stories help us make sense of the world and our place in it" and they help us understand why things happen the way they do. "We are constantly taking pieces of information and adding a layer of meaning to them; we couldn't function otherwise" (Smith, 2017, p. 104). Jerome Bruner (2002) has proposed that such narratives are fundamental to the human search for meaning. For Bruner, the human mind is best conceptualized not as a computer but as a creator of meaning. This is consistent with work discussed in the previous chapter by Dan McAdams (2008) who has studied intensively how building such coherent narratives is crucial for a stable adult identity and wellbeing.

Finally, fourth is "transcendence." By this Smith means having a sense of awe and recognizing that one is part of something much larger than oneself, a sentiment also strongly endorsed by William James and by Erik

Erikson, as discussed in Chapter 14. While we know of no studies linking attachment history to a sense of awe, our research did show a strong link between infant attachment and curiosity and an interest in exploration in the childhood years (e.g., Sroufe, 1983). Such curiosity, when taken to adulthood, is a likely foundation for the sense of wonder and awe.

Having surveyed the role of meaning in development, we do not feel that we can improve upon Smith's list. These do seem to be the critical components of a meaningful life. Moreover, except for the fourth key, each of these components is supported by developmental research. One's early attachment history, supplemented by subsequent social experiences, appears to determine the degree to which one feels a deep sense of connection with others and that close relationships have value. It is also related to agency, persistence, planfulness, and empathy, all of which bear on "purpose" as Smith defines it. And coherence of one's close relationships narrative is a key marker of a meaning network with security at its core. Such coherence is a central feature of the Adult Attachment Interview. Even though developmental research on meaning is in its early stages, there seems to be great promise in applying a developmental perspective for understanding the meaning systems that each of us creates.

Bibliography

Agarwal, P. (2020). Exposing unconscious bias. *New Scientist*, Aug. 29–Sept. 4.

Aguilar, B., Sroufe, L. A., Egeland, B., & Carlson, E. (2000). Distinguishing the early-onset/persistent and adolescent-onset anti-social behavior types: From birth to 16 years. *Development and Psychopathology, 12*, 109–132.

Ainsworth, M. D. S. (1967). *Infancy in Uganda: Infant Care and the Growth of Love.* Baltimore: Johns Hopkins University Press.

Ainsworth, M. D. S., Blehar, M., Waters, E., & Wall, S. (1978). *Patterns of Attachment.* Hillsdale, NJ: Erlbaum.

Appleyard, K., Egeland, B., van Dulmen, M., & Sroufe, L. A. (2005). When more is not better: The role of cumulative risk in child behavior outcomes. *Journal of Child Psychology and Psychiatry, 46*, 235–245.

Arnold, M. (1960). *Emotion and Personality.* New York: Columbia University Press.

Baldwin, J. M. (1897). *Social and Ethical Interpretations in Mental Development.* New York: Macmillan.

Barker, P. (1991) *Regeneration.* New York: Viking Press.

Bernier, A., Carlson, S. M., Deschênes, M., & Matte-Gagné, C. (2012). Social factors in the development of early executive functioning: A closer look at the caregiving environment. *Developmental Science, 15*(1), 12–24.

Block, J., & Block, J. H. (1980). The role of ego-control and ego-resiliency in the organization of behavior. In W. A. Collins (ed.), *Minnesota Symposia on Child Psychology: Vol. 13. Development of Cognition, Affect, and Social Relations* (pp. 39–101). Hillsdale, NJ: Erlbaum.

Bohannon, C. (2023). *Eve.* New York: Knopf.

Bollas, C. (2017). *The Shadow of the Object.* New York: Routledge.

Boszormenyi-Nagy, I., & Spark, G. (1973). *Invisible Loyalties.* New York: Bruner/Mazel.

Bowlby, J. (1946). Psychology and democracy. *The Political Quarterly, 17*, 61–75.

(1973). *Attachment and Loss: Vol. 2. Separation.* New York: Basic Books.

(1988). *A Secure Base.* New York: Basic Books.

Bransford, J. D. & Franks, J. J. (1971). The abstraction of linguistic ideas. *Cognitive Psychology, 2*, 331–350.

Brazelton, T. B., Kowslowski, B., & Main, M. (1974). The origins of reciprocity: The early mother–infant interaction. In M. Lewis & L. Rosenblum (eds.), *The Effect of the Infant on Its Caregiver* (pp. 49–76). New York: Wiley.

Breger, L. (1974). *From Instinct to Identity*. Englewood Cliffs, NJ: Prentice-Hall.

Brendgen, M., Vitaro, F., Bukowski, W., Doyle, A., & Markiewicz, D. (2001). Developmental profiles of peer social preference over the course of elementary school. *Developmental Psychology, 37*, 308–320.

Bretherton, I., & Munholland, K. A. (1999). Internal working models in attachment relationships: A construct revisited. In J. Cassidy & P. R. Shaver (eds.), *Handbook of Attachment: Theory, Research, and Clinical Applications* (pp. 89–111). New York: Guilford Press.

Bruce, J., Fisher, P. A., Pears, K. C., & Levine, S. (2009). Morning cortisol levels in preschool-aged foster children: Differential effects of maltreatment type. *Developmental Psychobiology, 51*, 14–23.

Bruner, J. (2002). *Making Stories: Law, Literature, Life*. Cambridge, MA: Harvard University Press.

Carlson, E. A. (1998). A prospective longitudinal study of attachment disorganization/disorientation. *Child Development, 69*(4), 1107–1128.

Carlson, E. A., Jacobvitz, D., & Sroufe, L. A. (1995). A developmental investigation of inattentiveness and hyperactivity. *Child Development, 66*, 37–54.

Carlson, E. A., Sroufe, L. A., & Egeland, B. (2004). The construction of experience: A longitudinal study of representation and behavior. *Child Development, 75*(1), 66–83.

Cole, M., Gay, J., Glick, J., & Sharp, D. (1971). *The Cultural Context of Learning and Thinking: An Exploration in Experimental Anthropology*: New York: Basic Books.

Collins, W. A., Hennighausen, K. H., Schmit, D. T., & Sroufe, L. A. (1997). Developmental precursors of romantic relationships: A longitudinal analysis. In S. Shulman & W. A. Collins (eds.), *Romantic Relationships in Adolescence: Developmental Perspectives* (pp. 69–84). San Francisco: Jossey-Bass.

Cooley, C. H. (1909). *Social Organization: A Study of the Larger Mind*. New York: Charles Scribner's Sons. https://doi.org/10.1037/14788-000

Coppola, G., Vaughn, B., Cassibba, R., & Costantini, A. (2006). The attachment script representation procedure in an Italian sample: Association with adult attachment interview scales and with maternal sensitivity. *Attachment and Human Development, 8*, 209–219.

Crowell, J. (2021). Measuring the security of attachment in adults. In R. A. Thompson, J. Simpson, & L. Berlin (eds.), *Attachment: The Fundamental Questions* (pp. 86–92). New York: Guildford Press.

Damasio, A. (2006). *Descartes' Error*. New York: Random House.

Dozier, M. (2019). *Coaching Parents of Vulnerable Infants*. New York: Guilford.

Duggal, S., & Sroufe, L. A. (1998). Recovered memory of childhood sexual trauma: A documented case from a longitudinal study. *Journal of Traumatic Stress, 11*, 301–321.

Dweck, C. (2017). *Mindset: Updated Edition: Changing the Way You Think to Fulfil Your Potential*. London: Hachette UK.

Egeland, B., Bosquet, M., & Levy-Chung, A. (2002). Continuities and discontinuities in the intergenerational transmission of child maltreatment: Implications for breaking the cycle of abuse. In K. D. Browne, H. Hanks, P. Stratton, & C. Hamilton (eds.), *Early Prediction and Prevention of Child Abuse: A Handbook* (pp. 217–232). Sussex, UK: Wiley.

Egeland, B., Carlson, E. A., & Sroufe, L. A. (1993). Resilience as process. *Development and Psychopathology*, *5*, 517–528.

Egeland, B., Jacobvitz, D., & Sroufe, L. A. (1988). Breaking the cycle of abuse: Relationship predictors. *Child Development*, 59(4), 1080–1088.

Egeland, B., & Susman-Stillman, A. (1996). Dissociation as a mediator of child abuse across generations. *Child Abuse & Neglect*, 20(11), 1123–1132.

Elicker, J., Englund, M., & Sroufe, L. A. (1992). Predicting peer competence and peer relationships in childhood from early parent–child relationships. In R. Parke & G. Ladd (eds.), *Family–Peer Relationships: Modes of Linkage* (pp. 77–106). Hillsdale, NJ: Erlbaum.

Englund, M., Levy, A., Hyson, D., & Sroufe, L. A. (2000). Adolescent social competence: Effectiveness in a group setting. *Child Development*, *71*, 1049–1060.

Erikson, E. (1963). *Childhood and Society* (2nd ed.). New York: W. W. Norton. (1984). Reflections on the last stage – and the first. *The Psychoanalytic Study of the Child*, *39*, 155–165.

Fairbanks, L. (1989). Early experience and cross-generational continuity of mother–infant contact in vervet monkeys. *Developmental Psychobiology*, *22*, 669–681.

Fingarette, H. (1963). *The Self in Transformation*. New York: Basic Books.

Fleeson, J. (1988). *Assessment of Parent–Adolescent Relationships*. Doctoral dissertation, University of Minnesota.

Fleeson, W. (2001). Toward a structure-and-process-integrated view of personality: Traits as density distributions of states. *Journal of Personality and Social Psychology*, *80*(6), 1011–1027.

Fonagy, P. (1999). Psychoanalytic theory from the viewpoint of attachment theory and research. In J. Cassidy & P. R. Shaver (eds.), *Handbook of Attachment* (pp. 595–624). New York: Guilford Press.

Frankl, V. (1985). *Man's Search for Meaning*. New York: Simon and Schuster.

Freud, S. (1926). Inhibitions, symptoms, and anxiety. In J. Strachey (ed.), *Standard Edition of the Complete Psychological Works of Sigmund Freud* (pp. 87–174). London: Hogarth Press.

Frijda, N. (1988). The laws of emotion. *American Psychologist*, *43*, 349–358.

Fury, G., Carlson, E. A., & Sroufe, L. A. (1997). Children's representations of attachment relationships in family drawings. *Child Development*, *68*, 1154–1164.

Garmezy, N., & Streitman, S. (1974). Children at risk: The search for the antecedents of schizophrenia. *Schizophrenia Bulletin*, *8*, 14–90.

Gianino, A., & Tronick, E. Z. (1988). The mutual regulation model: The infant's self and interactive regulation and coping and defensive capabilities. In T. M. Field, P. M. McCabe, & N. Schneiderman (eds.), *Stress and Coping across Development* (pp. 47–68). New York: Psychology Press.

Gojman-de-Millan, S., Herreman, C., & Sroufe, L. A. (2017). *Attachment across Clinical and Cultural Perspectives: A Relational Psychoanalytic Approach.* London: Routledge.

Gribneau Baum, N., Main, M., & Hesse, E. (2017). Unresolved/disorganized responses to the death of important persons: Relations to frightening parental behavior and infant disorganization. In S. Gojman-de-Millan, C. Herreman, & L. A. Sroufe (eds.), *Attachment across Clinical and Cultural Perspectives* (pp. 53–74). New York: Routledge.

Gunnar, M, & Stone, C. (1984). The effects of positive maternal affect on infant responses to pleasant, ambiguous, and fear-provoking toys. *Child Development, 55,* 1231–1236.

Habermas, T., & Bluck, S. (2000). Getting a life: The emergence of a life story in adolescence. *Psychological Bulletin, 126,* 748–769.

Haith, M. (1980). *Rules Newborns Look By.* Hillsdale, NJ: Erlbaum.

Harlow, H. (1966). Learning to love. *American Scientist, 54,* 244–272.

Jacobvitz, D., Hazen, N., Zaccagnino, M., Messina, S., & Beverung, L. (2011). Frightening maternal behavior, infant disorganization, and risks for psychopathology. In D. Cicchetti & G. Roisman (eds.), *The Minnesota Symposium on Child Psychology: The Origins and Organization of Adaptation and Maladaptation* (Vol. 36, pp. 283–322). New York: Wiley.

Jacobvitz, D., & Sroufe, L. A. (1987). The early caregiver–child relationship and attention deficit disorder with hyperactivity in kindergarten: A prospective study. *Child Development, 58,* 1496–1504.

James, P. D. (1975). *The Black Tower.* New York: Scribner.

James, W. (1884). *What Is an Emotion.* New York: Simon and Schuster.

Jung, C. G. (1990). *The Basic Writings of CG Jung: Revised Edition* (Vol. 20). Princeton: Princeton University Press.

Kagan, J. (2013). *The Second Year.* Cambridge, MA: Harvard University Press.

Kalsched, D. (1996). *The Inner World of Trauma: Archetypal Defenses of the Personal Spirit.* New York: Routledge.

Kegan, R. (1982). *The Evolving Self.* Cambridge, MA: Harvard University Press.

Keniston, K. (1966). *The Uncommitted: Alienated Youth in American Society.* New York: Harcourt, Brace, & World.

(1968). *Young Radicals.* New York: Harcourt, Brace, & World.

Kestenbaum, R., Farber, E., & Sroufe, L. A. (1989). Individual differences in empathy among preschoolers: Concurrent and predictive validity. In N. Eisenberg (ed.), *Empathy and Related Emotional Responses* (pp. 51–56). San Francisco: Jossey-Bass.

Kierkegaard, S. (1938). *Purity of Heart Is to Will One Thing.* New York: Harper & Row.

Kochanska, G., Boldt, L. J., & Goffin, K. C. (2019). Early relational experience: A foundation for the unfolding dynamics of parent–child socialization. *Child Development Perspectives*, *13*(1), 41–47.

van der Kolk, B. A. (2005). Developmental trauma disorder: Toward a rational diagnosis for children with complex trauma histories. *Psychiatric Annals*, *35*(5), 401–408.

Kovan, N., Levy-Chung, A., & Sroufe, L. A. (2009). The intergenerational continuity of observed early parenting: A prospective, longitudinal study. *Developmental Psychology*, *45*, 1205–1217.

Labella, M., Raby, K. L. Bourne, S., Trahan, A., Katz, D., & Dozier, M. (2024). Is attachment and biobehavioral catch-up effective for parents with insecure attachment states of mind. *Child Development*, *95*(2), 648–655.

Laing, R. D. (1965). *The Divided Self*. New York: Penguin Books.

Laing, R. D., & Esterson, A. (2016). *Sanity, Madness and the Family*. New York: Routledge.

Lazarus, R. S., & Folkman, S. (1984). *Stress, Appraisal, and Coping*. New York: Springer.

Lewis, M. (2016). *The Undoing Project: A Friendship that Changed Our Minds*. New York: W. W. Norton.

Lieberman, A. (2017). Attachment, trauma, and reality: Clinical integrations in the treatment of young children. In S. Gojman-de-Millan, C. Herreman, & L. A. Sroufe (eds.), *Attachment across Clinical and Cultural Perspectives* (pp. 205–220). New York: Routledge.

Lieberman, A., & van Horn, P. (2008). *Psychotherapy with Infants and Young Children: Repairing the Effects of Stress and Trauma on Early Attachment*. New York: Guilford Press.

Liotti, G. (1992). Disorganized/disoriented attachment in the etiology of the dissociative disorders. *Dissociation*, *4*, 196–204.

Loevinger, J. (1976). *Ego Development*. San Francisco, CA: Jossey-Bass.

Luborsky, L., & Crits-Christoph, P. (1998). *Understanding Transference: The Core Conflictual Relationship Theme Method*. Washington, DC: American Psychological Association.

Lyons-Ruth, K., Bronfman, E., & Parsons, E. (1999). Maternal disruptive affective communication, maternal frightened or frightening behavior, and disorganized infant attachment strategies. *Monographs of the Society for Research in Child Development*, *64*(3), 67–96.

MacKenzie, M., & McDonough, S. (2009). Transactions between perceptions and reality: Maternal beliefs and infant regulatory behaviors. In A. Sameroff (ed.), *The Transactional Model of Development* (pp. 35–54). Washington, DC: American Psychological Association.

Main, M., & Goldwyn, R. (1998). *Adult Attachment Interview Scoring and Classification Manual, 6th version*. Unpublished manuscript, University of California, Berkeley.

Main, M., & Hesse, E. (1990). Parents' unresolved traumatic experiences are related to infant disorganized attachment status: Is frightened and/or frightening parental behavior the linking mechanism? In M. Greenberg, D. Cicchetti, & M. Cummings (eds.), *Attachment in the Preschool Years* (pp. 161–182). Chicago: University of Chicago Press.

Main, M., Kaplan, N., & Cassidy, J. (1985). Security in infancy, childhood, and adulthood: A move to the level of representation. *Monographs of the Society for Research in Child Development, 50*(1–2, Serial No. 209), 66–104.

Main, M., & Weston, D. (1981). The quality of the toddlers' relationship to mother and to father: Related to conflict behavior and the readiness to establish new relationships. *Child Development, 52*, 932–940.

Mandler, G. (1975). *Mind and Emotion.* New York: Wiley.

Markus, H., & Kitayama, S. (2010). Cultures and selves: A cycle of mutual constitution. *Perspectives on Psychological Science, 5*, 420–430.

Maslow, A. (1954). *Motivation and Personality.* New York: Harper and Row.

Masten, A. S. (2001). Ordinary magic: Resilience processes in development. *American Psychologist, 56*, 227–238.

Mathews, T., Caspi, A., Danese, A., Fisher, H., Moffitt, T., & Arseneault, L. (2022). A longitudinal twin study of victimization and loneliness from childhood to young adulthood *Development and Psychopathology, 34*, 367–377.

McAdams, D. (2008). Personal narratives and the life story. In O. P. John, R. W. Robins, & L. A. Pervin (eds.), *Handbook of Personality: Theory and Research* (pp. 242–262). New York: The Guilford Press.

(2013). Life authorship: A psychological challenge for emerging adulthood. *Emerging Adulthood, 1*, 151–158.

McAdams, D., & Pals, J. (2006). A new big five: Fundamental principles for an integrative science of personality. *American Psychologist, 61*, 204–217.

McCrone, E. R., Egeland, B., Kalkoske, M., & Carlson, E. A. (1994). Relations between early maltreatment and mental representations of relationships assessed with projective storytelling in middle childhood. *Development and Psychopathology, 6*, 99–120.

Mead, G. H. (1913). The social self. *Journal of Philosophy, Psychology, and Scientific Methods, 10*, 374–380.

Mears, R. (2012). *A Dissociation Model of Borderline Personality Disorder.* New York: Norton.

Mischel, W., Shoda, Y., & Rodriguez, M. (1989). Delay of gratification in children. *Science, 244*, 933–937.

Moffitt, T. (1993). Adolescence-limited and life-course-persistent antisocial behavior: A developmental taxonomy. *Psychological Review, 100*, 674–701.

Morris, D. (1980). *Infant Attachment and Problem Solving in the Toddler: Relation to Mother's Family History.* Unpublished doctoral dissertation, University of Minnesota.

Murdoch, I. (1978). *The Sea, the Sea.* London: Chatto & Windus.

Nin, A. (1961). *Seduction of the Minotour.* Athens, OH: Swallow Press.

Ogawa, J. R., Sroufe, L. A., Weinfield, N. S., Carlson, E. A., & Egeland, B. (1997). Development and the fragmented self: Longitudinal study of

dissociative symptomatology in a nonclinical sample. *Development and Psychopathology, 9,* 855–879.
Osin, E., Voevodina, E., & Kostenko, V. (2023). A growing concern for meaning: Exploring the links between ego development and eudaimonia. *Frontiers in Psychology, 14,* 958721.
Pancake, V. (1988). *Quality of Attachment in Infancy as a Predictor of Hostility and Emotional Distance in Preschool Peer Relationships.* Unpublished doctoral dissertation, University of Minnesota, Minneapolis.
Parke, R. D. (1996). *Fatherhood,* Vol. 33. Cambridge, MA: Harvard University Press.
Pettit, G., Bates, J., Dodge, K., & Meece, D. (1999). The impact of after-school contact on early adolescent externalizing problems is moderated by parental monitoring, perceived neighborhood safety, and prior adjustment. *Child Development, 70,* 768–778.
Piaget, J. (1952). *The Origins of Intelligence.* New York: Routledge & Kegan Paul.
Pianta, R. C., Egeland, B., & Sroufe, L. A. (1990). Maternal stress and children's development: Prediction of school outcomes and identification of protective factors. In J. Rolf, A. S. Masten, D. Cicchetti, K. H. Neuchterlein, & S. Weintraub (eds.), *Risk and Protective Factors in the Development of Psychopathology* (pp. 215–235). New York: Cambridge University Press.
Pierce, S. (1999). *The Role of Fathers and Men in the Development of Child and Adolescent Externalizing Behavior.* Unpublished doctoral dissertation, University of Minnesota.
Posada, G., & Waters, H. (2018). The mother–child attachment partnership in early childhood: Secure base and representational processes. *Monographs of the Society for Research in Child Development, 83,* Serial No. 331.
Radke-Yarrow, M., & Zahn-Waxler, C. (1984). Roots, motives and patterns in children's pro-social behavior. In E. Staub, D. Bartal, J. Karylowski, & J. Reykowski (eds.), *The Development and Maintenance of Pro-social Behavior* (pp. 81–99). New York: Plenum Press.
Rosen, N. (1978). *John and Anzia: An American Romance.* New York: Dutton.
Salinger, J. D. (1951). *The Catcher in the Rye.* New York: Little, Brown, & Company.
Sameroff, A. (2000). Ecological perspectives on developmental risk. In J. Osofsky & H. Fitzgerald (eds.), *WAIMH Handbook of Infant Mental Health: Vol. 4: Infant Mental Health in Groups at High Risk* (pp. 1–33). New York: Wiley.
  (2009). *The Transactional Model of Development.* Washington, DC: American Psychological Association.
Sameroff, A. J., & Chandler, M. J. (1975). Reproductive risk and the continuum of caretaking casualty. In F. D. Horowitz, M. Hetherington, S. Scarr-Salapatek, & G. Siegel (eds.), *Review of Child Development Research* (Vol. 4, pp. 187–243). Chicago: Chicago University Press.
Sander, L. (1975). Infant and caretaking environment. In E. J. Anthony (ed.), *Explorations in Child Psychiatry* (pp. 129–165). New York: Plenum Press.

Sapolsky, R. (2010). Forward. In C. Worthman, P. Plotsky, D. Schechter, & C. Cummings (eds.), *Formative Experiences* (pp. xxiii–xxvi). New York: Cambridge University Press.

Schacter, S. (1966). The interaction of cognitive and physiological determinants of emotional state. In C. Spielberger (ed.), *Anxiety and Behavior* (pp. 193–224). New York: Academic Press.

Schore, A. (2003). Early relational trauma, disorganized attachment, and the development of a predisposition to violence. In M. Solomon & D. Siegel (eds.), *Healing Trauma* (pp. 107–167). New York: Norton.

Schuengel, C. Bakermans-Kranenburg, M., & Van IJzendoorn, M. (1999). Frightening maternal behavior linking unresolved loss and disorganized infant attachment. *Journal of Consulting and Clinical Psychology*, 67, 54–63.

Selman, R. (1980). *The Growth of Interpersonal Understanding*. New York: Academic Press.

Shulman, S. (2024). *A New Lens on Emerging Adulthood*. New York: Oxford University Press.

Shulman, S., Elicker, J., & Sroufe, L. A. (1994). Stages of friendship growth in preadolescence as related to attachment history. *Journal of Social and Personal Relationships*, 11, 341–361.

Siegel, D. J. (2003). The interpersonal neurobiology of psychotherapy: The developing mind and the resolution of trauma. In M. Solomon & D. J. Siegel (eds.), *Healing Trauma* (pp. 1–56). New York: Norton.

(2017). The integration of attachment, mindfulness, and neuroscience. In S. Gojman-de-Millan, C. Herreman, & L. A. Sroufe (eds.), *Attachment across Clinical and Cultural Perspectives* (pp. 165–181). New York: Routledge.

(2020). *The Developing Mind: How Relationships and the Brain Interact to Shape Who We Are* (3rd ed.). New York: Guilford Press.

Singer, J. (2004). Narrative identity and meaning making across the adult lifespan: An introduction. *Journal of Personality*, 72, 437–460.

Slade, A., & Holmes, J. (2018). *Attachment in Therapeutic Practice*. New York: Sage.

Slade, A., Sadler, L., Close, N., Fitzpatrick, S., Simpson, T., & Webb, D. (2017). Minding the baby: The impact of threat on the mother-baby and mother-clinician relationship. In S. Gojman-de-Millan, C. Herreman, & L. A. Sroufe (eds.), *Attachment across Clinical and Cultural Perspectives* (pp. 182–204). New York: Routledge.

Slade, A., Sadler, L., Eaves, T., & Webb, D. L. (2023). *Enhancing Attachment and Reflective Parenting in Clinical Practice: A Minding the Baby Approach*. New York: Guilford Press.

Smith, E. (2017). *The Power of Meaning*. New York: Broadway Books.

Spitz, R., Emde, R., & Metcalf, D. (1970). Further prototypes of ego formation. *The Psychoanalytic Study of the Child*, 25, 417–444.

Sroufe, L. A. (1983). Infant–caregiver attachment and patterns of adaptation in preschool. In M. Perlmutter (ed.), *Minnesota Symposia in Child Psychology:*

Vol. 16. The Roots of Maladaptation and Competence (pp. 129–135). Hillsdale, NJ: Erlbaum.

(1996). *Emotional Development: The Organization of Emotional Life in the Early Years*. New York: Cambridge University Press.

(1997). Psychopathology as an outcome of development. *Development and Psychopathology, 9*, 251–268.

(1999). Changing the odds: The development of resilience. *Paper presented at the meeting of the American Association for the Advancement of Science*, Anaheim, CA.

(2020). *A Compelling Idea: How We Become the Persons We Are*. Branden, VT: Safer Society Press.

Sroufe, L. A., Bennett, C., Englund, M., Urban, J., & Shulman, S. (1993). The significance of gender boundaries in preadolescence: Contemporary correlates and antecedents of boundary violation and maintenance. *Child Development, 64*(2), 455–466.

Sroufe, L. A., Cooper, R., & DeHart, G. (1992). *Child Development: Its Nature and Course* (2nd ed.). New York: McGraw-Hill.

Sroufe, L. A., Egeland, B., & Carlson, E. (1999). One social world: The integrated development of parent-child and peer relationships. In W. A. Collins & B. Laursen (eds.), *Relationships as Developmental Context: The 30th Minnesota Symposium on Child Psychology* (pp. 241–262). Hillsdale, NJ: Erlbaum.

Sroufe, L. A., Egeland, B., Carlson, E., & Collins, W. A. (2005). *The Development of the Person*. New York: Guilford Press.

Sroufe, L. A., Egeland, B., & Kreutzer, T. (1990). The fate of early experience following developmental change: Longitudinal approaches to individual adaptation in childhood. *Child Development, 61*, 1363–1373.

Sroufe, L. A., & Fleeson, J. (1988). The coherence of family relationships. In R. A. H. J. Stevenson-Hinde (ed.), *Relationships within Families: Mutual Influences* (pp. 27–47). Oxford: Oxford University Press.

Sroufe, L. A., Jacobvitz, J., Mangelsdorf, S., deAngelo, E., & Ward, M. J. (1985). Generational boundary dissolution between mothers and their preschool children: A relationships systems approach. *Child Development, 56*, 317–325.

Sroufe, L. A., Schork, E., Motti, F., Lawroski, N., & LaFreniere, P. (1984). The role of affect in social competence. In C. E. Izard, J. Kagan, & R. Zajonc (eds.), *Emotions, Cognition, and Behavior* (pp. 289–319). New York: Plenum Press.

Sroufe, L. A., Stuecher, H. U., & Stutzer, W. (1973). The functional significance of autistic behaviors for the psychotic child. *Journal of Abnormal Child Psychology, 1*, 225–240.

Sroufe, L. A., & Ward, M. J. (1980). Seductive behavior of mothers of toddlers: Occurrence, correlates, and family origins. *Child Development, 51*, 1222–1229.

Sroufe, L. A., & Waters, E. (1977). Attachment as an organizational construct. *Child Development, 48*, 1184–1199.

Sroufe, L. A., Waters, E., & Matas, L. (1974). Contextual determinants of infant affective response. In M. Lewis & L. Rosenblum (eds.), *Origins of Fear* (pp. 49–72). New York: Wiley.
Stechler, G., & Carpenter, G. (1967). A viewpoint on early affective development. In J. Hellmuth (ed.), *Exceptional Infant* (Vol. 1, pp. 163–190). Seattle, WA: Special Child Publications.
Steele, H., & Steele, M. (2008). *Clinical Applications of the Adult Attachment Interview.* New York: Guilford.
Stern, D. (1985). *The Interpersonal World of the Infant: A View from Psychoanalysis and Developmental Psychology.* New York: Basic Books.
  (1990). Joy and satisfaction in infancy. In R. Glick & S. Bone (eds.), *Pleasure beyond the Pleasure Principle.* New Haven: Yale University Press.
Stiles, J. (2008). *The Fundamentals of Brain Development.* Cambridge, MA: Harvard University Press.
Suess, G. J., Grossmann, K. E., & Sroufe, L. A. (1992). Effects of infant attachment to mother and father on quality of adaptation in preschool: From dyadic to individual organization of self. *International Journal of Behavioural Development, 15,* 43–65.
Szasz, T. (1961). *The Myth of Mental Illness.* New York: Harper & Row.
Teicher, M. H., Samson, J. A., Anderson, C. M., & Ohashi, K. (2016). The effects of childhood maltreatment on brain structure, function and connectivity. *Nature Reviews Neuroscience, 17*(10), 652–666.
Thelen, E. (1989). Self-organization in developmental processes: Can a systems approach work? In M. Gunnar & E. Thelen (eds.), *Minnesota Symposia in Child Psychology: Vol. 22. Systems and Development* (pp. 77–117). Hillsdale, NJ: Erlbaum.
Tobin, A., Condon, E., Sadler, L, Holland, M., Mayes, L., & Slade, A. (2022). School age effects of Minding the Baby: An attachment-based home-visiting intervention: On parenting and child behaviors. *Development and Psychopathology, 34,* 55–67.
Tomasello, M. (2019). *Becoming Human.* Cambridge, MA: Harvard University Press.
Tomkins, S. (1962). *Affect, Imagery, and Consciousness.* New York: Springer.
Troy, M., & Sroufe, L. A. (1987). Victimization among preschoolers: The role of attachment relationship history. *Journal of the American Academy of Child and Adolescent Psychiatry, 26*(2), 166–172.
Urban, J., Carlson, E., Egeland, B., & Sroufe, L. A. (1991). Patterns of individual adaptation across childhood. *Development and Psychopathology, 3,* 445–460.
Van IJzendoorn, M. H. (1995). Adult attachment representations, parental responsiveness, and infant attachment: A meta-analysis on the predictive validity of the Adult Attachment Interview. *Psychological Bulletin, 117*(3), 387.
Van IJzendoorn, M. H., Schuengel, C., Wang, Q., & Bakermans-Kronenburg, M. J. (2023). Improving child attachment and externalizing behaviors. *Development and Psychopathology, 35,* 241–256.

Varese, F., Smeerts, F., Drukker, M., Lieverse, R., Tineke, L., Viechtbauer, W., Read, J., van Os, J., & Bentall, R. (2012). Childhood adversities increase the risk of psychosis: A meta-analysis of patient-control, prospective and longitudinal studies. *Schizophrenia Bulletin*, *38*(4), 661–671.

Vaughn, B., & Bost, K. (1999). Attachment and temperament. In J. Cassidy & P. Shaver (eds.), *Handbook of Attachment* (pp. 198–225). New York: Guilford Press.

Vaughn, B., Waters, E., Egeland, B., & Sroufe, L. A. (1979). Individual differences in infant–mother attachment at 12 and 18 months. *Child Development*, *50*, 971–975.

Vygotsky, L. (1978). *Mind and Society*. Cambridge, MA: Harvard University Press.

Waldinger, R., & Schulz, M. (2016). The long reach of nurturing family environments: Links with midlife emotion-regulatory styles and late-life security in intimate relationships. *Psychological Science*, *27*(11), 1443–1450.

Waters, E. (1978). The stability of individual differences in infant-mother attachment. *Child Development*, *49*, 483–494.

Waters, E., & Sroufe, L. A. (1983). Social competence as a developmental construct. *Developmental Review*, *3*, 79–97.

Waters, E., Vaughn, B., & Waters, H. (2024). *Measuring Attachment*. New York: Guilford Press.

Waters, E., & Waters, T. (in press). Developmental change, bricolage, and how a lot of things development. *Development and Psychopathology*.

Waters, H., & Waters, E. (2006). The attachment working models concept: Among other things, we build script-like representations of secure base experiences. *Attachment and Human Development*, *9*, 185–197.

Waters, T. E. A., Facompré, C. R., Dagan, O., Martin, J., Johnson, W. F., Young, E. S., Shankman, J., Lee, Y., Simpson, J. A., & Roisman, G. I. (2021). Convergent validity and stability of secure base script knowledge from young adulthood to midlife. *Attachment and Human Development*, *23*(5), 740–760.

Wilson, D. S. (2019). *This View of Life*. New York: Vintage Books.

Yates, T. M. (2004). The developmental psychopathology of self-injurious behavior: Compensatory regulation in posttraumatic adaptation. *Clinical Psychology Review*, *24*(1), 35–74.

Youngblade, L. M., & Belsky, J. (1992). Parent–child antecedents of 5-year-olds' close friendships: A longitudinal analysis. *Developmental Psychology*, *28*(4), 700.

Zeanah, C. H., Benoit, D., Hirshberg, L., Barton, M. L., & Regan, C. (1994). Mothers' representations of their infants are concordant with infant attachment classifications. *Developmental Issues in Psychiatry and Psychology*, *1*, 9–18.

Index

ABC program, 136
ability to expect well, 143, 147, 187
adaptation, 125–127, 151
Adler, Alfred, 125, 188
adolescence
   abstract thinking in, 105
   challenges of, 114–116
   developmental changes in, 103–105
   expanding minds in, 105–107
   meaning, and, 192, 193, 198–200
   parental relationships in, 111–113
adrenalin, 9, 179
Adult Attachment Interview (AAI), 133–137, 141, 164
adulthood, 105
   meaning, and, 200
affect, 6
agency, sense of, 60
Ainsworth, Mary, 39, 40, 41, 42, 60, 133, 134, 135
anger, fear of, 172–173
anti-empathic responses, 74
appraisal theory, 9
Arnold, Magda, 9
attachment, 33, 36
   effective in infancy, 145
   measuring quality of, 41–46
attachment behaviors
   organization of, 119
attachment figures, 21, 25
   separation from, 36, 179
attachment patterns, 205
   anxious, 38, 58
      family drawings, 95
   avoidant, 39, 58
      family drawings, 95
   control, and, 162–163
   disorganized, 39
      in infancy, 139
      stability of, 137–139
   resistant, 39, 58
      family drawings, 95
   secure, 38, 44, 58, 60, 108, 148
      central meaning, 114–115
      challenges of adolescence, and, 116
      dependency, and, 166
      family drawings, 94
attachment relationships, 37–39
   continuity across generations, 132–133
   early, 182
   effective, 145
   stability of, 46
attachment theory, 36–37, 39, 62, 147, *See also* Bowlby, John
attention deficit hyperactivity disorder, 57
attractiveness and social competence, 195
attunement, 62
autism, 169–171
autonomous status, 134, 135
autonomy with connection, 111
avoidance, 42, 44
avoidant status, 135

baby talk, 28
Baldwin, James Mark, 62, 187
Barker, Pat, 146
Barrier Box task, 60
behavior and meaning, 8–9
behavior–punishment cycle, 15
belonging, sense of, 205, 206
blame, parental, 159–160
Block, Jeanne and Jack, 60, 76, 111, 120
Bollas, Christopher, 188
borderline disorder, 169
Boszormenyi-Nagy, Ivan, 129
boundaries, lack of, 140
boundary violations, 56–57
   in childhood, 140–141
Bowlby, John, 36, 37, 48, 62, 72, 125, 157, 161, 164, 166, 167, 179, 180, 205
brain development and trauma, 175–178

Bransford, John, 5
Brazelton, Berry, 29
Breger, Louis, 165
Bruner, Jerome, 206
bullying, 80–81

caregivers
  attentive, 33
  critical role in meaning making, 20, 182
  early origins of meaning, and, 29–31
  responsive, 21
  sensitive, 40–41
  toddlers, and, 51
category descriptions, 205
childhood disorders, 167–169
cognition, 6
  emotion, and, 10
coherence, 207
  of experience, 183
  at level of meaning, 132
Cole, Michael, 22
Collins, Andrew, 198
co-morbidity, 205
competence, 143, 144
  development of, 38
  established by preschool period, 146
  real-world, 88, 101
  social, 195
  in toddler period, 145
complex trauma, 175, 183
conduct disorder, 168
conflict-resolution ability, 121–122
conformity in middle childhood, 91
connection, sense of, 205
consistency at level of meaning, 132
continuity, 120
  of attachment relationships across generations, 132–133
  of experience, 183
  in individual development, 119
  of infant attachment, 139–140
  at level of meaning, 121, 131
  of parenting across generations, 128–132
  in personality, 120–121
control, sense of, 52
controlling behavior, 160–163
Cooley, Charles, 187
Cooper, Robert, 71
core values acquisition, 87
cortisol, 179, 180
cross-gender relationships, 121
crowds, 108
culture, acknowledging, 21–23

Damasio, Antonio, 7
dandelion children, 147
defensive exclusion of information, 125
delay of gratification, 83
dependency, 165–167
depression, 149
development
  how it works, 62–63, 83–84, 141–142
  nature of, 25
    cumulative, 15–16, 47–48
    transactional, 17–18, 193
developmental change and early experience, 149–151
developmental prototypes, 27
developmental psychopathology, 158
differentiation, 175–176
disengagement, 110
dismissing status, 134
disruptiveness, 110
dissociation, 5, 138, 139, 169, 182, 183
distress, recognition of, 74
disturbance
  cumulative nature of, 158
  meaningfulness of, 157–158, 169–172
Dozier, Mary, 136
drawings, *See* family drawings

early intervention programs, 136
early trauma, 175, 177, 180, 182, 183
earned secures, 141, 142
ego, 188
  autonomous level of development, 134
  resilience, 76
elementary school years, *See* middle childhood
emancipation in adolescence, 111
emotion
  cognition, and, 10
  regulation, 158–159
  thought, and, 9
emotional health, 35
emotional knowing, 48
engagement, 32
Erikson, Erik, 55, 71, 111, 189, 199, 205, 207
evolution, 8, 22
exogenous smiles, *See* social smiles
expectations, 48, 83
  acquired, 69
  behavior, and, 101
  confident, 147
  in preschoolers, 73–74
experience, 125
  continuity, wholeness, and coherence of, 183
  after developmental change, 149–151
  histories of, 205
  meaning, and, 15–18, 151–153

Index

Fairbanks, Lynn, 130
family
  drawings, 94–96
  understanding in adolescence, 110
family systems thinking, 129
fears, 161, 167
  regulation of, 178–180, 182
feelings in adolescence, 107
Fingarette, Herbert, 189
Fleeson, Will, 35
Fonagy, Peter, 136
Frankl, Viktor, 6
Franks, Jeffrey, 5
Freud, Sigmund, 32, 125, 157, 189
friendships, 123
  in adolescence, 108
  in middle childhood, 89, 93, 97, 98
future, conceptualizing in adolescence, 107, 113–114

Garmezy, Norman, 143
good developmental outcome, 144, 145
Grossmann, Klaus and Karin, 76
groups, 88, 90, 91–93, 109
guided self-regulation in toddlers, 52–54
guilt, 52

Hesse, Erik, 39, 139, 162, 182
hierarchy of needs, 189
Hodgson, Ralph, 187
Horowitz, Mardi, 124

idealization, 163–165
identity
  forging of, 111
  narrative, 200
  personal, 111
inconsistencies in adolescence, 108
infants, 13, 14, 18
  emergence of intentionality, 31–33
  meaning, and, 191
  sensitivity to social context, 20
institutional rearing, 25
integration, 6–8, 178, 181–182, 200
integrity, 199
intentionality
  emergence in infants, 31–33
  in preschoolers, 77
  in toddlers, 51
Internal Working Model (IWM) of the child, 136
investment, 32
  of individuals, 4

Jacobvitz, Deborah, 139
James, P. D., 190

James, William, 206
Jung, Carl, 157

Kagan, Jerome, 15
Kahneman, Daniel, 8
Kalsched, Donald, 182, 183
Kanner syndrome, *See* autism
Kegan, Robert, 11, 187
Keniston, Kenneth, 106
Kochanska, Grazyna, 17–18

Laing, R. D., 171
language and sense of reality, 72
Lazarus, Richard, 9
Lewis, Michael, 8
Lieberman, Alicia, 179
lifespan, meaning through, 190–193
limits, 62
Liotti, Giovanni, 138, 139
Loevinger, Jane, 125, 134, 188
looking glass self, 188
Luborsky, Lester, 124
Lyons-Ruth, Karlen, 162

Mackenzie, Michael, 18
Main, Mary, 39, 58, 94, 133, 136, 139, 141, 162, 182
maladaptation, 126, 151–153
Mandler, George, 9
Maslow, Abraham, 189
Masten, Ann, 147
Mayes, Linda, 136
McAdams, Dan, 200, 206
McDonough, Susan, 18
Mead, George Herbert, 187
meaning
  as active process, 12, 13–15
  in autonomy with connection, 111
  behavior, and, 8–9
  capturing in parent-infant interaction, 39–41
  as carrier of development, 122–124
  childhood disorders, and, 167–169
  compassion, and, 172
  creation of, 27–28
  derived from experience, 151–153
  development
    transactional nature of, 12
  disturbance, and, 157–158
    extreme, 169–172
  experience, and, 15–18
  individual variations across development, 193–194
  as inherent human motive, 13–15
  organization of, 183
  origins of, 28–31

meaning (cont.)
    from past to new, 57–60
    personal, 204–205
    place of, 23–24
    power of, 5–6
    processes in carrying forward, 139–141
    prototypes for, 33–34
    search for
        change and continuity in, 101–102
        seeking, 12
    social imbeddedness of, 18–21
    subjectivity of, 3
    through lifespan, 190–193
    trauma, and, 180–182
meaning analysis, 9
memory, 27, 47, 131, 181
    as constructive, 123
    in preschoolers, 72
mentalization, 136
middle childhood, 87–89
    major developments in, 87–94
    meaning, and, 192, 193, 196–198
Minding the Baby program, 136
mirroring, 62
Mischel, Walter, 83
mixed-gender relationships, 115
Moffitt, Terrie, 116
molecules, behavior of, 46
morality, 87
    developing code of, 91
    principled, 106
    system of, 22, 100
multiple personality disorder, 169
Murdoch, Iris, 21

narrative identity, 200
narratives, 206
negativism, 169–170, 171
newborns, 13, 28–29
    capacities for memory, 27
    meaning, and, 191
    smiles, 25–27
norms in middle childhood, 90–91

order, 8
organized self, 67, 183
overwhelming events, 175

parallel play, 80
parental monitoring, 86
parental relationships in adolescence, 111–113
parentification, 120
parent–infant interaction
    capturing meaning in, 39–41

parenting, *See also* seductive parenting
    blame, 159–160
    continuity across generations, 128–132
pattern recognition, 5
peer relationships, 145
    in middle childhood, 89–91, 93–94, 100–101
    perseverance in times of crisis, 143
personal identity, 111
personal meaning, 204–205
personality, 120
    organization of, 125
Piaget, Jean, 7, 10, 105, 125
play pairs, 80–82, 190
pre-adolescent children, *See* middle childhood
predictability, 48
preoccupied status, 135
preschoolers, 67–68
    connection to peer group in, 100
    emerging of person, 77–83
    meaning, and, 191–192, 193, 194–196
    minds of, 70–77
    world of, 69–70
prioritization, culturally based, 23
procedural learning, 30
procedural memory, 27, 47
proto-dissociation responses, 138
psychoanalysis, 188
psychological development and trauma, 178–180
psychopathology, developmental, 158
purpose, sense of, 71, 206, 207

radicals, among adolescents, 106
rebounding, 148
reciprocity, 30
recognition of distress in preschoolers, 74
reflection, in adolescence, 105, 107, 110
reflective function, 136
reflexive behavior, 29
reinforcement, 35
relationships, *See also* social relationships
    in adolescence, 107–111
    constancy, 52
    different views on, 100
    in middle childhood, 99
    with parents, 111–113
    with peers, 89–91, 93–94, 100–101, 145
    reality and power of, 46–49
    robustness of, 179
    systems, 128
resilience, 141, 142, 143, 146–149, 187
resistance, 43
resourcefulness, 143
responsibility, 111
responsiveness, 62
rules, importance in middle childhood, 90–91

Salinger, J. D., 164
Sameroff, Arnold, 15, 147
Sander, Louis, 30, 52, 83, 179, 188
Sapolsky, Robert, 176
Sartre, Jean-Paul, 6
Schacter, Stanley, 9
schizophrenia, 146, 171–172
school phobia, 167
Schore, Allan, 176
Schuengel, Carlo, 139
script theory, 124
scripts, 123
seductive parenting, 59, 128–130, 202
selective inattention, 125
self, 178, 179
   in adolescence, 107–111
   organized, 67, 183
   as search for meaning, 189
   sense of, 88
   social relationships, and, 187–188
self-actualization, 189
self-awareness in toddlers, 51
self-confidence, 89
self-control, 61
self-management, 67, 145
self-mutilation, 169
self-regulation, 52–54
Selman, Robert, 107
sensitivity in caregivers, 40–41, 60
sensory-affective meanings, 30
separation from attachment figures, 36, 179
shame, 52
Shulman, Shmuel, 197–198, 200
Siegel, Dan, 182
signal-response pattern, 31
Slade, Arietta, 136, 182
smiles, 124
   development of meaning-based, 25–27
Smith, Emily Esfahani, 5, 6, 205, 206
social competence and attractiveness, 195
social context, 19–20, 21
social referencing, 20
social relationships, 34, 187
   in adolescence, 108
   primary, 190
   self, and, 187–188
social smiles, 26, 27
Spark, Geraldine, 129
Spitz, René, 25, 27
Stechler, Gerald, 30
Stern, Daniel, 29
Stiles, Joan, 176

storytelling, 206
Strange Situation procedure, 41, 42
stress, regulation of, 178–180
Stuecher, Uwe, 170
subjectivity of meaning, 3
Suess, Gerhard, 76
Sullivan, Harry Stack, 125
surprise, 33
symbolic play, 14, 76–77
synthesis, 6–8

teachers, behavior of preschoolers with, 75–76
teenagers, *See* adolescence
Teicher, Martin H., 177
Thelen, Esther, 27
therapeutic change, 16
thought and emotion, 9
toddlers, 7, 13–14, 15, 17, 18, 50–52
   developmental change in, 57–60
   guided self-regulation in, 52–54
   meaning, and, 191, 193–194
   variations in experience, 55–57
Tomasello, Michael, 12
Tomkins, Sylvan, 124
transactional model of development, 15, 193
transactional processes, 17–18
transcendence, 206
transference, 123
trauma, 175
   brain development, and, 175–178
   meaning, and, 180–182
   psychological development, and, 178–180
turn-taking dialog, 29–30
Tversky, Amos, 8
Tyson, Neil deGrasse, 5

uncommitted, among adolescents, 106
uniqueness, understanding of, 107
unresolved status, 139

van der Kolk, Bessel, 175
Van IJzendoorn, Marinus, 135
vulnerability, sense of, 114

wholeness of experience, 183
Wilson, David Sloan, 18, 22
worldviews, 187, 189–190
   consolidation of, 99–101

Yarrow, Marian, 68
Yates, Tuppett, 169

Made in the USA
Monee, IL
03 May 2026